READING NARRATIVE
AS LITERATURE:
SIGNS OF LIFE

Open University Press

English, Language, and Education series

General Editor: Anthony Adams
Lecturer in Education, University of Cambridge

TITLES IN THE SERIES

Narrative and Argument
Richard Andrews (ed.)

The Problem with Poetry
Richard Andrews

Time for Drama
Roma Burgess and Pamela Gaudry

Computers and Literacy
Daniel Chandler and Stephen Marcus (eds)

Readers, Texts, Teachers
Bill Corcoran and Emrys Evans (eds)

Thinking Through English
Paddy Creber

Developing Response to Poetry
Patrick Dias and Michael Hayhoe

Developing English
Peter Dougill (ed.)

The Primary Language Book
Peter Dougill and Richard Knott

Children Talk About Books
Donald Fry

Literary Theory and English Teaching
Peter Griffith

Lesbian and Gay Issues in the English Classroom
Simon Harris

Reading and Response
Michael Hayhoe and Stephen Parker (eds)

Assessing English
Brian Johnston

Lipservice: The Story of Talk in Schools
Pat Jones

The English Department in a Changing World
Richard Knott

Oracy Matters
Margaret MacLure, Terry Phillips and Andrew Wilkinson (eds)

Language Awareness for Teachers
Bill Mittins

Beginning Writing
John Nichols *et al.*

Teaching Literature for Examinations
Robert Protherough

Developing Response to Fiction
Robert Protherough

Microcomputers and the Language Arts
Brent Robinson

English Teaching from A–Z
Wayne Sawyer, Anthony Adams and Ken Watson

Reconstructing 'A' Level English
Patrick Scott

School Writing
Yanina Sheeran and Douglas Barnes

Reading Narrative as Literature
Andrew Stibbs

Collaboration and Writing
Morag Styles (ed.)

Reading Within and Beyond the Classroom
Dan Taverner

Reading for Real
Barrie Wade (ed.)

English Teaching in Perspective
Ken Watson

The Quality of Writing
Andrew Wilkinson

The Writing of Writing
Andrew Wilkinson (ed.)

Spoken English Illuminated
Andrew Wilkinson, Alan Davies and Deborah Berrill

READING NARRATIVE AS LITERATURE: SIGNS OF LIFE

Andrew Stibbs

Open University Press
Milton Keynes · *Philadelphia*

Open University Press
Celtic Court
22 Ballmoor
Buckingham
MK18 1XW

and
1900 Frost Road, Suite 101
Bristol, PA 19007, USA

First Published 1991

British Library Cataloguing in Publication Data
Stibbs, Andrew
    Reading narrative as literature: signs of life. –
    (English language and education series).
    1. Literature. Narrative. Interpretation by readers
    I. Title.   II. Series
    809.923

    ISBN 0–335–09419–8

Library of Congress Cataloging-in-Publication Data
Stibbs, Andrew.
        Reading narrative as literature: signs of life/by Andrew Stibbs.
        p.   cm. – (English, language, and education series)
        Includes bibliographical references and index.
        ISBN 0–335–09419–8
        1. Literature – Study and teaching (Secondary)
        2. Narration (Rhetoric)   I. Title.   II. Series.
    PN59.385   1991
    809.3′0071′2 – dc20

Typeset by Scarborough Typesetting Services
Printed in Great Britain by Biddles Limited,
Guildford and King's Lynn

Contents

Figures

Lettered figures (model)

Numbered figures (illustrations)

Presentiments are strange things! and so are sympathies; and so are signs; and the three combined make one mystery to which humanity had not yet found the key.

Jane Eyre, Chapter 21

General editor's introduction

This is an unusual book. However, this should be no surprise, for his many friends in the world of English teaching will know the author as a most unusual man. The range of reference that is encompassed here is typical of Andrew Stibbs's agile mind and quick interest in all things literary. The 'doodle' presented as Figure 1 (p. 32) can perhaps stand as a symbol of the book as a whole. Here is a visual exploration (Stibbs says that he has 'a relatively sensitive eye but coarse ear') of a seemingly trivial text out of which grows a full explication that reveals the true complexity of a simple quatrain.

As Andrew Stibbs reminds us, as part of the same discussion, 'literary theorists often use "text" to mean more than words.' So this book begins with an extended discussion of Ambrose Bierce's short story 'An Occurrence at Owl Creek Bridge'. Later in the book it is explored as a film. The book also encompasses, amongst much else, discussion of texts as different in literary quality as *A Midsummer Night's Dream* and *Black Beauty*, and as different in form and audience as *All Creatures Great and Small* and Chaucer's *Knight's Tale*. It is, therefore, eclectic in the examples that it chooses and wide ranging in the interests it represents.

However, the examples (entertaining in themselves) are a means towards a more complex end. The eclecticism extends to a wide range of literary theory, mainly post-structuralist and narrative theory, on which the author draws and which he seeks to combine with his own original insights to suggest ways for the improvement of classroom practice. The evidence from the welcome for an earlier volume in this series, Peter Griffith's *Literary Theory and English Teaching*, demonstrates that many teachers are seeking to extend their understanding of recent approaches to literature and to apply these to their own teaching. The present volume makes a major contribution to this enterprise.

The requirements in the National Curriculum for English in England and Wales for the study of whole texts and of some pre-twentieth-century literature are ones that most English teachers will embrace whole-heartedly, but the question remains how best to approach such texts with students across the full ability range. The repertoire of techniques represented here, as a quick glance at the numbered figures will reveal, will assist all teachers in this endeavour by getting beyond the standard 'literary' approach and recognizing the range of enjoyment that narrative can provide. As Stibbs points out, we 'learn' many things from narrative, the uses of horses in the nineteenth century from *Black Beauty* and how to make a trolley from 'Spit Nolan'. Equally we 'enjoy' narrative in many different forms: story, film, television amongst them. All of these, and the different elements of narrative embedded in them, are explored in this book and applied to the demands of the mixed-ability classroom.

Andrew Stibbs, at the time of writing this book, is a Lecturer in Education at the University of Leeds. One of the requirements laid down for government approval of courses of initial teacher education is that lecturers teaching such courses should undertake what is termed 'recent and relevant experience in schools'. The value of this to individual lecturers varies considerably but, as the author's acknowledgements indicate, the research on which this book depends was partly the result of a recent term's work in a comprehensive school in the West Midlands. It is this sense of the reality of the classroom that informs the book as a whole: it brings together theory and practice in a most elegant ensemble.

The book is, therefore, the story of one man's exploration of the nature of text and narrative. It is, to the reader, a deeply satisfying personal statement and one that gradually unfolds a theory of narratology of its own, represented in large by the lettered figures in the text. The wide-ranging scholarship, the sensitive readings and the invigorating teaching are combined together to form a book that is a work of art in itself; throughout the text the personality and the personal voice of the author emerges with strength.

Andrew Stibbs is already a well-established author. He will be known to many teachers of English through his earlier work, *Assessing Children's Language* (Ward Lock Educational, 1979), published in association with the National Association for the Teaching of English. That book broke new ground in showing how 'assessment' could be made to serve and enhance the purposes of teaching; the current volume follows in this tradition and shows how much current literary theory can enhance the work of the classroom.

Anthony Adams

Acknowledgements

This book was written with the help of many people. I am grateful for the opportunities I had in spring 1989 to try out activities at Whitley Abbey School, Coventry, with pupils of Celia Rees, Jane Haldenby, Marion Imber and Avis Prior. I discussed the ideas with students of the Secondary English Diploma in Cleveland during summer 1989; Stephen Clarke helped me to think about *Tess*; colleagues who teach PGCE English Method at Leeds University allowed me to find time to write the text in spring 1990. John Catron, Jenny Burgoyne and Andrew Pierce allowed me to see and quote their pupils' work. Tom Stibbs made the index.

My first thoughts about *Black Beauty* and 'Spit Nolan' were trotted and trolleyed out in *Children's Literature in Education* (nos 7 and 22) to whose editors, especially Geoff Fox, I am grateful, and Section 5.2 derives from a piece I wrote in Michael Jones's and Alastair West's *Learning Me Your Language* (Mary Glasgow, 1987).

Spain, 1809 by F. L. Lucas, from *Many Times and Lands*, is reproduced with the permission of the estate of F. L. Lucas and The Bodley Head, and the Brecht fragment (translated by Humphrey Milnes) on p. 151 (section 5.4), from Willett and Mannheim's *Bertolt Brecht Poems 1913–56*, is reproduced with the permission of Methuen, London.

Introduction: stories and why they matter

We all remember stories we've been told, or read, or seen – probably better than we remember information. We use stories, too. We describe our friends by telling characteristic anecdotes about them; we remember our holidays by reminiscing; we plan our day by telling ourselves the future-story of what we'll do; and we sum up our philosophy, implicitly, in little stories we call jokes.

The power of stories has been recognized by different societies and story-tellers have been honoured as public servants. The Ancient Greeks enacted their myths as public ceremonies; the Vikings put their history into legends; Victorians provided children with improving tales; in our time newspaper stories can bring down governments. The Elizabethan theatre was censored because it could use a historical story such as Shakespeare's version of *Richard II* against a contemporary monarch and later *Henry V* was produced as part of a push to have Prinny made the Regent to George III. Some stories have played a part in changing public attitudes or even policies: *Uncle Tom's Cabin* fuelled indignation at slavery and helped to have it outlawed, and in the 1960s the TV play *Cathy Come Home* raised people's awareness about (and preparedness to act against) homelessness. The continued employment of story-tellers in schools and the success of books like Betty Rosen's *And None of It Was Nonsense* (1988) shows that story is still seen as important in education.

We actually get a lot of information from stories. From where have you got your knowledge about how the Romans fought or treated their slaves, about pirates, or about child-thieves in Victorian London? I know about the different uses of horses in the nineteenth century and about how to make a trolley, from two stories which will be referred to in this book: *Black Beauty* and 'Spit Nolan' respectively.

More importantly, and more subtly, we get explanations of life from stories. If you believe that virtue is its own reward, or that those who live by the sword die by the sword, or that God is not mocked, or that pride comes before a fall, or that it's better to outface what you fear than run away from it, or that girls were born to ripen then rot, – if you believe any of these platitudes, then it's probably because you've had them illustrated in stories you've read, rather than because you've had them proved in your real-life experience. Maybe you are still waiting for your patience to be as rewarded as Jane Eyre's. It's traditionally claimed that we 'suspend our disbelief' when we experience stories, and feel about the characters in them as if they were real characters, so that they provide us with models to emulate or imitate. Through the stories they tell, authors can make us feel about characters, or feel for them, or even feel as them, so that our real-life values are supplemented, reinforced or challenged.

Of course, to some extent we impose our existing values upon the stories we read (or hear or see). We find what we look for and see what we believe. We choose to read what we expect to like, and we evaluate characters according to systems of attitudes and beliefs that we have already developed. Also, by reading critically, we may spot an author's game and recognize the values he or she is trying to put on us and reject them. Nevertheless, stories have a power to engage us in anticipating, visualizing, celebrating and revelling in the events they purport to describe, and we may not stop to reflect on their nature as sign-systems and vehicles of values.

Stories are made available to us (or kept from us) by a social system which has a stake in our taking on certain values. That system works through what authors want to tell us, what publishers think will be popular, what censors are prepared to allow, what librarians stock, and what teachers think is worth the while of children to encounter or study. Later, for instance, I'll suggest that *Black Beauty* was, and remains, popular – especially with parents – because it reinforces pressures on genteel children to behave and conform.

In the context of possible classroom activities, this book sets out to explore the mental processes by which we recognize and read stories, the mechanisms by which stories work on us, and the means by which society and its cultures produce us as readers and produce the stories we read. The intention is not to represent stories as such insidiously dangerous pieces of propaganda that they are best avoided. Rather, I want to make stories seem more interesting to readers and teachers, and to make readers more knowing and discriminating, so that they can use their power to take, leave or use the narrative texts they encounter. If I seem to open a gap between the ways we see texts and life it's partly to make texts seem more interesting but also partly to make life seem more like text.

I try to deal with all the items in the process of reading narrative, and build up a model of the way they interact with each other. I suggest that different theories about reading have emphasized and explored different elements in the process: response theories have concentrated on the reader and the act of reading (Chapter 1); formalist theories have concentrated on features of the text (Chapter 2); and more recent theories have paid attention to some of the social influences on writing and reading narrative (Chapter 4).

I suggest that these changes of theoretical emphases are related to changing emphases in teaching literature – first in Higher Education, then, by a 'trickling down', in schools. So a concentration on authors had led to a biographical approach to literature teaching; an emphasis on the events which literature purports to describe was created by a fashion for 'comprehension'; a more child-centred approach developed attention to the act of reading and to the reader's role in making meaning; and – more recently – there has begun to be a recognition in schools of the nature of the text as a sign-system but also of the social significance of the way texts are made and construed by socially constructed young readers. The question of what is the relationship of literature to life also arises. What makes sign-systems interesting to young students, as well as to professional semioticians?

A second intention is to introduce some of the ideas of literary theorists that have gained currency since most of us last had the chance to study literature theoretically. It is a contentious field in which I have adopted a pragmatic and eclectic approach, though I have paid more attention to events than characters and tended to pick sensational – indeed ghoulish – stories to yield many striking illustrations. I am aware that I have done scant justice to psychoanalytical or deconstructive approaches, but Peter Griffith's earlier volume in this series (1987) deals thoroughly with deconstruction and its implications, and Tallack (1987) is an elegantly conceived demonstration of the explicit application of nine distinct approaches to three recurring texts.

Finally, I take a number of types and examples of classroom-applicable activities and relate these to particular elements in the model and the way those elements have been theorized. In some cases I suggest that the theorizing is providing rationales for techniques that teachers have already developed, often pragmatically or intuitively. In other cases I propose activities which derive directly from application of theoretical ideas. All this is against a background of belief in the values of attentive reading, of imaginative interpretation, of critical evaluation and of emulative creative writing. I am aware of the danger of seeming to present only a literary transposition of the discredited arguments for teaching the analysis of language in the hope that it will enhance the use of language. I should hope a more apt analogy is with recent developments in teaching language awareness which, often playfully, adopt a comparative, social and political dimension to language studies in schools and colleges.

My 'model' of the elements in the process of reading narrative which I am implying is a model of the way those elements interact, and relate to fashions in literature teaching, and generate classroom activities or their justifications. It is based on a model of communication in general from Jakobson (see Hawkes 1977: 83). I build the model up by representing parts of it in a sequence of developing figures in early chapters. These are labelled with letters, whereas the figures illustrating possible classroom activities are identified with numbers.

In choosing illustrative narrative literary texts I have tried to range from the short to the long, from the old to the new, and from children's to adult literature. I have tried to confine my illustrations to readily available stories, especially classics which are copyright-free and I can assume are familiar to teachers and likely to be read by students, but I have also thought it important to mention one or two contemporary novels for children or adolescents which I see as healthily challenging some of the traditions of the genre. Although, in accord with my advocacy of idiosyncratic and 'intertextual' reading, I have grabbed examples from whatever I happened to be reading at the time, I have centred my exposition round eight exemplary narrative texts – two novels (*Black Beauty*, *Jane Eyre*), two stories ('Spit Nolan', 'An Occurrence at Owl Creek Bridge'), two plays (*A Midsummer Night's Dream*, *The Caucasian Chalk Circle*), and two narrative poems (*Spain, 1809*, *Business News*). *Tess of the d'Urbervilles*, *The Hound of the Baskervilles*, *Bleak House* and *Black Jack* also receive more than passing reference.

I include a list of recommended readings and a fuller bibliography of mainly literary theory texts. You don't need to read the original theories to apply them intelligently, but be warned that the versions of them which I give in what follows are simplified and partial.

Finally, I have adopted a perverse solution to the problems posed by many literary theorists' use of jargon – often foreign or neologistic or coined merely to emphasize their originality. I have added to it by inventing my own.

1 Making a reading

1.1 Voyeurism at Owl Creek

A man stood upon a railroad bridge in Northern Alabama, looking down into the swift waters twenty feet below. The man's hands were behind his back, the wrists bound with a cord. A rope loosely encircled his neck . . .
. . . A sentinel at each end of the bridge stood with his rifle in the position known as 'support' . . . It did not appear to be the duty of these two men to know what was occurring at the centre of the bridge . . .
Beyond one of the sentinels nobody was in sight; the railroad ran straight away into a forest for a hundred yards, then, curving, was lost to view. Doubtless there was an outpost further along.

Where are we? Who is this man? What has he done? What are they going to do to him? Why?

If you are reading the first three sentences of Ambrose Bierce's 'An Occurrence at Owl Creek Bridge', some of these thoughts might go through your head.

First, you will have certain expectations of the story. You will know from its physical length that it is of the 'short story' genre, so you will probably expect it to describe in detail some single event of implied significance. The print is small – it is for experienced readers, so its subject is probably adult, and even difficult. The title, with its 'Occurrence' and 'Creek' may confirm your expectation about the genre and lead you to guess that it is set in America or Australia, and might even be a Western. The wording of that title will have told you that the story is modern, if not contemporary, and therefore likely to be realistic in style. All this before you have got beyond the title – but all this assuming you are an experienced reader who draws upon that experience to create a 'set' towards a reading.

'Alabama' may alert you to the issue of Abolition in the USA last century, and combined with the military references may point you to the American Civil War as a period. If so, you will be deploying your general knowledge. And your assumptions about the setting will help you begin that visualizing of details (only a fraction of which the verbal artist can provide) which is a feature of the reading-style of most of us.

Maybe the detailed description that fills the early part of this story would have begun to irritate you if you had a full text (it is an example of reading-time exceeding history-time, in the terminology of section 1.6). If so, that may be because of the operation of a 'hermeneutic code' by which the text creates an enigma, a curiosity, and an impatience for explanation in the reader (the term is from Barthes's S/Z – see Hawkes 1977: 116). You may also spot that the author has reinforced the curiosity by adopting the role of an ignorant, objective narrator here, and denied the reader any interpretation of, or background information about, what can be seen and heard. He says 'It did not appear . . .' and 'Doubtless . . .' (Later the narrator becomes omniscient and shares the knowledge with the reader, and later still the narrator adopts the viewpoint of the central character.)

With a noose in the third sentence, you may well anticipate that, early in the story, a central character will die, but there will have to be enough 'ado' to fill up the remaining pages. So you will guess that much of this story will consist of flashbacks.

But it is probable that, at the same time as you make this judgement – a technical judgement based on your consciousness that you are reading an author's manipulative artefact – you are also engaged with the central character as if, he were real.

> He looked a moment at his 'unsteadfast footing', then let his gaze wander to the swirling water of the stream racing madly beneath his feet. A piece of dancing driftwood caught his attention and his eyes followed it down the current. How slowly it appeared to move! What a sluggish stream!
>
> He closed his eyes in order to fix his last thoughts upon his wife and children . . .
>
> And now he became conscious of a new disturbance. Striking through the thought of his dear ones was a sound which he could neither ignore nor understand, a sharp, distinct, metallic percussion like the stroke of a blacksmith's hammer upon the anvil . . . The intervals of silence grew progressively longer; the delays became maddening. With their great infrequency the sounds increased in strength and sharpness. They hurt his ear like the thrust of a knife; he feared he would shriek. What he heard was the ticking of his watch . . .
>
> . . . As these thoughts, which have here to be set down in words, were flashed into the doomed man's brain rather than evolved from it, the captain nodded to the sergeant. The sergeant stepped aside.

Are you sorry for him now because he has a wife and children and he's about to die? You have been invited to 'enter his consciousness' by sharing his thoughts and sense-impressions. Or are you still antipathetic to him because he's on the side you'd disapprove of in the Civil War?

II

> Peyton Farquhar was a well-to-do planter, of an old and highly respected Alabama family. Being a slave owner, and, like other slave owners, a politician, he was naturally

an original secessionist and ardently devoted to the Southern cause. Circumstances of an imperious nature which it is unnecessary to relate here, had prevented him from taking service with the gallant army which had fought the disastrous campaigns ending with the fall of Corinth . . .

. . . One evening while Farquhar and his wife were sitting on a rustic bench near the entrance to his grounds, a grey-clad soldier rode up to the gate and asked for a drink of water. Mrs Farquhar was only too happy to serve him with her own white hands . . .

III

As Peyton Farquhar fell straight downward through the bridge, he lost consciousness and was as one already dead.

If you are a reader who needs 'the whole story', you will have to imagine – either when you reach the end of Part II or later – the events which make the bridge between the soldier's visit and Farquhar's hanging. (In II there's a short conversation which I have omitted: the soldier tells Farquhar how easy it would be to burn down the Yankees' bridgehead.) You will be filling one of those gaps which stories cannot avoid leaving and which are used in readings to engage the reader in an active role. You will be a very knowledgeable or alert reader to realize – at least on a first reading – that the grey-clad soldier was a Federal scout in disguise and an *agent provocateur* who was setting Farquhar up.

. . . From this state he was awakened – ages later, it seemed to him – by the pain of a sharp pressure upon his throat, followed by a sense of suffocation . . .

. . . Then all at once, with terrible suddenness, the light about him shot upward with the noise of a loud plash: a frightful roaring was in his ears, and all was cold and dark. The power of thought was restored; he knew that the rope had broken and he had fallen into the stream . . .

. . . He felt the ripples upon his face and heard their separate sounds as they struck. He looked at the forest on the bank of the stream, saw the individual trees, the leaves and the veining of each leaf – saw the very insects upon them, the locusts, the brilliant-bodied flies, the grey spiders stretching their webs from twig to twig . . . A fish slid along beneath his eyes and he heard the rush of its body parting the water.

. . . The man in the water saw the eye of the man on the bridge gazing into his own through the sights of the rifle. He observed that it was a grey eye, and remembered having read that grey eyes were keenest . . .

. . . The trees upon the bank were giant garden plants; he noted a definite order in their arrangement, inhaled the fragrance of their blooms. A strange, roseate light shone through the spaces among their trunks, and the wind made in their branches the music of aeolian harps. He had no wish to perfect his escape, was content to remain in that enchanting spot until retaken.

. . . All that day he travelled, laying his course by the rounding sun. The forest seemed interminable; nowhere did he discover a break in it, not even a woodman's road. He had not known that he lived in so wild a region . . .

. . . At last he found a road . . . as wide and straight as a city street, yet it seemed untravelled . . . Overhead, as he looked up through this rift in the wood, shone great golden stars looking unfamiliar and grouped in strange constellations.

When do you spot that Farquhar's 'escape' is a fantasy? When he heard the fish or saw the marksman's grey eye? Possibly not till he is walking the 'untravelled road' when you respond to a progressive change of style and realize that he is now in a landscape more characteristic of fantasies or fairy stories than of realistic short stories? Did you see snakes in the trees? Maybe your reading experience – of Golding's *Pincher Martin* for instance – has helped you to recognize that this story belongs to that small class of fictions in which the entire narrative purports to be the last thoughts of a dying person. At a second reading you might notice some of the clues to the instantness of his death: you might find horrible details of Farquhar's dying in the objective world intruding into the fantasy of his inner world.

> His tongue was swollen with thirst; he relieved its fever by thrusting it forward from between his teeth into the cool air. How softly the turf had carpeted the untravelled avenue! He could no longer feel the roadway beneath his feet! . . .
> . . . As he pushes upon the gate and passes up the wide white walk, he sees a flutter of female garments; his wife, looking fresh and cool and sweet, steps down from the verandah to meet him. . . . Ah, how beautiful she is! He springs forward . . .

Are you becoming annoyed with the author by now for playing with you when authors are supposed to play only with their characters? Certainly he adopts an unusual and baffling variety of narrational stances – a camera in Part I, omniscient in II, inside the character in III – and at some points not quoted he comes out of the role and has a sententious paragraph (or is it ironic?) about Death the dignitary or sly praise for a military code liberal enough to hang a gentleman. He never does tell you what 'imperious' circumstances kept Farquhar from the fighting, nor whether his capture had been caused by the Yankees' trap, his own carelessness, bravado or a desire to be a martyr. (Fuentes's *The Old Gringo* ascribes such a death-wish to Bierce himself.)

> As he is about to clasp her, he feels a stunning blow upon the back of the neck; a blinding white light blazes all about him, with a sound like the shock of a cannon – then all is darkness and silence!
> Peyton Farquhar was dead; his body, with a broken neck, swung gently from side to side beneath the timbers of the Owl Creek bridge.

It is time for each of you and Farquhar to get your own back. Authors have only a posthumous role in this reader-centred chapter.

1.2   Response theories: the reading process and what counts as literature

A naive view of literary reading might see an author collecting or inventing some messages for the reader – such as Farquhar's last thoughts – and conveying them

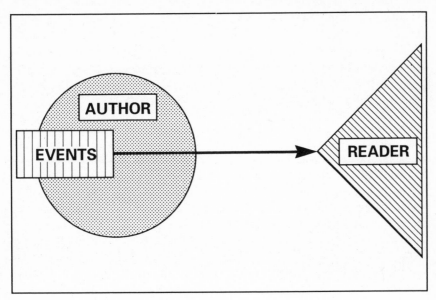

Figure A   A naive model of reading narrative

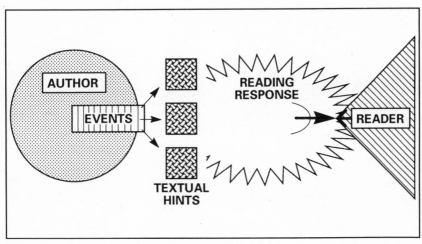

Figure B   A response model of reading narrative

directly and invariantly to a reader. Bradley, for instance, saw a proper reading of Shakespeare as an entering into the mind of the composing poet (see Hawkes 1986: 32). This simplistic model is represented in Figure A, where the message is labelled 'events' for the purpose of dealing with narrative literature. This diagram, and its subsequent developments, is adapted from Jakobson's six-part model of communication (see Hawkes 1977: 77, or Griffith 1987: 2). In this section, I concentrate on the reader and 'the act of reading', and develop a model of reading which is represented by Figure B.

Response theories and English teaching

Of the three main categories of theories of reading narrative that I use in this book, what I shall call the response theories are probably the ones most readily acceptable by English teachers.

First of all, by concentrating on individual readers and on the ways they make meaning, they share a central concern of teachers in classrooms. Most English teachers are practitioners of response theories whether they know it or not. And the pedagogical activities indicated by response theories – activities such as keeping reading journals or performing DARTs (Directed Activities Related to Texts – see Lunzer and Gardner 1984) – are familiar. In lists of Things to Do with Books, activities informed by response theories predominate, at least as I interpret them.

In Fox (1982) I estimate that about half the approaches he advocates are designed to elicit what response theories see as important components of literary experience – short-term anticipation, anticipating endings, refocusings, recappings, sharpening images, gap-fillings and monitoring one's own changing response. In the Northampton Heads of English *Approaches to the 'Class Novel'* reproduced as Appendix 6 of the Cox Report (1989) over a third of the suggestions would fit the 'applications' of this chapter (with a useful handful on the structures of my Chapter 2, the narrational rhetoric of my Chapter 3 and the cultural content of my Chapter 4).

The rationale for Benton and Fox's excellent *Teaching Literature 9–14* (1985) is explicitly response-centred, deriving a pedagogy from their estimate of a predominating thrust in literary theory ('Our approach reflects a dominant emphasis in modern literary theory that the reader's response is fundamental to the meaning of the text . . .', p. vii). Another of the most influential and admirable recent books on literature teaching (Protherough 1983) has 'Response' in its title and an index with many references to 'response' (but only 'structuring response' on 'structure').

English teachers' own education in English and English teaching may well have given prominence to two pieces of field-work in the best empirical traditions of Anglophones, which were precursors of more intellectual Continental response theory. I. A. Richards's work (1929) on the attitudes, ignorances, habits and misconceptions that led students to 'misread' poems was seminal in establishing the Practical Criticism movement in English studies which influenced a whole generation of literature students. Because of its association with the Leavisite tendency within English Studies (a tendency itself very influential in determining what texts are read in school), practical criticism was likely to have most deeply influenced those most likely to go in for schoolteaching. Although Practical Criticism is best classed as 'text-centred' practice, and Richards took the text to be authoritative, he was discussing naive students' responses to text, so he was original and influential in taking those responses into consideration.

For the second piece of influential field-work, Squire's pioneering work on adolescents' responses to stories was disseminated through the American and then English voluntary associations for English teachers in a way which has shaped much examination of secondary children's encounters with literature (Squire 1964).

To give a taste of the concerns of response theorists and how these might inform classroom teachers, I shall mention simplified versions of some ideas from three of them.

Iser's act of reading

Wolfgang Iser is heavy going (though *The Implied Reader* entertainingly deals with readings of specific English novels). But the mental processes his books examine are ones which we will all recognize, if in different terms. We recognize them from our own reading experience, from our pupils' reading and – I hope – from my outline of reading 'Occurrence at Owl Creek Bridge' above.

To simplify Iser, in his book of that (action-emphasizing) name, he characterizes 'The Act of Reading' as a search for 'consistency', within the text (pp. 118–25 of Iser 1978, to which the following references all are). The 'Implied Reader', complicit with the 'Implied Author' (terms from Booth 1961), seeks to cope with the contradictions, ambiguities and gaps in the text which they encounter, by constantly reconstructing the text in the head to make meaning. Two sets of processes in this constantly active, revising process of reading will be readily recognized.

First: gap-filling. Iser discusses many ways in which we cope with blanks and negations in the text, on different scales and on different levels of abstraction (e.g. pp. 168–9). We bridge the gaps in the narrative so that our reconstruction of events more nearly resembles the seamlessness ascribed to 'real-life'. With the crudity of words and the limited number of them available, no verbal artefact could represent the infinite extent and divisibility of our perception, never mind of the 'real-life' we infer to lie behind our perception. Obviously, the reader, complicit with the implied author, accepts and bridges sudden jumps in time and place, just as we have learned to 'read' cuts in films and videos. You probably provided a very strong example of this in your reading of 'Occurrence at Owl Creek Bridge' when you guessed that Farquhar, enticed by the Federal scout in the grey uniform, went to the bridge with the intention of burning it and got caught. More subtly, and probably subconsciously, you filled a gap when you inferred that the rope round Farquhar's neck was a noose.

'Owl Creek' has very detailed description but it has great gaps of context. In contrast, the poem *Spain, 1809* – reproduced in the Appendix – is relatively straightforward, but coarse in its description '. . . two blackened mills . . .') Here, the gap-filling which the text invites is more a fleshing out than a providing of explanation. Students with whom I've read this have written such items as the ambush which had provoked the raid, the speech with which a Spanish resistance leader would have persuaded the woman to sacrifice herself and the reasons why she might accept.

One easily understood type of gap-filling which the reader constantly performs, according to Iser, is the supplementing of inadequate information in the text. For instance, in visualization, upon a few hints from an implied author, the reader builds up a picture of a setting or character (or rather a sense of having a picture – the 'pictures in our head' turn out not to be susceptible to the same sort of scrutiny as real visual images) (Iser 1978: 135–9). Right from the start you probably gave the man in the noose a physique, a physiognomy and a costume. Maybe you visualized Farquhar on his verandah, or the fairy-tale wood through which he appeared to be travelling home. (Interestingly, in ways I'll suggest further in Chapter 2, this apparent limitation in the ability of verbal narrative to create images gives it a special power. Unlike a visual medium, it can leave out elements of a picture and thereby concentrate the visualization upon such single, chosen features as the rose petals lying around the dying Spit Nolan.) Fry (1985) suggests how this power of visualization is necessary for competent reading of fiction (pp. 104–5). Despite Iser's proviso that imaging in reading creates a feeling of seeing rather than an image we can scrutinize on the back of the forehead, I believe that getting students to draw their visualizations of characters and settings in the narratives that they read can help them into the habit of visualizing.

Iser says we constantly reconstruct our sense of the whole meaning of a text by revising both our retrospect of what we have already read and our prospect of what we anticipate reading, again in the search for consistency. In a 'continual interplay between modified expectations and transformed memories' (p. 111) what Iser calls 'a wandering viewpoint' (pp. 109–11) is sucked into the gaps and vacancies of the text, and sees what has just been read as foreground moving back to be the background of the next foregrounded section of the text. The word 'view' is apt, not just because visualization plays a part in most readers' interplay with text but because there's an analogy between the way we scan a text in time and 'read' a picture in space. In the latter process (which does take some time), the significance of what we see is continually modified by juxtaposition with memories of what we have just seen elsewhere in the picture or of viewings from other points.

I think these self-adjusting processes will be readily recognizable from your experience of reading 'Owl Creek'. Strikingly, teenage students to whom I showed Enrico's film *Incident at Owl Creek* (now unavailable) would gasp at the ending and immediately demand a re-run in order to confirm their new construings of the main action so lately and drastically modified by their experience of the ending.

Iser implies that the appeal of literary texts lies in the dynamic between having expectations confounded and re-established. We read on because we think we know what will happen, but then we find that – without it being so absurd as to frustrate our expectations – it's not quite how we expected, so we redefine our expectation and want to read on again to check that (see Iser 1978: 68–73). We need to know there is something in the attic, but we need to be a bit unsure or get it a bit wrong. Whereas a criterion for a reference book would be that it constantly eliminates doubt and ambiguities and progressively closes down alternatives, a literary text opens us out. If the author of a literary text has got it right for the implied reader of a literary text, then the reader is sufficiently tantalized into making predictions but never disappointed to discover the predictions are so accurate that reading on was a waste of time which yielded no new experience.

This active, demanding, but rewarding model of the reading process appeals to English teachers and reminds us to be patient. Evans (1981), writing about Iser and English teaching, stresses the need for us to 'cultivate this forward probing of the reading mind' by avoiding 'constant correction' or 'too ready a supply of facile interpretation' (p. 38). Iser's model assumes a rather straightforward linear reading of a narrative. In fact educators have done some sensitive fieldwork on styles of reading literature, especially Benton *et al.* (1988) – though they refer to adolescents reading poetry, where linear reading would hardly be expected.

Although Iser is primarily interested in the 'phenomenology' of reading literature, that hint about the difference between 'closed', non-literary texts and 'open', literary ones, does raise the questions of what is literature and why do we enjoy it. These questions are tackled more directly by two American response theorists, Norman Holland and Stanley Fish.

Holland and whatever turns you on

In *The Dynamics of Literary Response* (1968), Holland – taking many of his examples from poetry and film and drawing on Freud's explanations of jokes – explains literary works as defensive displacements. They act as vehicles into which we insert our fantasies and thereby manage them. So if an analysis of plots, for instance, showed them to cover a small range of themes and patterns which are also found in jokes, myths, or anecdotes, this would be explained by their appealing to (and being generated by) a small range of common subconscious and unconscious fantasies, However, readers at different periods of history or maturity might rationalize the appeal of *The Wife of Bath's Tale* as an allegory, an expression of Oedipal sexuality, or a nature myth respectively (or simultaneously) according to their age, taste, education, self-knowledge (or versatility) (pp. 12–26).

What makes the literary versions of these expressions of our fantasies count as 'literature', as high art rather than low art such as dirty jokes or comic strips, is nothing inherent in their meaning, but just the way the content is presented or the context in which it is presented. For one thing, works of literature flatter their readers by disguising their coarse armatures of archetypal fears and lusts under a superstructure of intellectualizing – symbols, arcane references, or historical displacements. So we accept the Bierce story as a puzzle, a daring experiment in proto-stream-of-consciousness writing, rather than as a sadistic piece of voyeurism. The sensational contents of stories appeal to our ids, their structures (patterning our expectations) gratify our egos, but their providing 'a feeling that we are engaged in a socially, morally, or intellectually responsible enterprise' is a sop to our superegos (pp. 184–5). From this one could guess that Holland would say *Jane Eyre* appeals because its content titillates our sexual fantasizing, its structure teases our curiosity, and its status as classic and set-book dignifies our enjoyment.

This is helpful to teachers: we need only provide the settings for authors who provide the structures and leave the students' rich fantasies to do the rest! However, as well as expounding this universal appeal of literature, Holland recognizes that one essential ingredient a reader brings to a reading is their own individuality: 'we . . . [enrich] the central fantasy with our own associations and expressions that relate to it' (p. 30). Later I'll discuss the part that a reader's unique repertory of previous reading plays in the process of making meaning of a new text. Here it's appropriate to mention the part played by individual reading styles in the reader's response.

As part of a wider study of the ways adolescents engaged with characters in the stories they read, I identified four girls who appeared, on the evidence of their talk and writing, to have clearly distinguished styles of engaging with the secondary worlds of the fiction they read, though I should stress that this refers to their styles of discussing (and, by inference, thinking about) characters in fiction, not of engaging directly with the words on the page. Jackie, for instance, was more likely than Caroline to imagine or speculate about undescribed events in the characters' lives, whereas Caroline made more pithy generalizations about the characters, categorizing them and taking her evidence from a gist of the text which she had clearly constructed.

I gave them three short stories to discuss which seemed as if they might impose three different styles of engaging with character, since one was an opaque, unrealistic, telling of a legend from a distant time and place (Borges's 'The Encounter'), one a realistic Victorian story in which more than one character's thoughts were described or hinted at (Saki's 'The Open Window'), and one a contemporary suspenseful first-person narrative (Richard Hughes' 'A Night in a Cottage'). Despite these contrasts in the respective accessibilities, viewpoints and narrational stances of the stories, they seemed to make very little difference to the styles of the girls' discussion of them, which retained their mutually distinguished qualities. As I believe almost all teenage readers of fiction do, the girls predominantly engaged with the characters they were reading about by projecting into their world, as onlookers (rather than identifying with them on the one hand or literary-theorizing about them on the other). Comparatively, however, Jackie and Dawn 'expanded' the characters in the text, while Caroline and Sue 'placed' them. The peculiarities of the readers seemed to have more influence on the styles of readings than did the peculiarities of authors' narrating styles. On the other hand, sharing their responses made the girls more versatile readers.

Fish's uncertain readers in interpretative communities

Stanley Fish is a saucy, combative writer whom it is unfair to represent, as I do here, as if his views have been unchanging. Nevertheless, the essays in Fish (1980) give further support for validating students' first impressions, tentativenesses and idiosyncrasies, and to teachers who encourage them to think aloud about texts, discuss them openly, keep reading journals and so on. Fish valuably points out the truism for response theory that there is no reading without a reader because readings are temporal but texts are spatial: a text is a meaningless object until it becomes part of a reading. Its meaning is not some metaphysical entity hidden like a ghost in the physical text: its meaning is the actual process of the reader's reading (pp. 2–3 and 21–67). If that reading includes uncertainties and contradictions, then they are part of the meaning too, for that reader, because they are part of the reading: critics or theorists who try to iron out the inconsistencies and paper the cracks which readers find in works are misconceived in their assumption that there must be essential and impersonal coherences hidden in great works which are potentially available to all properly instructed readers (pp. 112–35).

Fish, like Holland and Iser, has an explanation of why some texts count as literature and some do not. As do some Marxists (e.g. Eagleton 1983, in his Introduction, reprinted in Lee), Fish suggests that 'literature' is merely those texts which are defined as literature by those with power and influence, though Fish would define that power and influence as coming from the culture of an 'interpretative community' rather than from the hegemonic power of a self-perpetuating ruling class. (Holub 1984: 157 asks whether we agree on a reading because we are part of an interpretative community or are part of an interpretative community because we agree on a reading!) We find 'literary' qualities in literature because we go to it expecting from the context of our reading and the packaging of the text that it will be defined as 'literature' (pp. 10–11). When we go to the texts which are defined as literary by our 'interpretative communities' we attend to them in particular 'literary' ways. Fish illustrates this by showing how his students were misled to read a list of names on his blackboard as a gnomic poem (pp. 322–37). So, for Fish, *Jane Eyre* would be literature but a bodice-ripper wouldn't, because *Jane Eyre* is forced on us in school but bodice-rippers aren't.

Fish's ideas should appeal to teachers because he represents an idea of initiation into reading and – unlike some Marxist and other post-structuralist theorists – he does not question the individuality, singularity and coherence of the (student-)reader.

I now examine one component of learning and teaching narrative – dialogue in stories – in terms of reader's response. Then I look at some response-legitimized activities more generally. Finally I take two other aspects of reading – reading through previous reading and reading-time – both as illustrations of response theory and as introductions to later chapters of this book.

1.3   Reading who says what

'No! No!' screamed Hatch, outraged and panic-stricken. 'I told him it was suicide! I never said more! I never said –'

He stopped. Terrible looks were exchanged. The giant's eyes widened. His great fists clenched. Hatch made wretched attempts to undo the damage he'd done himself.

'Suicide . . . suicide . . . dead and buried now. All over with. Buried . . .'

'Buried,' repeated Dr Jones soothingly – and hoped the savage fellow hadn't understood.

But Parson Hall was not deceived. His eyes, ever-burning and prophetical on account of a malformation of the lids, sought out the giant's soul. He grew pale . . .

'Black Jack!' came Tolly's urgent voice. But Black Jack shook his head. There was a greater urgency now.

'Where – is – he – buried?'

The madhouse guardians stared at the giant in dread as they understood what he was intending.

'It – it's months! There'd be nought left to see. That is, even supposing –'

'Where is he buried?'

'Would you raise the dead?' muttered the parson desperately. 'Oh, you are damned indeed!'

'*Where is he buried?*'

'What can he find now? It don't signify –'

'Not at Tyburn!' cried Mitchell of a sudden, knowing nothing of the terrible undercurrents and only wanting her hall to be cleared. 'You murderous great pig, you! Nor in quicklime at Christchurch, neither! He's buried good and respectable at Old Street – and long may he rest till Judgement –'

'Black Jack! Black Jack!'

'Scoundrel!' shouted the parson as the giant lumbered after Tolly's cry. 'Would you interfere with them whom God has cursed? Would you set yourself against the Almighty?'

But Black Jack had gone from the hallway and the next that was heard of him –
in the midst of the ceaseless shouts and shrieks of Dr Jones's ladies and gentlemen –
was the crash . . .

(Garfield 1971: 166)

Reading dialogue plays an important part in both the apprenticeship of competent silent readers and in classroom activities to support the development of reading literary narrative.

I asked a mixed-ability third year to check that they could tell who said what in the passage above (from p. 166 of the 1971 Puffin edition of Leon Garfield's *Black Jack*). They underlined speeches in coloured felt-tip pens according to the different speakers, shriekers, or mutterers. They had some knowledge of the book because I had read them extracts, episodically. In most cases they performed the exercise with both enough accuracy and enough difficulty to make it worth while, and with some pleasure at using the pens. Then they prepared group readings-aloud.

Although I did not labour the point (because there is a degree of self-examination and explication of one's implicit working knowledge which secures it and increases its availability, but a further degree which muscle-binds it) I had them think and explain how they had known the speakers. Most could do that, if not easily.

Of the first four words, 'No! No!' are speech and 'screamed Hatch' are narration. This is signalled by the inverted commas, a system which a competent reader has learned. Common as the system is in modern texts, it is not universal, even in English. Some authors use dashes instead of flying tadpoles, and some continentals use double chevrons. If you learned to read on the Authorized Version of the Bible you learned to distinguish speech without the help of this system, which had not been invented in 1611. So that proves that modern standard punctuation isn't God-given.

The first utterance ('No! No!') is tagged with both the utterer's name and the manner of its utterance, as are all examples of direct tagging in this passage. The textual information is unambiguous, but it comes after what it operates on, so in a close word-by-word and left-to-right reading the reader would either have to guess the speaker when the 'No! No!' was reached or 're-read' it dramatically in a retrospect.

The second part of Hatch's first speech ('I told him . . .') will intuitively be ascribed to Hatch by any reader who has learned the 'new speaker/new paragraph; same speaker/same paragraph' convention (for instance by trans-ferring more easily understood playscripts into direct speech) and detected that this convention is used in this text.

The third speech ('Suicide . . .') would be ascribed to Hatch on assuming that it is one of his 'wretched attempts to undo the damage . . .' (Perhaps an exemplary one – the reader imagining other ones for which this stands.)

The next two speeches are like the first in form, but the sixth ('Where – is – . . .') introduces new sorts of clues. First there is information before and after it which suggests Black Jack is the speaker ('Black Jack shook his head' and 'The madhouse guardians stared at the giant'). Secondly, the layout of the quotation suggests a slow delivery which readers should by now associate with the big man.

'It – it's months . . .' is another free stander, but again there is a weak clue to its source – in the previous paragraph's mention of 'madhouse guardians'. But do both speak or only one? Even though transcripted speech is taken to be the most mimetic form of narration (see section 3.3 on 'showing and telling'), it leaves an active, creative role for the reader and scope for debate between different readers about their different readings.

The repetition of 'Where is he buried?' can confidently be ascribed to Black Jack because his first question was never answered, so the author, subconsciously assuming this, has taken the chance to drop the indicative layout to make room to use another convention of layout – italicization for increased volume.

An alert reader might find a clue to whether only one of the guardians asks the next question, and if so which. The unstandard grammar of 'It don't signify –' does not accord with the voice of the parson who had used 'Would' and 'indeed' in his tagged response to Black Jack's second 'Where is he buried?'

Then there's (Mrs) Mitchell's outburst, and the cry of 'Black Jack! Black Jack!' which we can ascribe to Tolly with confidence only after we have read of 'Tolly's cry' in the next paragraph, though a reader sensitive to relationships and modes of address in the book might intuit that Tolly is the only one of the dramatis personae in this scene who would address Black Jack by his name.

The last, unfinished, paragraph, with its reported shouts and shrieks is the only example here of a way of representing speech alternative to direct transcription. Although not strictly relevant to response, it is sometimes worth having students speculate on the reasons why texts report rather than transcribe speech and other utterance. Brevity? Phonetics? An unwillingness to quote swearwords? Or a fair division of labour between author and reader?

Most young readers cope automatically and swiftly with the inferences which are necessary to recreate the drama of a passage like this. Nevertheless I think such close analysis may sometimes help to explain the misunderstandings and confusions which some learner-readers have. Readers who can't 'hear' literary texts when that is appropriate are as deprived as those who can't 'see' them. Some explicit on-site analysis may show that readers who find passages like the above 'boring' do not know some of the conventions (like the paragraph-changing one) or have been allowed to learn some unhelpful reading style (such as a reluctance to read on past an ambiguity to collect a retrospective or cohesive clue).

Here, I hope the analysis showed just how remarkably various are the strategies we need to deploy in order to construe narrative texts with dialogue – a feature often thought to make them popular with young readers. Textual representation of speech, even in a novel which comes from a naturalistic fashion, is not so much a time-traveller's bug for overhearing virtual people as a sketch to guide a creative reader. To list some of the components in an ascribing of speeches to speakers in the *Black Jack* passage, the students used: the implication of inverted commas; tags, including retroactive ones; paragraphing; the implications of information other than tags; layout; representations of dialect and other speech mannerisms; the probability of characters saying things with certain meanings or assuming certain relationships.

All this at the same time as – for this passage – visualizing the dramatis personae, anticipating the consequences of this conversation, completing unfinished utterances, imagining characters' thoughts, and so on.

Three main implications for teaching occur to me. First, if and only if a student clearly has difficulties in recognizing speakers in dialogue, an exercise in coloured underlining and/or reading-aloud and conversation with a teacher or peers might expose an ignorance of convention or quirk of reading style which a quick explanation and demonstration, transferable to subsequent reading, could correct.

Secondly, for competent readers to bring their competences into the open (for instance by using them to dramatize passages) might help them to apply those competences to harder passages (see Newbould and Stibbs 1983). This is in line with my assumption throughout this book that judiciously encouraging a degree of public performance and demonstration will service private reading. It should go without saying that I should want any such classroom activities to take place in a convivial and playful atmosphere, and not to impede readers' enjoyment of a text or proper pursuit of an ending. In the case of this passage, however, the drama and characterization seemed to justify some dwelling on it to realize it communally by the exercise I described. Another possibility would have been to rewrite it as a playscript, complete with stage directions and 'thinks balloons'.

A third justification for examining how these reading processes act on textual conventions is that they may aid students' use of the conventions in their own writing and help them to imagine the effect of their writing on readers. Realizing the writer's responsibility to supply clues without clogging up the progress of story-telling may help students to understand at least some aspects of the artificiality of conversation in novels and stories. One example would be the unnatural frequency of the vocative which makes it easy to keep track of who's saying what in duologues, as in the speakers' overdoing the 'Miss Jane's and 'Bessie's in Jane Eyre's goodbye to Gateshead in *Jane Eyre* (Chapter 5).

Of course there are many more conventions for representing aspects of speech in narrative than I have illustrated here, and all need learning. One I hinted at above is the economical device of moving the speaker's person back to third and their speech's tense back one degree for reporting speech. Again, this is a device which had to be developed. In *Jane Eyre* what we would call 'reported speech' sometimes still appears in inverted commas, oddly to the modern reader and maybe confusingly to young readers (for instance in the destitute Jane's conversation with the Whitcross shopkeeper in Chapter 28).

Without going into such complexities as the narrator's voice growing up with Stephen Daedalus in *A Portrait of the Artist as a Young Man*, the representation of the thoughts of a dying man in 'An Occurrence at Owl Creek Bridge', or Anna Sewell's talking horse, one important potential cause of misunderstanding is the representation of thought in modern narratives. Narrators often stop narrating in their own voices and start to 'quote' a character's thoughts with no warning tag or quotation marks (sometimes called 'free indirect discourse'), as when Farquhar thought how slowly the stream flowed under Owl Creek Bridge. A good example of this is in the first chapter of *Black Jack* where the apprentice Tolly, incarcerated with what he thinks is the corpse of the eponymous giant, first realizes the 'corpse' is waking up.

> The silver moonlight, very bright now, seemed to lend the dingy room an odd beauty – as if it was intricately fashioned out of shining grey lead. Even the coffin and the still ruffian within it seemed carved and moulded by a master hand.
>
> How finely done was the tangled hair – the knotted brow – the powerful, thick nose . . . how lifelike were the deep grey lips. How – how miraculously shone the moon in the profound eyes –
>
> In the eyes? In the *eyes*? Sure to God those eyes had been shut before?
>
> Those eyes! They were open wide! They were moving! They were staring at him!
>
> Bartholomew Dorking, sent from Shoreham to London to be spared the perils of the sea, stood almost dead of terror.
>
> 'Alive!' he moaned. 'He's alive!'
>
> (p. 17)

There the narration slowly modulates into quoted thought (fully realized by 'In the eyes . . .'), then abruptly back into the narrator's story-telling, complete with tagged direct speech, at 'Bartholomew Dorking, sent . . .' Another peculiarity is the speaking aloud of what would not normally be spoken to maintain the fiction of narrating in one character's voice, as when Rochester speaks aloud to Jane what would more plausibly be described as the author's narration of his thought – for instance his account of his first marriage in Chapter 27.

If you turn to literature for adults (as you should, with teenage readers) you can find many crafty techniques which may baffle inexperienced readers too long before they are explained or understood with self-help. I needed Iser (1974) to give me the clue to the artificiality of dialogue in Ivy Compton-Burnett's novels. Others might be baffled, in Elizabeth Bowen's 1948 novel *The Heat of the Day*, by a flashback to an inquest where all you get embedded in the narration is one character's memory of the answers she gave to questions which are not reported:

> Two years and two months; we met in September 1940 . . . Yes, we saw one another frequently . . . Yes, I have always tried to keep some drink in my flat . . .
>
> (p. 302)

For students to write literary dialogue, to convert it into performance, and to appreciate both its full import and limitations, they have to learn how unrealistic and artefactual it is. Comparing transcripts of our own conversations with our written recounts of them can show this up. One way in which this is so can be in literary overuse of the vocative, mentioned above. Some other unnaturalistic features of dialogue in even naturalistic stories and novels are as follows: its length; its polite turn-taking; its prosiness (even when the transcription tries to reproduce dialect or phonetic mannerisms); its reproduction of foreign talk in English (as in *Spain, 1809* or Chapter 26 of *Jane Eyre*); its frequent restriction to two speakers (if I could have found a good example of a plurilogue in *Jane Eyre* instead of *Black Jack* I would have used one); its relevance and purposiveness and maybe ominousness (readers have learned to find significance in everything, even the apparently arbitrary or digressive; and we shall see what unnatural freight of significance is carried by the 'rose' exchange in 'Spit Nolan'). One way to make students aware of these artificialities is to have them improvise conversations in literature, record and transcribe them, and compare their transcriptions to the originals. The differences will be as great for 'Spit Nolan' as they will for the blank verse of *A Midsummer Night's Dream*.

Those are differences between the forms of 'real-life' conversations and those of the conversations which purport to lie behind literary representations of conversations. Now add the differences between the relative situations: in 'real-life' conversations you are usually a participant but in literary ones you are an eavesdropper; the progress of 'real-life' conversations is controlled by the speakers but of literary ones by authors; speakers' accents, vocal and facial expressions, gestures, clothing and so on influence our perceptions of 'real-life' conversations, but for literary ones we rely on the printed words.

1.4   Implications and applications: public models of private reading

Some of the pedagogical implications of response theory have been hinted at incidentally above: teachers' withholding correction or ready-made interpretations; gap-filling by fleshing out reported or implied events; drawing visualizations; making predictions about texts on the bases of opening lines, and so on. And the possibilities of developing responsive reading in the small area of dialogue was illustrated in the last section. In this section I discuss three general classroom approaches which response theory would support; using reading journals; using group discussion; DARTs, especially prediction.

Literary theories suggest their relevance to reading, interpreting and criticizing narrative texts. Their relevance to teaching reading, interpreting and criticizing needs some pedagogical theory.

I advocate these practices because I assume that they can develop literary competence by crystallizing readers' literary skills so that they come to know, explicitly, what they know implicitly, and so that they come to use that knowledge more discriminately and effectively. They are the skills which competent literary readers use, unconsciously, when they predict, re-assess, visualize, compare, etc. Teachers can help to develop these competences by putting students into situations where they have to go through these processes openly, publicly, maybe accountably and self-consciously. Thus they practise these processes, get models and support from peers, and some criticism and encouragement and suggestion for their practice. In most cases, the practices will be internalized with their refinements and critiques and will transfer to subsequent private reading, and make for more attentive, alert, accurate, interpretative and eventually critical literary readings. (Fox 1982 implies a rationale which includes finding ways to bring into class the processes which characterize good silent reading.)

In many students we cannot rely on attentive and rewarding active reading developing, just with practice, as fully or as fast as it could with some teaching. Thomson (1987) suggests that Australian teenagers lack strategies for active reading and need more help than they get from teachers, in order to develop those strategies (pp. 27–30). Just as we draw in order to see what we look at, and sing in order to hear what we're listening to, so we should write or talk in order to read the texts we go through. It is noteworthy that Fox's list of teaching approaches (1982) has a title which stresses activity and collaboration. One of Jackson's students (in Minns *et al.* 1981) reflects in her reading journal after a reading during which she'd kept a journal and taken part in group discussions:

> Looking at *Nancekuke* in such a deep and detailed way has helped me to understand the book in a way I had never thought before . . . This new way of looking at a book will help me to look at other books and find things out about the book that I otherwise wouldn't have been able to do before.
>
> (p. 65)

Fry (1985) would agree:

> . . . if we can encourage children to talk about what happens as *they* read . . . they will grow into an awareness of themselves reading, which is another way of coming to understand how they learn, how they live, how they are.
>
> (p. 107)

The teacher's skill lies in the timing and structuring of the requirements for these artificial outward expressions of the reading process so that the benefits accrue without the disadvantages of impeding or frustrating narrative reading or bringing the trees into such focal awareness that the wood is missed. So I'd always advocate that practices such as keeping reading journals, group discussion, or DARTs are an accompaniment to, and enhancement of, reading for meaning and pleasure, rather than self-justifying exercises which use reading for their excuses and occasions. I'd want teachers reading aloud to keep the interruptions to that minimum which they judge necessary to elicit the episodically modified hindsights and foresights which should become habitual in silent reading of novels, for instance. Nevertheless, I think that the pleasures and meaningful-nesses of reading narrative literature are enhanced by attentive, speculative, critical reading, and include the pleasures of analysis and criticism. The teachers cited above and below seem to have got it right.

John Catron had 13-year-olds reflect directly on their reading processes, especially visualization. They made charts of their experience as they read Margaret Mahy's *The Changeover*, to some extent structured by John's instruc-tions to record things which 'stuck in their minds'. These charts had some of the features of both reading journals and the 'total doodles' mentioned in the next section. They wrote comments on what they were reading; they copied quotations; they asked genuine later-to-be-answered questions about the text ('Will Sorry and Laura save him?' 'What is a vespa?'); they drew pictures of or made remarks about how they were imagining settings and characters ('Sorry's house makes me think of the big house where I live with big trees outside and a big front and back garden'); they wrote down little anecdotes of personal memories provoked by the text and incorporated into the meaning; they recognized objects in the text as being like objects owned by members of their families; they noted other texts they were reminded of (e.g. pop songs, TV programmes, *Sleeping Beauty*, *Macbeth*); they recorded their own developing understandings ('at first I thought it was a teddy bear but when I brought the subject up i was not the only one but we were put on the wright track . . .'; 'It made me think twice to what he was up to and that there was a hidden meaning to what he said'; 'it sounded disgusting at the time, but when I thought about it, I understood what she meant').

On the right-hand sides of their A3 sheets, these students wrote accounts called 'What Happens When We Read'. There are complaints that it hurts their eyes, notes that they learn new words and spellings, and remarks relevant to what I say about 'art and life' in Chapter 5. There are also confirmations of some of what Iser suggests about the experience of reading: 'when a house or road is described I imagine a house/road I know or I just make one up but always in really good detail'; 'We all imagine whats going to happen which makes reading exciting as you want to know exactly what does happen, were you right! Therefore you read on!'

Reading journals

One simple way of getting students to explicate the processes by which they read, and interpret and criticize what they read, is for them to keep journals of their literary reading. Maybe these provide the 'written equivalents of exploratory discussion' which Barnes *et al.* (1984) would want to replace the 'ubiquitous comprehension exercises' and 'detailed exposition of texts' which they found as the staple of fifth-year literary study. Jackson (in Minns *et al.* 1981) shows Kim modifying her estimate of a character's age and making sense of a house-moving in a novel she's reading by remembering her own move (pp. 57–8). Benton and

Fox (1985) has exemplary quotations from reading journals (p. 122), and so has Corcoran (in Corcoran and Evans 1987: 60–4).

Pierce (1985) makes the point, with ample illustration, that the use of reading journals in A-level teaching can 'raise practical knowledge to consciousness' and 'lead to the more explicit awareness of how literary language works and means . . .' (p. 76). He also illustrates many of the features of the phenomenology of reading from the reading journal which a 14-year-old kept, chapter by chapter, as she read *Jane Eyre* for the second time. The entries were partly prompted by her teacher's suggestions to record: first impressions; likeable passages; frustrations with the text; questions; personal links; expectations; talking points (Pierce 1985: 128). The entries (pp. 82–3) illustrate anticipation informed by some knowledge of the genre:

> I think the presence of Mr Rochester, as the stranger, will change things a great deal.
>
> (Chapter 12)

The reader finds enigmas and eventual explanations:

> Why does he call her 'Janet'?
>
> I now understand Mrs Fairfax's fear.
>
> (both Chapter 24)

She gropes towards an understanding of specifically literary signification:

> The horse-chestnut tree being struck by lighting seems to signify something – maybe a split between Jane and Rochester.
>
> (Chapter 23)
>
> Rochester does appear like the tree that was burnt down.
>
> (Chapter 37)

It is interesting to note how, on the evidence of extracts from their journals on *Jane Eyre*, this writer's classmates have slightly different emphases from hers as they record their reading experience and to a more or less degree than she, speculate about characters' feelings, or express their expectations or describe their visualizations. These may reflect differences in their reading styles (such as was suggested for the four girls discussing character to whom I referred in section 1.2) or it may just reflect what individually they find easy to write about. Benton and Fox (1985) also point out that particular readers' responses are different in style (pp. 16, 17) and draw support from Holland (1968) in saying so. To their justifications for reading journals I should want to add that they seem the best site for exercising an oscillation between engagement and detachment which makes for keen but critical readers.

Group discussion

Group discussion should need no advocacy: many of its efficacies were first demonstrated using pupils' group discussions about literary texts (e.g. Barnes *et al.* 1971). But it is worth pointing out that when students talk to each other about books they have read, they formulate, and mutually examine, notions about the story. They draw each other's attention to features of the text they may not have noticed during their own, partial readings, and they exemplify for each other the legitimacy of alternative readings. Sharing readings enlarges the repertory of ways of reading. Group discussion exemplifies how text is not a repository of clues to a single 'correct' meaning such as Richards (1929) implies, but nevertheless acts as a restraint on eccentric interpretations. The discussion acts as a critique of its participants' individual readings.

Jackson (1983: 71–3 or in Minns *et al.* 1981: 60–2) shows how pupils discussing an appropriate cover for a book they have read are led to consider interpretative issues such as which are the most important characters in the book. Another feature of such discussions is a tendency to refer to other texts they have read. A valuable possibility is to get them to see if their differences in interpretation which they clarify and specify, might be related to differences in their respective previous reading experiences. This possibility is suggested in the next section.

DARTs

Group discussion is central to Direct Activities Related to Texts. DARTs are thoroughly dealt with in Lunzer and Gardner (1984), in which many of the examples are taken from secondary English lessons, including work on stories and novels. Some of the activities I advocate for work on character or on language in novels and stories could be described as DARTs, and it is worth any literature teacher's while to look at Lunzer and Gardner's cross-curricular suggestions for activities which encourage students to 'interrogate the text'.

In my own teaching of 'An Occurrence at Owl Creek Bridge' to 14-year-olds, as well as having them fill the biggest gap with their own stories of how Farquhar came to be at the bridge or having them watch and 'write' the film for comparison with the text, I've had them tell each other what they see at the beginning, and DARTily predict what will happen. I've had them tabulate what the reader senses and what Farquhar senses. And, with relevance to Chapter 3 on narration, I've had them divide the text into description, narrator's story-telling and Farquhar's consciousness.

Some DARTs are more appropriate than others for work on literary narrative. Sequence being the essence of narrative, sequencing jumbled sections of text appears in many of the 'Things To Do' lists, though this is one activity where there is the danger of merely mystifying the already understood. A class of 14-year-olds I taught enjoyed sequencing the separated verses of *Frankie and Johnny* to perpetuate their pleasure at hearing it performed, and they made some use of discussing possible variants in sequence. But when I asked them to lay out the events behind the song and text (in what section 1.6 calls 'history-time') all I could claim for the results was that some were pleased to find what a complicated feat of chronological inference they had performed in so easily understanding the narration at a first hearing and restoring the text from its scrambled version. Some were also able to rewrite the story clearly in the random order in which I'd given it to them, using skills with parentheses, prepositions and tense-changes which neither they nor I realized they possessed.

Prediction is a DART specially relevant to studying narrative. As mentioned, progressive predicting based on the accumulating evidence of early text fits Iser's model of effective reading. So does deploying beforehand readers' knowledge of other texts and genres. Jackson (1983) shows 11- and 12-year-olds discussing *The Turbulent Term of Tyke Tiler* predictively (pp. 111–19). Exton (in Miller 1984) shows how he used prediction to get 13-year-olds to use and recognize their skills in, and knowledge about, literature and genre without being 'intimidated by feelings that they lacked sensitivity' (p. 72). In the next section I raise the question of how much we know about a text such as *Spain, 1809* from its opening words. But consider what would happen if readers only had the first half of the poem (printed on pp. 159–61), ending at

> . . . At his sign
> One filled a cup.

Readers or groups of readers discussing what happens next will be informed by a sense of scale and ending – how long a story like this and in this form will last. Such a sense will be developed by being explicated and disciplined by the contributions of other discussants – their references to other texts, their questions about others' opinions. (This increasing theme of the contribution to a reading of other readings is one of the subjects of the next section.) Maybe someone in the group will pick up the significance of the first-person narration, suggesting a survivor. Maybe some will pick up the hint of 'death's-head hovels watched us'. The need to predict will ensure close reading. The search for clues and signs will form an interpretation. These will open out into discussion that performs more paraliterary functions than strictly 'interpretation'. There will be debate about whether the woman would or wouldn't sacrifice herself and child, and perhaps at the end, when the poet's ending has been provided – whether she was credible, and whether she did right. Such debates would lead on to a beginning of criticism.

1.5   Reading as expectation and recognition: context, quotation and reference

'Once there was a little rabbit. Now look how many there are.' This joke depends on its second section debunking the expectation set up by the first sentence – the expectation that an anecdote will follow the opening statement. We expect an anecdote because of all the other anecdotes we have heard which begin with that form of words.

Yet the anecdotal expectation is not fixed by the words themselves. There are literal meanings inherent in the words which do allow that meaning surprisingly taken up by 'Now look how many there are.' So, with hindsight: 'Once' could be taken quite literally as 'at one historical moment' (rather than 'in an indefinite story-time we are inventing for the sake of sharing a story about a rabbit') and 'a' could mean either 'only one rabbit' (as in the joke), or the rabbit we are about to focus on for the sake of this story (as we expect) – even the indefinite article is ambiguous, versatile and dependent on context for meaning.

The opening form of words is part of a convention which leads readers or hearers to know what sort of text and meanings will follow it. And also to know what meanings to ascribe to the words within the formulation. Such formulations are parts of a code which define genres, for those who can recognize those formulations of words and their usual provenances. Fry (1985: 45–6) shows an inexperienced reader being thrown by a tricksy opening which confounds the reader's expectations. To work – to create the correct anticipations and expectations and 'mental set' in its implied readers – that little formula 'Once' needs readers who have read or heard many other stories beginning like that and who therefore share the convention of reading 'once' as the beginning of a story.

Readings of stories depend for their meaning on previous readings of other texts, especially stories. People only begin stories with 'Once' because they know that a story is the sort of text which that formula usually introduces. So someone who had never heard a 'Once' story would not find the opening of this section funny, because the first sentence would not have created an expectation to be debunked by the second.

In a bar, 'Once there was a little rabbit' would lead us to expect a dirty joke. In a classroom a sentimental tale. In a church, a parable. Bars, classrooms and churches provide different 'interpretative communities'. But what about in a scientific lecture or monograph – especially if we knew that the title was *The spread of lapine dwarfisms from chance genetic mutation in a single individual – a case-study*? Is Tess's story a love story, a parable, a social critique or a palatable treatment of the socio-economic consequences of agricultural mechanization? It depends on the social context. (And that dependence has classroom implications. What will having the book given out in school tell the recipients about the contents of the text? How does having a text provided on a duplicated sheet influence their approach to it? But here I want to confine myself to the expectations created in readers by the text, rather than by social contexts.)

Students reflecting on the contexts of their readings

Many students' recognitions in a text are teetering on the brink of becoming active because they have done just enough reading of comparable texts to recognize clues, but not enough to take for granted some of the things their teachers take for granted (such as that a play beginning in the way that *A Midsummer Night's Dream* begins will be a comedy or that Jane Eyre is an unreliable narrator of the events of *Jane Eyre*).

What have cover illustrations and titles told them? Do they recognize some books as items in series and approach them accordingly, as they did when they collected Enid Blyton books? Do they ever bother to look at the date or place of publication and take that into account (as I learned to do when I was shocked by what seemed an anti-British – at least anti-Redcoat – historical adventure sent to me as a boy by an ex-neighbour who'd emigrated to Canada)? What differences does it make to their reading whether or not the text is illustrated? How do illustrations influence their approach to words?

And when we come to the words, how are their meaning-makings successively modified by what they assume, anticipate, and remember? Our Brecht begins 'In an olden time . . .' – ah! – '. . . in a bloody time . . .' – oh! The possible generic function of 'Alabama' in 'Owl Creek' was alluded to on the first page of this chapter. The function of the opening of 'Spit Nolan' will be dismembered in a later chapter. For now, let's look more closely at *Spain, 1809* (see Appendix) and see what secondary students might do with it.

Some of the phenomenology of reading the opening line will be discussed in the section on 'showing and telling'. But suppose the line had been read aloud:

All day we had ridden through scarred, tawny hills.

Would it be recognized as verse? If not, what sort of story might it introduce? A Western, a travel memoir, a traveller's tall tale? Would it matter whether or not you met the story in school in a sombre hardback, or out of school in a garish paperback?

Does it make any difference to know the author – Hank Janson, Paul Theroux, Graham Greene, Sandy Gall, a class-mate, or anon? Or someone you've never heard of called Dick Burke, Anthony Julian Grenfell, or José Ribera? Does the gender of the author make a difference to expectation? And what about the effect of the title? Do the words of the line read different ways – do they not connote and even denote different meanings – according to whether they are preceded by 'BLAZING GUNS!', *Spain, 1809*; AFGHAN REBELS FIGHT ON! *from our own correspondent*; 'A Martini refreshes you worldwide'? By 'Are you sitting comfortably?', by 'Something like that happened to me once', or by nothing?

Moving into the text, words like 'mills', 'mule', 'San Pedro', 'convoys', 'ambushed' will begin to set up a rich network of associations for most young readers, and add a set of competing provenances and geographies to the enigma of the title: all material for an 'interplay between modified expectations and transformed memories', or for a flattering historico-geographical displacement of some reprehensible wish-fulfilment, or for an experience of contradiction and uncertainty which is part of a literary reading, to read with Iser, Holland, or Fish, respectively. Putting these suggestions into operation in the classroom clearly relates to many of the notions of response theory.

Expectations of a text are created in a reader by interactions between previous readings and elements which the reader recognizes in the present text – like 'San Pedro' being a likely (probably Mexican) site for some heroic violence. In a wide sense, or some extreme cases, these recognitions are 'quotations'. The notion that each text presents a reader with a unique web of quotations from other texts is related to the literary theoretical concept of 'intertextuality' though the literary theoretical proponents of the concept use it in a more technical sense than I do here (see, for instance, Kristeva 1980: 15). The term will be useful in discussing the cultural contexts of narrative reading in Chapter 4. From now on, I shall use it for the nature of texts, and the perception of texts, as collages of references to other texts, not just overtly (like Fuentes' references to Bierce in his *The Old Gringo*, 1988), but by the very nature of using words and phrases used before. And I shall begin to expand the use of the word text, as do some theorists, to include not only non-literary texts such as newspapers, but even non-verbal artefacts such as pictures, and even, at an extreme for which there are precedents, such artefacts as life!

Here's an illustration.

Reading from recognitions of quotations from a personal reading history

A little narrative poem by my colleague Eric Turnbull has been under my skin:

> Daedalus and Son
> pioneers of man-powered flight
> have gone
> into liquidation.

The last line, apart from being an apt dissolving of the spidery sounds of the foregoing, provides the clue for why Icarus is, by name at least, missing. 'Into liquidation' means drowned (or swimming, or commemorated in an eponymous sea). And it is also, like the appellation 'and Son' (with a capital) a phrase from the domain of business.

The poem, to help us get the joke in this pun, is called *Business News*. To appreciate the joke of describing Daedalus' Son as 'liquidated' you need to know some of the vocabulary of business, such as that 'Business News' might be a standard title for a subdivision of a newscast or newspaper supplement. In other words, you need some of the cultural knowledge of an English-speaking, late-twentieth-century Westerner.

Such knowledge will also help you with the resonances of 'pioneers of man-powered flight', so that Daedalus and Icarus are seen as fellows of the Wright Brothers and other instigators of our technological, boundary-pushing, capitalist, masculinist society.

And then, of course, you need to know who Daedalus and Icarus were. Most teachers do, if only from having classical myths told as stories in their own school-days. And, despite philippics about the decline of classical education, many contemporary schoolchildren will remember them, with prompting, from Ladybird books or BBC broadcasts. They may also be familiar with the names from knowing the genre of hi-tec thriller which, since *The Andromeda Principle* or something like that (maybe the Oedipus Complex started the fashion!) has used titles generated by combining a classical name with a technical word: as *The Hyperion Factor*, *The Icarus Syndrome*, or *The Daedalus Hypothesis*.

So far, so cultural. I've expounded the ways I think the poem depends on general knowledge from other readings to make its meaning.

When I think about my own idiosyncratic responses I find that as well as that general cultural network of references, a quite individual history of knowledge, interest and reading which I have built up over years is brought to bear on this modest text and helps to create and explain its fascination and richness for me. At its most idiosyncratic: 'pioneer' evokes an early pre-literate trauma in being taken to what I thought was called the Iron Ear Hospital (though I now suspect it may have been the 'Eye and Ear'). For a war-baby like me, too, 'pioneer' is redolent of troops who dig trenches and embankments – thus hinting how an aspirant to the element of air originated in the element of earth before the elements of fire and water did for him. (If you pointed out that only Icarus drowned, I'd reply that only the 'Son' is rhymed with 'gone', but that Daedalus also went 'into liquidation' in the sense that he flew on weeping, as the myth tells us!)

One of the sources of the meaning in anyone's reading of anything is their previous reading. Every word of every text signifies only by virtue of the reader having experienced its use somewhere else. In a sense, every word must be experienced as a quotation in order for it to signify, a phenomenon which can be particularly frustrating in would-be sincere verbal love-making. I make a meaning out of *Business News* because I have read and heard the myth of Icarus and read or seen examples of 'Business news' in newspapers. But also because I've read other poems about *hubris*, falls and liquidations. When I first read *Business News* I already knew Auden's and Carlos Williams' poems about the fall of Icarus. I was reminded by Icarus' liquidation of Shakespeare's 'Full fathom five . . .' Also of Milton's *Lycidas*, though I knew that not so much directly as via Norman MacCaig's reference to it in his *Sea Change*, a poem which also resonated into my reading of *Business News*.

These other readings of other texts constitute the 'intertextuality' of my reading of *Business News*. For other readers the intertextuality would be different according to their other reading histories. So their readings of the text would be different, according to the different references and their relative saliences which contributed to the readings. Another reader has told me that she immediately thought of Stevie Smith's *Not Waving But Drowning* when she read *Business News*. Others may think of Lucifer or Gibreel. To refer to considerations raised elsewhere in the book, who you are and what you've read and experienced would determine which binarities or associated ideologies you'd find first in the poem. For any reader, a reading is like a body in space distorted by the far or near presences and movements of other bodies which provide its gravity and determine its shape and trajectory.

Responding to this poem perhaps provides a good example of why literary theorists often use 'text' to mean more than words. For me, *Business News* generates images. Breughel's 'Icarus' and its hubristic galleon; Millais' liqui-dated 'Ophelia'; Hockney's 'Splash'; frogmen. My rapid move into reminders of images may be because, compared to most people, I think I have a relatively sensitive eye but coarse ear (so that, for instance, compared to other people of the same overall knowledge and experience of a foreign language I am good at reading it but poor at understanding it spoken). However, I cannot imagine any reader not visualizing while reading this poem, even though the soonness, salience and 'vocabulary' of your images may not be mine.

My visual sensitivity but aural insensitivity may extend to my personal responding to the words of the poem and the subconscious associations they provoke. So the four occurrences of the diagraph 'on' work powerfully on me in this poem of exploration, even though they are buried in different sound-clusters and pronunciations. Similarly, I was immediately sensitive to the sight of letters on the page and their potential rearrangements into new but associated meanings which are not embodied in the sounds they make in the original. 'Daedalus' signals 'dead' to me and I spot 'sand' and 'sea' in the letters of that first line at once; 'maps', 'fire', 'light' and 'remains' announce themselves to me in line two; and 'into liquidation' even signals its near-anagram of 'laid on a tidal quilt'! If you protested that this is far-fetched, I'd reply that our responses to poetry do go far, and deep, and act at an unconscious level. Also that only the reader is an authority on his/her own, idiosyncratic response.

Some puns which depend on sound do work in my response, too. When I did a 'total doodle' for my first exploration (see Figure 1) the sun featured prominently (though of course it is Icarus' destroyer as much as a homophone of 'Son'). More significantly I picked on a suggestion of 'Anson' in 'and Son', because I knew Anson was a sea-going explorer and also that there was a Second World War aircraft of that name (I was obsessed by aircraft as a child).

Another very particular response may be the one I had to the recurrent trigraph '-ion'. Where someone with a classical education may have picked up the 'Io' in this and related the Daedalus myth to the myth of Io (of which I know nothing), I – on the evidence of my doodle – related 'ion' to the ionosphere which Icarus approached too nearly and we now know, with current science, is responsible for quasi-magical radio which, like myth and flight, communicates over distances.

This flickering from word to word is a small-scale version of the passing on of references from one text to a previously read one (where it may itself have signified by referring to an even earlier reading, and so on). It gives some idea of

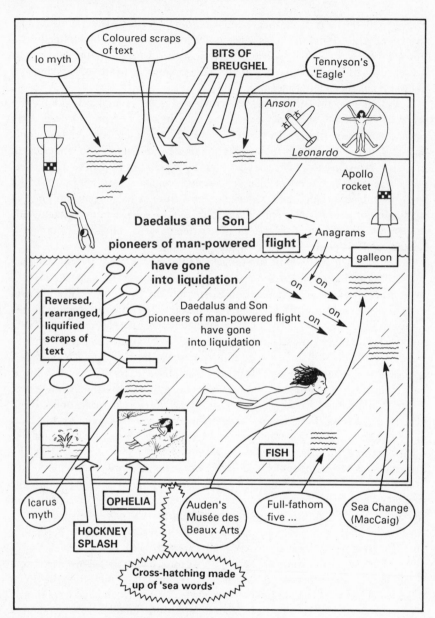

Figure 1   Total doodle of *Business News*

what radical deconstructionists like Derrida mean by saying that meaning-taking is always postponed because every signifier (e.g. 'mills') refers to other signifiers (e.g. Blake's dark satanic or Brighouse's Black Dyke) rather than a signified (i.e. the ?corn mills in San Pedro). So literature, say the radicals, can only be about other literature and never life. In writing what follows I have been struck by the degree to which the illustrative texts I chose for their mutual differences have begun to resonate with each other in my second readings of them: unsuspected common themes (like exposure of family secrets), events (hangings) and even little details (black gloves, bridges) have started to show up.

Applications

I've tried to tease out some factors in my own response to this poem as an illustration of one particular reader's creative reconstruction of a text and how that meaning-making depends on the text activating certain literary references, both predictable and unpredictable, in the reader. This cultural knowledge may act not just to make detail explicable but also to structure the reading experience, as when readers who know about Bluebeard will have a sense of direction and foreboding when they read of Jane Eyre's first sight of the upper floors of Thornfield (Chapter 11). The influence of this sort if intertextuality is added to the response model in Figure C.

There are implications in such an analysis for teachers. First, it acts as a reminder of our dependence on cultural knowledge in order to read at all. Pupils may have less of our cultural knowledge (e.g. the Bible, Greek myths or the personalities and geography of the Second World War) than we assume. On the other hand, pupils may have lots of cultural knowledge which they can deploy in their reading which we haven't (relevantly to *Business News* – of Superman and other flying heroes, perhaps?). For some readers it will be *Black Beauty*'s Chapters 3 and 13 which illuminate Chapter 9 of *Women in Love*. For Joanne in Fry (1985: 85–6) the intertextuality of *Lord of the Flies* included Blyton and two recent TV documentaries. It's unlikely to have included *Coral Island*.

Second, the illustration shows how teachers cannot predict exactly how any student will respond to any story. Third, the importance of encouraging wide reading is as obvious as studies like those of Fader and McNeil (1969) and Ingham (1982) have shown. How it can be promoted in English classes is demonstrated by Brown (in Corcoran and Evans 1987). Previous readings construct present readings (and the extremists would say our previous readings are all we can read about). A work of literature read in isolation would be nonsensical and meaningless. Wide reading is not only an alternative to close reading: it is an enhancer, an enabler and an essential, of close reading.

Here's one suggestion for a practical application. To explore my response to *Business News*, I placed the text in the middle of a large sheet of paper. Then I got to work ringing, boxing, colouring, annotating and generally defacing the text in

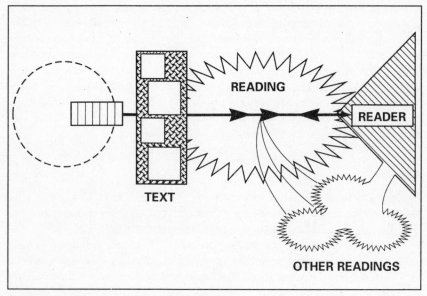

Figure C   Reading a text through other readings

the best traditions of DARTs. Then I went collecting copies of other poems and pictures to stick around the edges and supplement my marginal drawings and medieval-type illuminations. In the end I had a display which was a cross between a doodle and a collage and made an effective non-linear display of all my responses to the text and possibly (as Eric Turnbull pointed out to me) responses to my responses (Derridean postponement in reverse?) and certainly it would be hard to disentangle the initial responses which the display represented and new responses generated in the course of making the display (see Figure 1).

Benton and Fox (1985) justify doodling as a means to develop response to literature in schools (p. 119). I certainly find this sort of free-association doodling and collaging useful. It provokes a deployment of other readings of other texts into an intertextual reading of the target text. At the same time it does provoke a closer reading of the target text, if only for the low reason of offering the vainglorious a challenge to find further- and further-fetched references and fill more and more of the margins. And if extended free association begins to lead to centrifugal responses so much the better for making the reader self-conscious about reading processes and linking reading with thinking, seeing, feeling, dreaming and – dare one say? – living.

1.6   Reading-time and reading Time

Fiction does not hesitate to accelerate time, to slow it down, project it forward or run it backward, cause it to skip over itself or repeat itself; it can freeze an action in the middle of its performance. I can expand a single moment like the skin of a balloon or bite off a life like a thread.

(Welty 1987: 166)

A literary reading is a mental experience. It takes place within a certain period – an all-night sitting, twelve consecutive English lessons, half an hour a day on the bus for a fortnight, or whatever. The inability to specify the circumstances of a reading is another reason for insisting on the individuality of reading.

A text, on the other hand, is an object. So, in Figure D, the response model set in time, the text has been represented vertically. Like a musical score, it exists in space, not time, waiting to be 'played'. But it does relate to temporal sequences: two different ones set horizontally. An exploration of these two relationships, implicit in an intelligently responsive reading, will serve as a link to Chapter 2 which explores the relationships and structures inherent in texts.

First, just as a score guides a musical performance – an accurate, interpretative or critical performance – so a text acts as a template to a reading. The spatial arrangement of the text influences the temporal arrangement of the way it is played. Conventional texts have a sequence (left to right, top to bottom, in English) which suggests a sequence (in time) for their readings once it has been realized that it's a narrative and not a recipe book, directory, map, concrete poem, or Arabic scripture. Chapter divisions suggest segmentations of the reading in time; the bottom right corner of the last page suggests an end to the reading. So although you can scan texts backwards, read alternate pages, or at random, or read exactly ten pages a day starting and finishing at page corners in mid-sentence, those are uncommon styles and usually we allow our readings to be subjected to the same manipulations of time which Eudora Welty ascribes to the text in the head-quotation. (However, the reading illustrated in the simplified diagram of these transformations of chronology in Figure 2A includes a very common quirk of reading: the reader has read the end (D) before the beginning, perhaps to see who is going to have done it.)

Spatial arrangements in text don't correspond only to time in a reading: the sequence in which items in the setting are described can structure a reader's visualizing, expectations and interpretations – at the start of 'Owl Creek' for instance, or in Hardy's zooming in on the reapers in Chapter 14 of *Tess*.

If the text is a story, it also refers to a second sort of temporal sequence: the sequence of events in the story as they would have happened in history if the story were true – in what I shall call 'history-time'. (There is a musical analogy only if it is 'programme music'.)

Text misrepresents experience and events in historical time both by pressing them into a space and by separating the single. Although in one sense text makes events in history simultaneous by putting them into a single spatial text, in another sense it must separate and space out elements of single experiences and events when it tries to describe them, because in history – in 'real' time – many

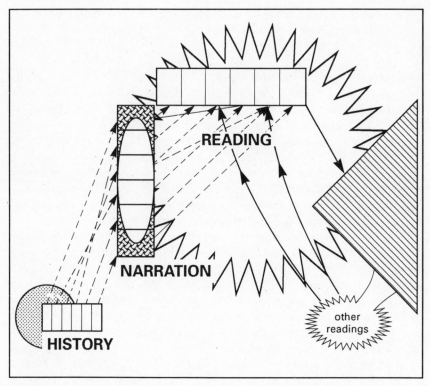

Figure D   Making a reading experience in time from a narrative text in space

complex experiences and events are single. So things which are simultaneous in reality are separated and sequenced when they are represented in text. This is because text is made up of words which unnaturally conceptualize inseparable aspects of synaesthetic experience as separate, sequenced, words. In 'Owl Creek', Farquhar's 'looking' comes a line below his 'standing', but in history both were simultaneous. In the *Black Jack* passage, the 'who said' information of tags would come simultaneously with the 'what said' of quotations, not before or after according to whether the tags act forward or backward. And in *Spain, 1809* the hills are 'scarred' at the same time as they are 'tawny', or indeed that they are 'hills'.

What are the relationships between these three times – the reading-time in which all the mental processes in the act of reading take place (the visualizations, reconsiderings, rememberings, recognizings and so on), the narrative 'time' (which is really space), and the history-time in which it is implied the events of the story take place?

I shall consider two features of these different times – sequence and duration.

These, along with iteration, are explored and illustrated with examples from *Tom Sawyer* in Griffith (1987: 15–18). Definitive and exhaustive treatments of these, as of the 'viewpoint' and modalities ('showing and telling') are in Genette (1980) and Chatman (1978) which provide classifications of the features of the way narrative works. I shall simplify these classifications and change their terminology, and – since Genette uses Proust for his illustrations – use our own examples.

Sequence

> A novel with a straightforward chronological organisation is likely to be less demanding than one which makes use of flashbacks (this is one reason why young readers generally find *Jane Eyre* easier than *Wuthering Heights*, for example).
>
> (Cox 1989: 7, 17)

Most educated readings produce a chronology of events structured by the textual, narrative sequence, though modified by the anticipations and reconsiderations which characterize active reading. In all but the simplest tales (and Fry 1985 suggests part of Blyton's appeal might be her 'adherence to a continuous one-track narrative line', p. 49), the sequence of events in history-time is not the same as the sequence of references to them, in the text. In an extreme case, Pinter's *Betrayal* of 1978 (Pinter 1981) narrates events in the opposite order of their occurrence.

It's thought-provoking to represent these differences visually (Figure 2A does so generally and Figure 8 – section 5.2 – does it for 'Spit Nolan').

Despite what I said in 1.4 about sequencing *Frankie and Johnny*, it is also sometimes necessary to help confused readers with sequence in stories, plots and reading-experience. In my experience the chronology of *Kes* can cause problems for otherwise keen readers, and constructing a time-line which reveals that its events are those of one-day-plus-memories surprises and helps them. I'd contend that for students to explicate their readings of chronology and to explicate the processes by which they make the decisions, would help them to read texts more difficult than those we commonly read in school and to read by themselves texts as confusing as those we help them with in school. Discussing what is lost or gained by reading in different sequences will also help them appreciate the literary reasons for narratives not always corresponding in sequence to the sequence of events in history-time. (To create an enigma is one obvious reason, for instance.)

The commonest differences between narrative and history is the use in narrative of those flashbacks referred to in the Cox quotation. In Figure 2A, segment A is a flashback. The commonest flashbacks are probably those which provide a brief history for a newly introduced character. Anna Sewell uses the tellings of their early experiences by Ginger, Peggy and Captain to show the range of things that can happen to horses. We, like her, get Jane Eyre's family

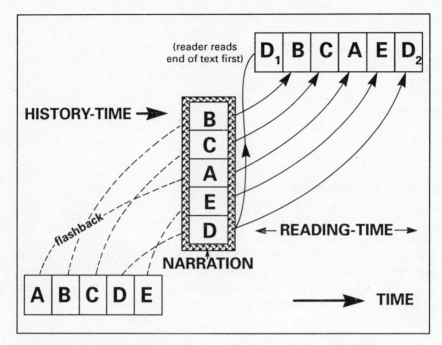

Figure 2A Transformations between events, narration, and reading: sequence

background from Bessie (Chapter 3), or Adela's from Mrs Fairfax (Chapter 11). Despite the justice of Cox's comparison between *Jane Eyre* and *Wuthering Heights*, *Jane Eyre* does use many flashbacks. Rochester's sensational early life, for instance, is fed into the mainstream of his acquaintance with Jane at regular intervals in each of which we take a brief trip up the tributary to its source in long-gone Paris or Jamaica, or wherever (e.g. the Varens affair, Chapter 15 or the first marriage, Chapter 27). The information comes to us after its time, like floods from distant springs.

The events of *Spain, 1809* take place in one night. The first line describes the soldiers travelling to the village on the day before the night's events.

All day we had ridden through scarred, tawny hills.

The next item in the narrative marks the arrival.

At last the cool
Of splashing water.

So far, so corresponding in sequence to history-time. But in the next stanza we are taken back to an event before the journey and the arrival.

(Two convoys ambushed in the gorge below.
They had to learn.)

And in the next stanza: 'They had been wise.'

Those are explanatory flashbacks to events before the 'main' events of the poem. It is as well for a reader to understand that they are flashbacks if they are to realize their import. Not all students do so unaided. Later in the narrative of the poem there are flashbacked hints to earlier events within the history-time of earlier main events narrated in the poem. An explicit one is

> I never loved their wine,
> Had tasted none.

Flashforwards are also common enough in literary texts. In *Jane Eyre* we get Georgiana's and Eliza's fate cleared up in a flashforward from the history-time of the narrative's events to the present history-time in which Jane purports to narrate her story (Chapter 22). With myths, stories evolved in cultures which believed in predestination and now recycled in cultures which know how they end, flashforwards may be explicit: some, like Oedipus, depend on prophecies. A knowing reader of *Business News* will mentally flash forward to Icarus' fate at the mention of his father in the first word. In more modern stories, especially in genres such as thrillers or detective stories, flashforwards may be more allusive and elusive, deliberately placed in the narrative to create suspense and enigmas and keep the reader's interest. A reader who misses these will make an impoverished reading of such a text. (A withholding of an expected flashback can also create an enigma – as with Rochester's marriage, suppressed until the altar rail.) A weak case of flashforward is the sort of 'time-bomb' detail which only assumes significance in retrospect. In *Spain, 1809* the 'death's-head hovels' may not have been so 'blind' as they appeared at first sight to both narrator and reader.

The last two lines of *Spain, 1809* create a difficulty.

> But I remember one pale woman's face
> In San Pedro.

Here the intrusion of the present tense could justify you calling this the single main event of the poem, and designating all the foregoing as flashback with flashbacks-in-flashback and flashforwards-in-flashback. This would be like saying the main – the one – event in *Jane Eyre* is Jane's narrating her story and the story is just an embedded flashback. In *Spain, 1809* it's easier to treat the reprisal raid, the poisoning and the consequent massacre as the main events and the intrusive ending as a flashforward (containing – since it's 'I remember' – a flashback!).

At a second reading, we know the narrator is a survivor remembering, so the second reading must have some of the quality of 'I remember how all day we had . . .', thus putting the event which comes last in the text and the history-time (the remembering) first in the reading-time of a second reading. Any diagram of a *second* reading ought to arrow the last part of the narration to the first part of the reading-time. *Spain, 1809* is a poem, and most poems deserve, and get, repeated readings. So the processes of anticipation and re-ordering which have been suggested by response theorists will be secured here and the sequence in reading-time may gradually align with that of history-time rather than narration. You can never read the same text twice: intertextuality ensures that. In my experience, repeated reading is necessary with this poem. Students are engaged by the horrific and heroic themes in the poem but confused about what happened, literally, in the history-time implied by the text. They enjoy sorting that out by re-reading, discussing, diagramming and writing.

How do they recognize flashbacks and flashforwards? Tense is one indicator: 'we had ridden', 'I had tasted none', 'I remember'. Time phrases are also indicators, though there are none to indicate flashes back or forwards in *Spain, 1809*. And then there is a sense of what sequences of events make a 'story', a sense which will be referred to in the next chapter on narratology, and which is developed through wide reading and secured by explication and discussion.

Duration

> By the way, I think I should mention that all of this (I mean all of Bit 37) took no more than ten seconds, which only goes to show how much faster real life can happen than reading about it (or, worse still, writing about it . . .)
>
> (Chambers 1982: 146)

A second way that there are differences in time between readings, texts and events is in their speed and duration. If you exclude the remembering, *Spain, 1809*, like Joyce's *Ulysses*, covers the events of about 24 hours. Unlike *Ulysses*, the text of *Spain, 1809* can be read in five minutes. But, like that of *Ulysses*, its text occupies no time at all – only space.

Within a whole reading, the duration of different parts can differ very much from the duration of the events they evoke, especially if you allow for a particular reader's skimming, dwelling, re-reading, backtracking and so on. 'Jane Eyre', the narrator of *Jane Eyre*, is explicit about this in Chapter 10: 'Hitherto I have recorded in detail . . . I now pass a space of eight years almost in silence' (p. 115). Part I of 'Owl Creek' occupies four sides in the edition I use and takes a few minutes to read silently or ten or so to read aloud. (I had my class calibrate these times and discuss their significance.) Yet it describes a scene which 'takes' no time at all (or could be scanned and 'taken in' in a few seconds) plus events which take only a few seconds (a stepping-aside, a salute, a look, a hearing the watch, and a thought). Part II flashes back to describe the events of some weeks in the time it takes to read two pages. Part III describes at length events which at first seem to occupy a day of history but, with hindsight, an instant. Maybe the slowing down of the ticking of the watch in Part I would have alerted you to the fact that soon Farquhar would be swinging like a pendulum in clock-time. In Figure 2B, the segment B is a description which takes up no history-time, a lot of text-space,

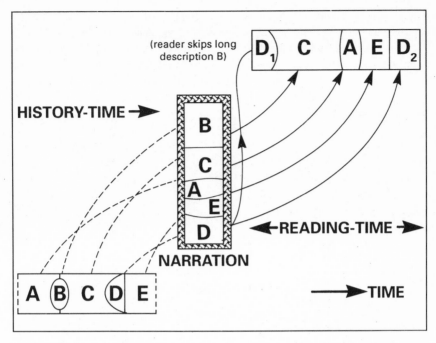

(reader skips long description B)

HISTORY-TIME ➔

READING-TIME ➔

NARRATION

➔ TIME

Figure 2B   Transformations between events, narration, and reading: duration

and is skipped by a reader who doesn't like descriptions. Segments A and E extend into a distant past and up to the present, respectively.

Whereas dialogue usually takes up about as much reading-time as history-time (at least in a reading-aloud), flashbacks are characteristically much more compressed. That will be one support for my using dialogue and flashback as relatively uncontentious examples of 'showing' and 'telling', respectively, in section 3.3. *Spain, 1809* uses only two words to get through the 'All day' during which they *had* ridden.

What is the effect of taking up the time it takes to read a page to experience the brief race between Spit Nolan and Leslie Duckett when Spit's earlier sojourn in Southport Sanatorium is conveyed in less? What is the effect of taking longer to read how the charabanc hits Spit than it would take for that to happen in 'real life'? Such questions are specially interesting when we consider (as in section 3.1) the effects of transferring quasi-historical events in their history-time from one narrative medium (print) to another (film). How can text deal with instantaneous events (Spit's collision or Farquhar's death) or non-events (the scene at the bridge) compared to film? How can time-based narrative like that of film allow the reader chances to track back, flash back, pause, re-model memory and so on, as readers do in a reading-experience? How far should teachers use their awareness of complexity in the representation of time when assessing the comprehensibility and intelligibility of texts for inexperienced readers?

A third aspect of time in narrative which Genette examines is frequency. By definition an event occurs only once in history-time, but a reader may replay it often, and a text may narrate it more than once – from different viewpoints or by a narrator at first innocent but later knowing. (Prompted by the text we experience from Rochester's point of view events we earlier saw only from Jane's.) Frequency (and Genette discusses many varieties other than the one-event-narrated-many-times variety) becomes an interesting topic in considering many sophisticated modern novels (e.g. of Conrad, Durrell, Robbe-Grillet) but it is not so important in many novels read in schools.

Types of time and reading-time

Bakhtin (1981) suggests the very nature of represented time can differ in genres from different periods and societies. So, using our examples and extending beyond Bakhtin's thesis, *Business News* uses anachronisms with mythical figures to set a matter of recent public knowledge (bankruptcy and manned flight) into a universal time where universal truths operate. The time of *The Caucasian Chalk Circle* is a historical time where individual events illustrate military and political events in epic episodes. In *Black Beauty* and *Jane Eyre*, the focus is on the individual's personal – even inner – life (a concept improper in epic and unthinkable in myth), so the time is biographical. The span of biographical time is a life and the cruces are personal events (birth, leaving home, marriage, etc.), whereas in epic time the span would be a war or a dynasty, an age, perhaps, like the Golden Age that Azdak's reign almost was: the cruces would be political ones like revolutions. You could have a folk time, too, distinguished by being cyclical, like the seasons and the agricultural calendar. I would venture that the three interpreters of *A Midsummer Night's Dream* discussed in section 4.2 would set that play's narrative in an agricultural time (Kott), a psychological time (Girard) and a historical time (Eagleton).

Bakhtin (1981) also suggests (pp. 146–51) that the progression of events represented in a narrative may betray a sense of time in a metaphysical context. In Arcadian literature, time looks backwards or a life is in a continual decay from paradise, as is the case in *Black Beauty* or 'Spit Nolan'. In Utopian or millenial literature, time looks forward to a fulfilled potential, to progress, or to some climax, as does *Jane Eyre* or *A Midsummer Night's Dream* (you may choose to which goal the play aspires according to your own taste or Kott's or Girard's or Eagleton's and debate whether in this respect it differs from the similarly shaped *As You Like It* where the forest – being English rather than Greek? – is Arcadian). Kermode (1966) says 'there must be a link between the forms of literature and other ways in which, to quote Erich Auerbach, "We try to give some kind of order and design to the past, the present and the future"' (p. 93).

Reading about time

Those are public, cultural types of time. But there is also a private, personal sense of time which is specially strong in children who are bound in the present, orientated towards the future and struggling to come to terms with the past, especially their own past which they can often get at only through other people's memories and stories. Literature for children has a special responsibility to embody the textures of that sort of existential time-experience.

Meek (in Meek and Miller 1984) discusses how children learn about time, about succession, duration and simultaneity. Learning about time starts with their language development and with their negotiation of the confusing vocabulary of common talk about time: (clock-time which is 'told'; times as the separate recurrences of 'how many times have I told you . . .'; the times which barely prompt events happen 'just in'; times how many of which things have happened; 'time' which is wasted – or, in my childhood, was saved by the confusingly metaphorical 'looking sharp').

In demonstrating the intertextuality of children's story-making she shows how their stories include two pasts – the past of the events narrated and the past of the time they heard them narrated by someone else. She suggests that children's writers (and illustrators) take the opportunity which their readers' inexperience offers to them to create alternative times in their narratives, such as dream-time and fantasy-time.

She shows how Philippa Pearce, in her two great novels *Tom's Midnight Garden* of 1958 and the later *The Way to Sattin Shore* of 1983, uses experience-imitating narration, flashback, tense-change and all the rich vocabulary of time in everyday speech to explore a child's developing consciousness of times past, present and future. So, in the latter, we have Kate's immediate phenomenological experience and we see how Kate learns how to use her own and others' memories to discover the past so that she can face the future.

In that text, time with its different meanings and textures becomes a subject as well as a medium for the narrative. Meek makes it seem a Proust for juveniles.

2 Interpreting a text

Introduction

> The attraction of tales lies in their capacity to present a reality that human beings *can* bear: to paper over the cracks, resolve, explain and make coherent the contradictions.
>
> (Hawkes 1986: 21)

In the last chapter, it was suggested that theories centred on the reading and reader of literary narrative should have a special interest for literature teachers because they legitimate existing good practice. In this chapter I concentrate on what I call text-centred theories and suggest they may generate new classroom practices. I don't want to exaggerate the difference between these groups of theories (or between them and the culture-centred theories I discuss in Chapter 4). Iser's 'implied reader' is a feature of the text, the Practical and New Criticisms which fetishized the text stemmed from Richards' investigations of readers' responses, and the transformations of time which I discussed in the last chapter are clearly structural. Furthermore, the 'structures' which I discuss in this chapter are abstract, not physical, qualities of texts, and only operate when they are discerned by a reader. At the level of classwork, many of Protherough's admirably comprehensive and eclectic suggestions of activities for 'developing response' are, in my sense, text-centred. For instance, they include: charting plots; making purposive plot summaries; comparing characters; listing clues to denouements and characters; comparing films and novels; writing alternative endings (Protherough 1983: 185–98). Perhaps it's most useful to regard readers and texts as two poles of what Rosenblatt (1978) – writing of poetry – calls a 'transactional' model of reading.

However, it might be useful to align the qualified distinctions I make between the matter of my Chapters 1, 2 and 4, with Robert Scholes's categorization of literary teaching. He divides it into teaching reading; teaching interpretation; and teaching criticism (Scholes 1985: 21–4). Without committing myself to Scholes's

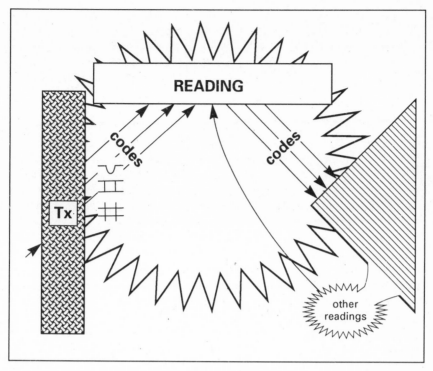

Figure E   Making meaning by reading through the codes

precise usages of these three terms, I'd say that the emphases of the practical applications of my three sections correspond to ones on: reading (in its wide sense of consciously and subconsciously apprehending clues in literary texts); interpretation (in the sense of consciously recognizing patterns and their significances); criticism (in the sense of actively evaluating the values discerned in attentive, interpretative reading).

The events which authors intend to convey to readers, and the events which responsive readers create in their work on literary texts, come in code. The reader has to decode and recode not just the language but also many abstract features of that language – cultural references, symbols, significant sequences and correspondences, absences, contrasts and so on.

Some signifying conventions are specialist codes confined to a particular work (like a pervasive metaphor), or to a particular writer (like a way of signalling direct speech), or to a current literary fashion, or they may be more general, in a genre, or common to narrative in a literary culture; it has even been argued that some of these signifying conventions are so pervasive that they are features of all human meaning-making.

These conventions are implicit in texts – from spellings of words to shapes of myths. For brevity I call them 'codes' (but not in a special sense such as Barthes 1970 uses – see Hawkes 1977: 116). They are placed on Figure E in a way which shows how texts are read through them. Figure E also shows how texts are written through these codes.

2.1   Storyshapes and summaries

When teachers read or discuss texts with pupils it is easy to forget that whereas the teachers – hopefully! – have read the texts before and know who's who and what happens, the students – by and large – have not and do not. In the terms of the last chapter, the students' readings have not had so much benefit from what Iser calls the search for consistency. The settings are more unfamiliar, the names more strange, the internal relationships more obscure, and the outcomes more surprising to inexperienced readers than their teachers ever remember them being. A pupil once explained that he assumed Hamlet – whom he knew to be a character in a Shakespeare play he had not seen or read – was a woman. Never having come across the name elsewhere and going on the only other name ending in '-et' which he knew – also from a Shakespeare play – Hamlet would be the same sex as Juliet.

Furthermore, young readers need – perhaps more than we need – the security of knowing what's going on in a narrative. They need to know the genre, to know who's important and who's not, what category characters belong to (male or female; goody or baddy; low-born or high-born); where they've gone when they're off-stage or off-page. This is a primitive version of what I mean by 'interpreting' the text – a discerning, or inferring, of more than is on the passing surface of a stream of words. (If you are keen to secure pupils' knowledge of the names of the characters in *A Midsummer Night's Dream* and to which groups they belong you can make the characters into cards in a 'Happy Families' type game and make the objective to be the first one to secure full sets of Lovers, Workmen, or whatever with no spares. Puck would be the joker, the odd card – the card about which you can lie, and which you can pass on instead of another card for which you've been asked. Possessing the Puck would prevent you declaring yourself the winner.

Another way we could help students get the events and characters of *A Midsummer Night's Dream* under their control is by using one or both of the following procedures. (Although my suggestions would help to secure a knowledge of the action, I am not proposing them as initial activities. Where response-based activities are often of most use for first readings, text-centred activities are often best for the reflections and analyses – the interpretations – that go with re-readings.) Both of these depend on some prior knowledge of the play obtained some other way, such as a read-through or reading a prose-retelling at the very least, though one would hope that no students would any longer begin to read a Shakespeare text, however playfully, before they had seen a live or video performance. However, I have seen the chart-making which follows used by a mixed-ability fourth year as a progressive visual aid to chart the action as they read through the play in class.

First, imagine that you are required to produce a one-hour version of the play for some school festival with only ten actors: which scenes (maybe drastically cut) would you retain? Which characters (maybe with some doubling-up by actors) would you retain? Whom would you cast as whom (either from your class or from well-known TV stars supposing they were available)? And in each case what principles would guide your choices? This, of course, could be a real exercise with a workshop production as an outcome. It could also be developed to provoke other elements of understanding the structure of the story – for instance choosing colours or other features of costume to demarcate groups of characters.

3W diagrams

A second exercise is aimed at focusing pupils on the text in a purposive manner and helping them to grasp the overall structure of this baffling but prestigious artefact, a Shakespeare play. Groups, using their simplified versions of the plot and dramatis personae, construct '3W charts' (so-called because they show 'Who's Where When' – they are a sort of combination of mapping and time-lining). Figure 3A is a very simple 3W chart for *Spain, 1809*, and an overlap of the four lines in Figure 3B would be the basis for one for *A Midsummer Night's Dream*. Students find these charts difficult at first, but many find them useful when they are familiar with them. (It helps if they have practised both mapping and time-lining separately.) They enjoy being able to work on a text graphically and create something which, however coarsely, encapsulates the whole plot in one image.

An important part of designing these 3W charts is the choice of the symbols. Which characters can be aggregated so that one symbol can represent them? How will symbols be chosen so that they embody certain similarities or contrasts between what they symbolize, or can convey such changes in characters as temporary infatuation, invisibility, or asininity? Again, could the colouring of time-columns or place-rows be made significant, as an aid to discovering the functional importance of night-time, wilderness or weather? Would it be worth sticking in examples of other narrative items (e.g. confessions in a novel, or reversals of nature in Shakespeare)?

However, the primary purpose is to establish a visual representation of the plot as a 'storyshape' which distributes the characters within a space representing, in its vertical dimension, the setting of the purported events of the story, and, in its horizontal dimension, the history-time of the events in the sequence in which they are described. Other forms of diagramming are in Jackson (1983: 173–7) and Thomson (1987: 278–82), and examples of different ways in which

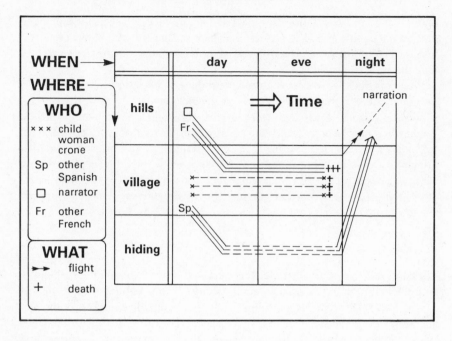

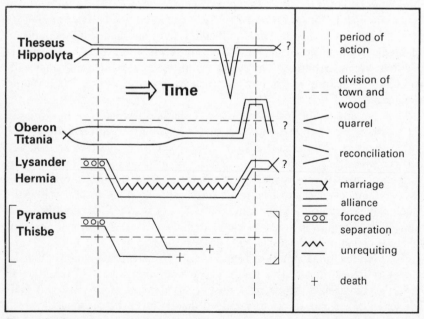

Figure 3   Storyshapes: (A) Simplified 3W diagram of *Spain, 1809*; (B) Storyshapes in *A Midsummer Night's Dream*

sixth-formers produced visual displays of their interests in *The Great Gatsby* are in section 5.4.

I have chosen a play for this example because in plays, certainly in *A Midsummer Night's Dream*, the sequence of events in narrative-time (the order of the events as they occur on the pages of a script or in order of enacting on the stage) usually corresponds to the order of the quasi-historical events they purport to represent, apart from a few flashbacks (though Azdak's and Grusha's stories overlap in *The Caucasian Chalk Circle*, as a 3W diagram will reveal). The sequence of events in novels, short stories and narrative poems is more likely to differ as between the history-time and the narration. However, 3W charts can be constructed for novels, and converting the narrative-sequence into history-sequence is a valuable exercise in drawing attention to this element in the constructedness of novels. From now on, I shall call the sequence of events in narration 'plot', and reserve 'story' for the sequence of the purported events in history-time which the plot narrates. The 3W diagrams I describe are of stories. In some cases it is possible and worth while to draw and compare the alternative 3W diagrams of stories and plots.

What storyshapes show

There is always a temptation to use drawing as a study-method in school, because students enjoy it and it produces decorative results. Not all forms of diagramming (such as many of those in Lunzer and Gardner 1984) are apt for studying literary narrative, but 3W diagrams, like storyboarding, accord with the nature of narrative. One feature of many of the narrative types popular in schools is the part played by coincidence of character, time and place in the mechanisms of certain sorts of adventures. This is not a problem in a myth or bourgeois *Bildungsroman*, but if servant girls are to meet princes, or shopgirls fall in love with tycoons, or all Estates and Orders of mortals and spirits are to get on stage together, then we have to enable characters from different worlds to intersect – on journeys, in wars, at conferences, or in jaunts to woods in order to elope, rehearse, or hunt. 3W charts show how that's done. They can also show how implausible coincidence and unlikely chance in narrative moves the meaning on – not just in Hardy but in narratives where trolleys lose control at a junction just as a charabanc is passing, a sex-maddened fairy queen wakes just as a donkey-headed weaver is standing by, a landowner falls off his horse as a governess approaches, and an adoptive mother has to swear the child is hers to save it from soldiers just as her long-lost fiancé turns up.

Looking forward to Chapter 4, the storyshapes which these 3W charts throw up can graphically reveal certain values and ideologies implicit in the text but not normally made obvious in a reading or viewing. Having to show where off-stage or off-page characters are can show up the powerlessness, passivity, or trophy-status of women, for instance. The parallels or differences between main plots and sub-plots can be politically or sociologically instructive. In the case of *A Midsummer Night's Dream*, the storyshape suggests how discord and mismatch are characteristic of the early, court-centred, part of the narration when the aristocracy, the plebs, and the immortals are busy about their separate and separated affairs. At the end of the narration, however, after the main characters from all three walks of life have been purged and educated by painful and magical experiences in the wood at night, harmonies are restored in the microcosm of the benevolent despot's court – a sort of Leavisite organic community where mutual marital agreement and contempt/respect across classes has replaced the despotism of the father and the duke, and the supernatural powers who had been hell-bent on inverting the old order now legitimize the new one with their final blessing.

Students could find particular messages from the storyshape of a 3W chart of *A Midsummer Night's Dream*: that you should run away from home to get your elder's attention but then return to enjoy their blessing, perhaps? More relevant at this stage are such formal parallels as those between the stories of the human and superhuman rulers (Theseus and Hippolyta; Oberon and Titania). In the terms of section 2.3, the horizontal relationships which tell their stories are themselves vertically related. Similarly for the lovers and for the story of Pyramus and Thisbe.

Students who prefer algebra to geometry could construct (or complete) a summary of the main development of each character's main relationship in the story at each of the four stages: the prequel; the start; the agon of Acts II and III; the reconciliations and marriages of Acts IV and V.

	Prequel	Start	Agon	Reconciliation
Ob:	+Tt.	−*Tt*	−*Tt*	+Tt
Tt:	+Ob.	−*Ob*	−*Ob*	+Ob
Th:	−*Hp.*	+Hp	+Hp	+Hp
Hp:	−*Th.*	+Th	+Th	+Th
Ly:	+Hm.	+Hm	+*Hl*	+Hm
Hm:	+Ly.	+Ly	+Ly	+Ly
Dm:	+Hl.	+*Hm*	+Hl	+*Hl*
Hl:	+Dm.	+Dm	+Dm	+Dm

These rows of symbols make clear that: the supernaturals' quarrel and reconciliation coincide with (and cause?) the start and finish of the lovers' instability; the royals set a good example by settling their quarrel early; the men lovers each change allegiance at sufficiently separate times to ensure they are rivals for long enough to liven up the action with a four-way quarrel; the women lovers are constant.

Drawing or symbolizing storyshapes, or other diagrams of relationships in

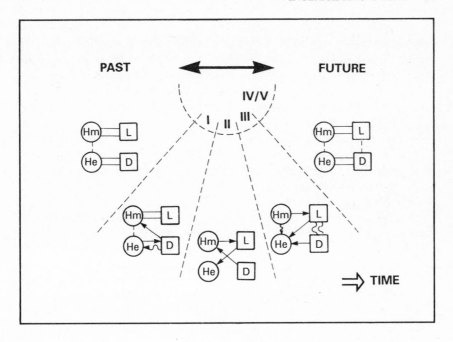

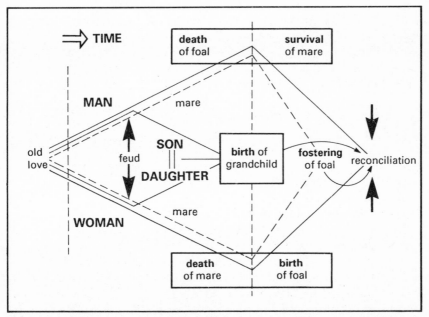

Figure 4 Diagramming relationships in stories: (A) Couplings and uncouplings in *A Midsummer Night's Dream*; (B) Fearful symmetry in *All Creatures Great and Small*

narratives, is to expose the abstract symmetries and correspondences which underlie the surfaces of narrative and constitute part of their universal appeal (see Figure 4A for the country-dance sequence of couplings and uncouplings of the lovers in *A Midsummer Night's Dream*). Such simple geometric structuring is not a feature of 'high art' only. To use symmetry as an example, a Saturday prime-time episode of a serial on a popular TV channel (*All Creatures Great and Small*, BBC1 21 October 1989) culminated in the resolution of a feud between two horse-breeders, once lovers. On the same night as the woman's daughter, married to the man's adoptive son, gave birth to a shared grandchild, her beloved mare died while giving birth to a foal which had to be fostered to the man's mare which that same night gave birth to a still-born foal (Figure 4B). Never be told that Shakespeare's plots are far-fetched!

Storyshapes which can be drawn to represent the action of the characters in these dramas relate to those of other narratives. Mapping the moves of *As You Like It*, in which social and sexual education is again represented by a running away to a forest with an alternative polity and conducted through misalliance, helps to expose underlying ideological values. Social, dynastic and sexual harmony is threatened in the over-sophistication of the machiavellian court of the usurping duke, not to be had on a long-term satisfactory basis in Arcadian slumming, but only in the suburban community of the One Nation High Tory legitimate duke.

Representing it graphically could help pupils to recognize the common features of works which more experienced readers than them have allocated to a single genre-category – namely early Shakespeare comedies.

Plot summaries

Words could do it too. If you were to set the challenge of representing the plot of a Shakespeare comedy in a brief statement, you might come up with one which, without the names, could apply to more than one work. Which comedy is this?

(A/a) low-**born**, **loves** (B/b), high-**born**, with whom (she/he) was **raised**.
The King **forces/thwarts** their **marrying**.
(B/a) **escapes/is banished** to Italy.
(A/b) **follows/is imprisoned**.
(B/a) **believes** (A/b) has **been betrayed/betrayed him** because of the **giving** of a ring.
(B/b) **meets** (A/a), disguised, whom [he]/who **believed** [had]/(she) **died**.
(B/b) **lies** with (A/c), who **loves** him/her, **believing** her/him to be (C/a) whom he/she **loves**.

Well, it could be *All's Well That Ends Well* (with A as Helena, B as Bertram, and C as Diana) or *Cymbeline* (with a as Posthumus, b as Imogen and c as Cloten), just showing that even dramatic narratives of different genres (an early 'comedy' and a late 'romance') have much in common.

If, further, the challenge (and it's one which schoolteachers could set to older and abler pupils) was to state the plot in only proper names and twenty words (which could be used more than once and in more than one inflection) the struggle to say as much as possible with as few words as possible might produce a verbal summary where the components – the words which did most relevant work – listed and represented the central *themes* of the work. In other words, an attempt to reveal the essential form would reveal the central meaning. This is suggested by the common usefulness of words for birth, upbringing, force, marriage, escape, belief, betrayal, giving, meeting, disguising, death and sex for purposes of compressing and comparing *All's Well That Ends Well* and *Cymbeline* .

For A Midsummer Night's Dream, for instance, one could make a terser and more accurate summary of the plot with words such as 'blind', 'love', 'quarrel', 'tell', 'follow' and 'deceive' than with 'tall', 'flower' and 'rehearse'. To have six groups (or six members of a group) come up with their own versions of a 20-word plot, then discuss what words they have in common and what they differ over will provoke them to reflect on what they think are, for them, the main meanings of the plot, and will discipline and enrich their readings and interpretations by awarenesses of alternative readings and interpretations. The concepts for which you have had to invent visual equivalences on a 3W chart give a clue.

I ought to make clear at this point that I'm not suggesting replacing works of literature by bluffers' summaries. The meanings of literary works – as Fish (1980) suggests – are their effects, and no one would expect a 20-word summary to have the same effect as reading a novel or watching a play. Indeed, a bonus of students' making a plot-precis is to provoke them to discuss and therefore dis- cover what's lost by summary. Nor am I suggesting that any narrative is little more than a kernel-story drawn from a small repertory. The variations which may be played upon the components of story structures are as infinite as those which genes play with a few molecules and chemistry, or language plays with a few words and rules for combining them. Even the most enduring storyshapes of fairy tales (linked by some to universal psychoanalytical archetypes or complexes – see Bettelheim 1977) are subject to great changes in their meanings. Zipes (1979 and 1983) shows how, by choosing and changing, Perrault and his like kept the struc- tures of fairy tales but changed the genre from tales about power told for adult peasants into tales about manners written for bourgeois children. Such material- ists would argue that the unconscious, through which 'archetypes' are said to work, is itself culturally constructed and changes with history (see Chapter 4).

Definitive stories?

Our ability to recognize the similarities between storyshapes, indeed to recognize that they are storyshapes, comes from our having experienced many works of a similar genre. This is relevant to the argument for wide reading as a pedagogy, and a further support for arguing that 'intertextuality' works in meaning-making. To give one obvious example, students cannot appreciate parody in literature (as they do in TV, film and comics) unless they can recognize genre by recognizing common features.

From Aristotle to Zipes (with an important detour through Frye – see Chatman 1978: 85–6) theorists have tried to define and taxonomize literature and its genres in terms of its forms and contents. There are your redemptive self-sacrifice stories (Oedipus, Jesus, Spit Nolan) your self-redemptive sacrifices (Sidney Carton, Farquhar, Oedipus again), your underworld journeyer (Orpheus, Marlow, Tom Sawyer, Black Beauty), your biter bit (Chaucer's Pardoner's three, the French in *Spain, 1809*, Viz's Johnny Fartpants, Dahl's antique-dealer in *Parson's Pleasure*, Oedipus again), your love-changed beast (the Wife of Bath's, Perrault's, Mr Rochester), your riddle-solver (the miller's daughter in *Rumpelstiltkin*, Sherlock Holmes, Oedipus again), your transforming stranger (Theseus, Shane, the Iron Man, Oedipus again). All these are my examples: Frye and Aristotle have little to say about Johnny Fartpants. Let the students find such recurrences in children's literature, soap operas, set books, or 'Listen with Mother'. This can and should make for fine sport in the classroom, but the recurrence of Oedipus suggests we don't have any distinct and irreducible paradigms here.

The central part that structural plot-patterns play in defining a genre and providing a text which we can recognize and make meaningful has been a concern of formalist – and more precisely 'structuralist' – literary theoreticians. One of the classic exemplars of structuralist method is Levi-Strauss's explanation of myths from many cultures as various combinations and transformations of equivalent items and relationships (in Pugh *et al.* 1980). In the first half of the century, Eastern European 'narratologists' were pioneers in attempts to discover what it is about a story that allows us to recognize it as a story, Typically, and most prominently, Propp (1958) worked on the 'morphology' of the Russian folk-tale in a manner like the one we suggested for finding the top 20 words with which to summarize a particular Shakespeare play (except he was pursuing the most common, rather than the most affecting, elements). In this, he identified a repertory of 31 'functions' with which he was able to summarize each member of his corpus of tales. Functions might be expected to consist of characters of recognizable type (e.g. villains) and events of recognizable type (e.g. discoveries or betrayals), but Propp had more success with functions which were more like relationships between characters or objects and events, as, for example, the violation of an interdiction. So, in different stories, a function could be 'played' by different characters of different age, class, gender or species. The interdiction could be violated by a princess, peasant or polecat, and a princess could be part of different functions in different stories. Propp showed how all his tales were describable by selecting and combining his functions. Incidentally, the need to reinterpret the function of stereotypical items of the genre story-by-story supports another argument, that summaries are not enough. Just as you can only interpret the surface structure of a story by knowing its deep structure, so you can only interpret the deep structure – i.e. identify the functions – if you have the surface structure too. Is Grusha's flight with the baby an escape, a sacrifice, a liberation, a theft? To decide which, you need to know something about Grusha and the baby's family and what was going on round Grusha when she picked the baby up. All those are in the text, not the summary.

The possibility of finding a repertory of ingredients and recipes which account for Shakespeare comedies should now be apparent from the possibility of writing the plot of one with a finite language and then finding how nearly it represents another. To revert to pre-Proppian ingredients, take a duke, an unsympathetic parent, and an unrequited lover; arrange a flight, a disguise, a mismatch, a change of heart . . . and so on. Find a court, a wilderness . . . The components are spans of time, places, characters, relationships, types of events. Other genres; other components: a country house, a cryptic servant, a locked attic, a scream in the night? Students can do that.

So far the examples have been of narratologies of particular genres – folk-tales, myths, Shakespearean comedies. But the strong structuralist argument would see even genres as only surface variations on deep similarities. Lodge (1981) has an account of how Oedipus insidiously inserted himself into a realist little radio story about a cat.

Look at *A Midsummer Night's Dream* as the story of Hermia and you have a young woman escaping domestic oppression to endure ordeals of physical exposure, betrayal and near-mismatch before achieving marriage, just as if she was in a Victorian novel like *Jane Eyre*. Extract Demetrius's story and you could have *Gregory's Girl*. Or take a horse . . .

So if only we use the right analytic terms, can we find a few ur-plot-structures which go right across cultures and genres such as Holland's (1968) common fantasies? Human beings have in-built tendencies to perceive experience in certain patterns. For instance we look for movements from one stable state to another, as with Black Beauty's move from innocent rural youth through a troubled displacement to a wise rural age, or *A Midsummer Night's Dream*'s move from patriarchy through anarchy to matrimony. We also tend to see people as doers or done-tos and objects as agents or gifts, and so on. The reason for calling analyses of stories in particular genres 'narrative grammars' has become apparent: they are explanations of how meaningful stories are generated by systematically organizing a limited number of category-items in a certain limited number of ways. The items are equivalent to 'parts of speech' and the forms they can take are their morphology; the limited sequences and juxtapositions with which they can be combined are the equivalent of syntax. And they don't make sense written backwards.

Some theorists (e.g. Fowler 1977: 23–4) would suggest that one-sentence synopses of novels are possible because novels have the same structures as sentences. Maybe the equivalence of the grammar of stories and the grammar of sentences is no coincidence. Structuralist linguists such as Chomsky have suggested that because some standard combinations are common to many languages and some possible ones are never found, then the particular grammars of particular languages are only forms of some universal, biological 'wired in' mental structure. If that is so, the universal appeal of stories and their cross-cultural similarities could be explained by the same mental structure. The appeal of structure – with its implication of economy and clarity – would then be linked to the appeal of neat epigrams, well-formed limericks or sonnets, powerful parables, elegant mathematical proofs and modernist buildings.

There's a snag. Culler (in Fowler 1975) describes and evaluates some attempts to define the story in linguistic terms. At its most radical (and least helpful?) the model is of story as subject and predicate. Genette's taxonomy of narrative discourse (1980) can be seen as all the variations of the verb (in tense, mood and voice). But Culler finds that all the models are, ultimately, bootstrap jobs which leave definition to intuition. We can say what is not a story and we can describe the elements and workings of stories when we find them, but as for defining stories we're still at the stage of looking round for them and agreeing that we recognize them. One of the subtlest (and slipperiest) models of the story is one of Barthes's (see Pugh *et al.* 1980). I shall use an adaptation of part of that in section 2.5.

Recognizing the operation of narrative grammar in a plot can help students to make meaning of them. This argues for encounters with a range of literature both within and between genres. To some extent it seems to require a degree of explication too. However, I am not arguing for 'narrative parsing' or explicit knowledge of narratological terms in classrooms, any more than I would for formal grammar as an aid to developing students' ability to recognize and generate meaning. But for teachers to know something of it would help them devise playful approaches which familiarize and empower their pupils.

One model is the pair of students' books on 'making' and 'changing' stories (Mellor and Raleigh 1984) which look at the changing manifestations of folk and fairy tales such as those referred to above, and invite students to identify the components of the basic forms and recognize the possibility of devising other versions (e.g. feminist ones). And I have always found that students have enjoyed using their explicit knowledge of the grammar of pop genres such as soap operas by inserting incongruous elements into them, inventing their own versions, parodying or pastiching them, and so on.

2.2   Binary structures: comparisons and contrasts

Barbara Hardy is often quoted to the effect that narrative is a primary act of mind. The title of her piece which opens Meek *et al.* (1977) says so. So is comparing: it structures our concepts, our language, and our thinking and narration. Comparing played a part in recognizing story shapes. Oberon/Titania and Theseus/Hippolyta were alike in being powerful pairs who quarrelled and made up. They were unlike in being spiritual on the one hand and mortal on the other and in visiting the court from their woodland home-base on the one hand and visiting the wood from the courtly home-base on the other. Comparing – in the sense of finding similarities and differences – gives students an easy purchase on literature in their first attempts to explore its mechanisms.

Comparing one work with another emerges in reading journals. A way teachers can help students to grasp the (often neglected) overall qualities of short literary works (most obviously poems but it can be used of short stories, too) is to have them divide the pieces in a mini-anthology into two contrasting groups within each of which the pieces have something in common, then discuss this with rival anthologizers. (The procedure gives a lot of scope for instructive titling too – see section 2.4.) I have found that an easy way for students required (e.g. by external exams) to make their first tentative explorations of writing about poetry is simply for them to take two poems and list things they have in common and things about them that are different. In some work on recognizing the characteristic features of different genres (broadly defined) – such as the use of conflicts in plays and images in poems – 13-year-old Graham Harvey's classmates made lists like his of the differences between Brecht's poem *The Children's Crusade* (in Brecht 1976) on the one hand and Brecht's play *The Exception and the Rule* (in Brecht 1977) on the other:

> *Similarities*: written by same person; both run out of stores; someone provides something for the other; someone killed; nothing to show the way.

> *Differences*: play and poem; battle and journey; snow and sand; one story cold, one hot; one story was to go somewhere, the other was running away.

There's material for plot summary there, of course: a journey; a dearth; a gift; a death. I have helped younger students prepare their own autobiographical writing by getting them to classify the autobiographical passages and poems we had read together (Gorky, Dylan Thomas, Hitchman, Joyce, Spender, pieces from ILEA's *Our Lives*) according to whether they were: verse or prose; first or third person; home or away; contemporary or period; wide-ranging or concentrated on a few incidents.

All those practical applications of comparing deal with different works. But students can recognize comparisons within works, too, like those within *A Midsummer Night's Dream*, or within the episode of *All Creatures Great and Small* in which the whole action hinges round births and deaths and every character can be classified as being horse or human, male or female, young or old, or – eventually – alive or dead. In another horsey classic there is an embedded contrast between town and country (see section 4.3). O'Toole (in Fowler 1975) shows how Sherlock Holmes stories are characterized and structured by an antithesis between security and adventure which can be detected at the levels of plot, of characterization, and sometimes even at the levels of individual paragraphs and sentences. Lunzer and Gardner (1984) have examples of diagrammatic comparings of the reactions of characters in a short story (p. 48) and in *The Pearl* (p. 79). In both cases the relatively detailed work involved seems to me as if it could be justified by its concentration on a central, pervasive and important theme of the whole work. Similarly, just to identify and illustrate the contradictions in Jane Eyre's character (passionate and rational, assertive and submissive) or situation (socially inferior, morally superior) would be a way for students to understand the novel's progress (and historical originality?). Such making of comparisons deploys recognitions of formal, abstract features of texts which are the concerns of formalist literary theories, including those described as 'structuralist'. Propp's narratology is one example.

Levi-Strauss's comparing, analysing and explaining myths from many cultures depended on his use of binary relationships like those so obvious in the *All Creatures Great and Small* episode (see Pugh *et al.* 1980, or Leach 1970, Chapter 4). A binary relationship is one in which there are only two possibilities: switches are on or off in electronic circuits; digits are one or zero in the binary arithmetic on which computers work; and each stage in an algorithm gives you the choice of doing something or not doing it.

Modern phonetics depends on the proto-structuralist perception that you can describe any phoneme by ascribing it to one or other of two attributes in each of a few categories. Thus a phoneme is voiced or unvoiced, dental or not dental, and so on.

This may seem very dry, but – at least for many of us – perceiving, thinking, feeling, playing and acting in binarities extends into all aspects of our lives. You can fill your square with a nought or a cross; your chess piece (which is white or black whatever its colour) is on or off a square (wherever it is); you can be with me or against me ('my enemy's enemy is my friend'); you're either 'us' or 'them'; it's either 'hip' or 'square', 'in' or 'out'. Male or female, left wing or right wing, guilty or not guilty, sacred or profane: we are socialized to construe much of our experience in binary terms. Before Socrates, Parmenides classified the fundamental nature of the universe with binary attributes, and now the classification, combination and prediction of quarks proceeds in binary dimensions. Indeed it has been suggested that the whole of language and therefore of experience could be classified with binaries if you thought up enough of them (Harland 1987: 86–7). Just two binaries of produced/received and written/spoken are enough to generate four modes of language. And if you introduce the 'or-not' ploy, three (of wet-or-not, nutritious-or-not and hot-or-not) would distinguish beer, crisps, sand, oil, bathwater, tea, embers and toast. And so on, geometrically.

My example of comparing autobiographical poems and pieces illustrated binaries. I've implied binaries to categorize the characters and their relationships in *A Midsummer Night's Dream*: low-born or high-born; mortal or immortal; female or male; lover or hater. A binary comparison will be used in the next section to discuss power inequalities; and a binary comparison will also be used in Chapter 4 to discuss embedded ideological values. But here is one suggestion for a classroom activity for secondary children using binaries to analyse characters in literature. This is a more elaborate version of a procedure which Exton (in Miller 1984: 73) used fruitfully in his work on the structure of a short story. My suggestion is based on the repertory grids used by the psychologist George Kelly and his followers to identify the constructs with which people operate in order to make sense of their experience (see Bannister and Fransella 1971: 66–71).

To make 'attribute grids' of characters in narratives, pupils list the main characters (as headings for columns, for instance). Take three of the characters and identify one respect in which two are alike and the third is unlike: e.g. Oberon and Lysander are male, but Titania's female. Can you say if each of the other characters is male or female and put a sign in their column accordingly? (Of course you can, but if the attribute that paired Oberon and Lysander and excluded Titania had been 'ruthlessness', the decisions and discussions to classify other characters according to this attribute would have been harder and more interesting.) Now take another trio of characters and identify a respect in which two are like each other but unlike the other: e.g. Egeus is mortal, like Lysander, but Oberon is immortal; Titania is immortal too; Helena isn't; is Puck? Helena is passionate, like Lysander but unlike Oberon: Titania seems passionate too, and so does Egeus from the way he introduces himself; what about Hippolyta?

And so on. Building up a grid like this has certain teaching uses. It provokes students to talk and argue, to scrutinize the text, to define the terms in which they conduct their arguing, and to make qualifications. It's centred round a straightforward active task (constructing the grid and filling it in). In the case of *Jane Eyre*, gridding the attributes of Jane, Rochester and Rivers alone might lead to the central ideological structure of the work.

It also teaches something about both the constructedness and the ideologies of literature. The discovery that characters are relatively simple combinations of attributes, even in Shakespeare or a Victorian novel, demonstrates that they are literary functions, limited artefacts, and not to be mistaken for unpredictable and ultimately unknowable human beings with lives outside and before and after the narrative. On the evidence of text it's simply impossible to ascribe some attributes to some characters, as group discussion will remind some over-expansive readers and as Caroline might remind Jackie (see section 1.2 on Holland). Of course, the effectiveness and complexity of the process varies according to period and genre. Sixth-formers referred to in Chapter 5 found it was frustrating to grid the attributes of characters in *The Great Gatsby* because the characters were complex and the reader's perceptions of them changed: but that was worth finding out. Characters in early, simple, or epic narratives are easier to grid than those in novels. In a novel, characters are defined psychologically rather than behaviourly, and where the story is about their development rather than about how events move them about or bring out their pre-existing nature. In some genres it might be impossible to grid the characters because they are nothing more than functions with names on them. In other genres, characters change too fast to be gridded. The 'gridding technique' is effective with Brecht. (It also helps to reveal the common and different features of separate works of Brecht, as adding *The Caucasian Chalk Circle* to the comparison of *The Children's Crusade* and *The Exception and the Rule* above will show.)

Just as making 3W diagrams exposes the necessary contributions to plot of functions such as partings and meetings, thefts and gifts, enmities and alliances, so does constructing attribute grids expose the necessary contribution to plot of characters which can be compared or contrasted or put into such mutual relationships as actor/sufferer, giver/receiver, lover/rejecter. Secondly, making attribute grids may reveal that certain attributes are related to each other, because the patterns of pluses and minuses in some rows may resemble others. If being male seems to get a plus in most of the columns in which 'power' gets a plus, there's a moral there.

Structuralist poetics provide a rationale for such practices, as well as hints for further applications. Theorists such as Saussure recognized and explicated what we instinctively and operationally know – that signification relies on difference.

Figure 5A takes a hint from Robert Scholes's *Textual Power* (Scholes 1985: 26–38) to represent Hemingway's *Interchapter VII* from *In Our Time* as a diagram. The diagram is structured on a number of binary oppositions which resonate with each other: sacred and profane; love and war; going up and going down; speaking and keeping silent; and – for the intertextual reader – Paradiso and Inferno. (The story tells how a soldier in Italy lies in a trench fearing death and promising to Jesus that if he survives he'll tell everyone about Him; but, next week when he lies upstairs at a brothel making love, he does not tell the girl. Again, I need the surface – 'soldier', 'Italy' to discern the structure.) The point I (and Scholes I hope) would wish to make here is that such a diagrammatic representation of the binarities at work within the text do not merely reveal the unspoken structure of the story, but they also reveal – in a sense they are – the meaning of the story.

Figure 5B is a representation of another tale of how Theseus goes to the woods and by chance finds runaway lovers at odds – Chaucer's *Knight's Tale*. Here the symmetries provide a very obvious armature for the plot, and the deviation from it is a thereby emphasized statement about metaphysical and theological priorities in the Middle Ages. In my experience, retellings of this story, episodically, are very appealing to younger secondary pupils. I also believe that hearers and readers enjoy and understand these tales largely because of these binary structural principles. Modern retellings which attempt to make the story attractive by adding realistic detail or modernisms, as distinct from laying bare

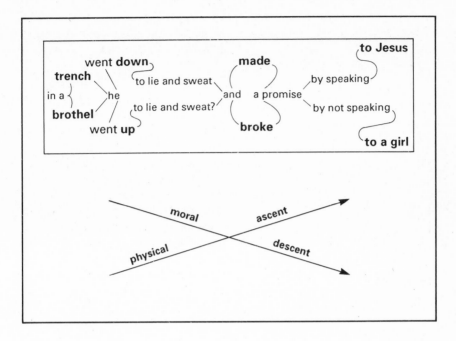

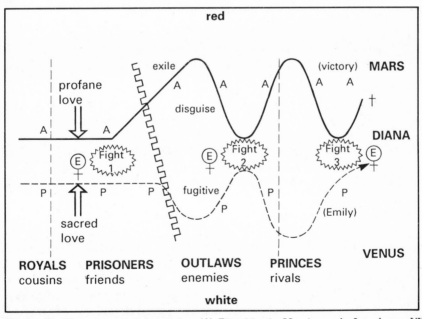

Figure 5   Binary structure in stories: (A) Binarities in Hemingway's *Interchapter VII* (from Scholes 1985); (B) Symmetry in Chaucer's *Knight's Tale*

the formal qualities, miss the point, I think. The story's attraction – and its recognizability – lie not in its surface but in its deep structure. Although I drew the diagram, the idea came from a 12-year-old student, who in her poem about the story, fastened on to the red and white binarity.

To turn to our central texts, we've already seen how *A Midsummer Night's Dream* can be conceived as structured along binary axes: concord and discord; nature and culture; love and war; human and supernatural. *Jane Eyre* can be understood as Jane's progress between two asymptotes, oscillating towards a synthesis (remember that a line finally meets an asymptote only at infinity!). The asymptotes could be conceived (and drawn on a diagramming of the plot's progress) in such over-arching terms as force and love (Jane alternating from the violent Reeds to the loving Helen to the violent Rochester I to the loving St John Rivers and homing in on the strong but loving Rochester II), or as subservience and independence (after some macro-segmenting as a preliminary DART). The asymptotes could be conceived as pure spirituality (left in Helen's grave at Lowood) and pure sensuality (left in Bertha's ashes at Thornfield), as male and female, or fantasy and reason or in more particularly instanced symbols, such as the warm and cold introduced by the colour-languaged imagery of the opening and suggested by the recurrence of binarily absent and present fires, which binarily heal or hurt. *Spain, 1809* has an action, and consciousness, that alternates between conqueror and conquered, French and Spanish, Life and Death. *Business News*, being about hubris, is a straight instantiation of human technology defying, but falling to, the gods of nature.

2.3   Paths and choices: sequences and correspondences

Structuralist literary theorists have claimed there are formal patterns in texts which influence intelligent readers' interpretations and, as we saw in the last section, binary analysis can lead on to simple but powerful ways of formally representing story structures. The distinction between horizontal and vertical relationships is an organizing principle of structural analyses of literature and another deeply epistemological procedure which goes beyond literature; for instance Freud's grammar of dreams uses axes of combination and substitution like the axes I describe below.

From their work in maths, many pupils will know about inequalities. It is easy for them to construct little statements of inequality with respect to certain aspects of literary works which they are studying: pecking orders are an example. In *A Midsummer Night's Dream*, for instance, and staying with the 'power' we thought we might find associated with other more obvious attributes in the 'character attribute grids' they will probably judge that, on the immortal plane, the following represents the respective abilities of characters to get their way over others:

Oberon > Titania > Puck > Fairies

It is worth getting them to cite an event or quotation which justifies each relative position, both as a means to the different end of getting them to scrutinize the text and become familiar with it, and also more relevantly to think through and qualify their judgements about relative power. It is also important to check whether these inequalities stay the same throughout the action, or whether the pecking orders change scene-by scene, like Top Twenty charts do week-by-week. (Students enjoy representing the changing relationships in plays and novels by changing lists of pop song titles.)

Are there any principles at work which might explain these inequalities? Comparing the inequality-statement with the corresponding one for mortals might help to answer that. If the two inequality-statements – the one for immortals and the one for mortals – are combined or set alongside each other, is it possible to decide the relative positions of characters in every case? Puck seems to have more power than Demetrius, but would he have more than Hippolyta? (I should suggest that the impossibility of answering that from textual evidence alone is another useful reminder that characters are limited literary constructs and not human – or even superhuman – beings.)

The inequalities are examples of what, at this stage, I am going to call horizontal relationships (to avoid jargon and having to decide between the different terminologies of different theorists). The comparisons between the inequality of the immortals and the inequality of the mortals is an example of what I am going to call, for now, a vertical relationship. Theseus's relationship with Hippolyta is horizontal. Theseus's relationship with Oberon is vertical. And Theseus's horizontal relationship with Hippolyta is vertically related to Oberon's horizontal relationship with Titania!

Theorists often use the example of meals to illustrate this second fundamental organizing principle of literature (and language – and thought). A menu is a horizontal relationship between certain dishes. In general, a slap-up meal might be:

a starter; a main course; a dessert.

In particular, it might be:

garlic bread; vegetable lasagne with spinach; trifle.

Or:

mushroom soup; stuffed turkey with sprouts; Christmas pudding.

Starter; main course; dessert: those items stand in horizontal relationships to each other and that relationship is their sequence – the order in which they follow each other across the page or in time. Similarly for the items in each of the particular examples of a slap-up meal.

Now the particular meals – the sequences – stand in vertical relationships to each other. The vegetarian meal corresponds – as a slap-up meal – to the

Christmas dinner, and each is a sequence of items which correspond to items in the other.

To take another example: cricket teams, written out in batting order, are two sets of horizontal relationships. Individual members of the team relate with each other horizontally: the bowlers need the batsmen to give them a target of runs to bowl at; they need the wicket-keeper to take catches off their bowling; the stroke-making batsmen need the opening batsmen to wear out and survive the opposition's opening bowlers so that they have scope for their flashy strokes and easy-pickings; and so on.

But the two sequences – the two teams – are vertically related to each other, by virtue of both being cricket teams in batting order. Similarly, at a more detailed level, individual members of the two opposing teams are related to each other vertically. The opening batsman who was related with his wicket-keeping team-mate horizontally, is vertically related to the opposition's opening batsman.

What I have been calling horizontal relationships exist by virtue of relative position in sequences – by combinations, contiguities and connections. In a Christmas dinner: turkey comes with sprouts; turkey and sprouts come next to, and before, Christmas pudding. Turkey is connected with Christmas pudding by being part of a traditional meal. Horizontal relationships are characterized by the association, succession and sequence of items which have distinct functions. What I have been calling vertical relationships, on the other hand, are characterized by comparisons, correspondences and the possibilities of mutual substitutions (you could substitute lasagne for turkey, for the sake of vegetarian celebrants, but you would not juxtapose them in the same meal).

Here we have a gastronomic grammar: a wide choice of items but in prescribed and limited categories with only one allowable sequence. Horizontal relationships, in my sense, are like those which connect words of a sentence syntactically. Vertical relationships are like those which allocate words of a sentence to the categories we call 'parts of speech'. Symptomatically, Saussure, one of the prominent theoreticians to work with this distinction, called these two contrasting types of recurrent semiotic structurings the *syntagmatic* (for what I have been calling 'horizontal') and the *paradigmatic* (Culler 1981: 23, Hawkes 1977: 26).

Now, on that large scale of relating linguistic items which we call literature, the horizontal relationships have been central to stories, plots and reading experiences. The 'history-time', 'narration', and 'reading-time' of the previous chapter were all perceptions of horizontally related events. The story shapes on the 3W diagrams, the plots and sub-plots, and the power inequalities extracted from *A Midsummer Night's Dream* were all examples. Horizontal relationships are characteristic of narrative. But from now on, especially as two of the exemplary instances I used to introduce the concept – menus and batting orders – can be written out vertically(!), I shall call these 'horizontal' relationships *sequences*.

Vertical relationships appear as the correspondence between events, characters or motifs which the reader or author provides. These can be obviously parallel functions between items within a work (as that between Theseus's dominance of the court and Oberon's dominance of the wood; or the lovers' running away and Pyramus's and Thisbe's running away in the vertically related 'play within a play'). They can be parallels between the items and their sequences in different works (as those between *A Midsummer Night's Dream* and *As You Like It*) which help us to allocate a work to a genre, or help us recognize the function of an item in an unfamiliar work by its correspondence to an item in a familiar work. They can be parallels between the items and sequences in the fictional world and items and sequences we recognize from real worlds, including our own experience, which help us recognize a setting or relevance for the fiction (so that we see *A Midsummer Night's Dream* as an expression of Shakespeare's political conservatism, as an example of folk-beliefs, or as a confirmation of our own experience of the blindness of teenage sexual infatuation).

These vertical relationships play a part in story-telling, as I intend to show by these examples and the ones to follow. But their simplest forms are metaphors, which I shall say more about in the next section. Metaphors are most characteristic of poetry. In *My luve is like a red, red rose . . .* there are elements of sequence (the rose sprung in June and Burns will love till a' the seas gang dry) but far more of correspondence (his love is like a rose, and a melody; he is 'deep' in; the love will last as long as the conceivable survival of the seas). From now on, I shall call these formerly 'vertical' relationships *correspondences*.

Menus and batting orders should have been enough, but Burns and metaphor suggest one, last, irresistible analogy for this pervasive structural distinction in the way we order our experiencing and understanding of linguistic and literary phenomena. Horizontal sequences make tunes; vertical correspondences are chords.

The examples already given should provide enough material to illustrate how sequences and correspondences provide the 'ados' which we count as narrative and the meanings which make them interesting to us. It is the sequencing of narrative functions and motifs – of violations, flights, exiles, returns, revenges and so on – which provide narratologists with their fundamental storyshapes. Spit champion; Spit challenged; Spit dead: like tunes and Black Beauty, storyshapes tend to move through changes from one stable state to another (bell tunes are called 'changes'). What make these shapes recognizable and meaningful are the correspondences between separate functions and motifs in different stories, and correspondences between the overall shapes of different stories.

While correspondences supply commentary, sequences imply consequence and consequences imply causes. That assumption is one of those 'codes' shared by readers and writers which make for literary meaning. In 'Occurrence at Owl Creek Bridge' we assume: that Farquhar's background causes his susceptibility to the Scout's temptation; that the temptation leads to him raiding the bridge, that that leads to his being hung, and so on. In *Spain, 1809* we assume: that the ambush has caused the retaliatory raid; that forewarning has caused the village's desertion (and – with reader's hindsight – the planting of the poisoned wine bait); that suspicion causes the Captain's forcing the woman to drink; that poison causes the scream, the pain and the massacre; that abstention has caused the narrator's survival to tell the tale; and that a plan by the Spaniards causes him to be fleeing across the sierra with their balls whizzing wide. Demetrius's first change of allegiance and Hermia's love for Lysander have led to Egeus's demand which Theseus's impending marriage makes him careless in satisfying, which leads to the flight to the wood where Oberon's earlier quarrel with Titania puts him in a position to interfere with the lovers whose plot intersects the woodlanders – and so on.

All this is interpretation: those causes have to be inferred by the gap-filling reader, and that they are causal relationships is inferred simply by their succession in the history-time which the reader constructs from the narration of the plot. Sometimes it is worth helping students into this code of causes by having them represent the causes and their consequences by drawing 'cause arrows' between different parts of event-sequences, especially in 'fugued' plots (see section 2.5) where, as with Azdak's sheltering the fugitive Grand Duke and thus surviving the counter-coup, the causes and consequences may be widely separated.

As I suggested in what I said about *All Creatures Great and Small* and different retellings of Chaucer, I think that such embedded structural relationships appeal in themselves to many readers, including young readers, and especially if you take into account Holland's claim that literature appeals through a 'puzzle' element. However, for most readers, these sequences are chiefly interesting because of the correspondences to them which we recognize. In *A Midsummer Night's Dream* the correspondences, as in the examples of the Hemingway story or Chaucer's *Knight's Tale*, include internal ones which give the plots intriguing contrasts and parallels. There are also, for some readers, the correspondences between items in the work, or sequences in the work, and similar ones in other works, which help to allocate it to a genre or enjoy a more informed prediction of outcomes such as the response theorists use to explain at least part of the appeal of literature.

2.4   Symptoms and symbols: metonyms and metaphors; names and titles

I said that metaphor was an obvious example of a correspondence, and that explicit expressions of that form of relationship were most characteristic of poetry (I am including the simile which can be taken to be a metaphor that is being honest about itself). Figure 6A gives a simple illustration, using a descriptive poem popular with juniors and lower secondary pupils. For James Reeves's poem *The Sea* (in Graham 1958, p. 82), the sequence – what there is of it – is represented by a succession of cartoons of the sea's implied behaviour. A corresponding sequence of cartoons represents the succession of the statements Reeves makes about the dog to which he has compared the sea. Each dog-frame

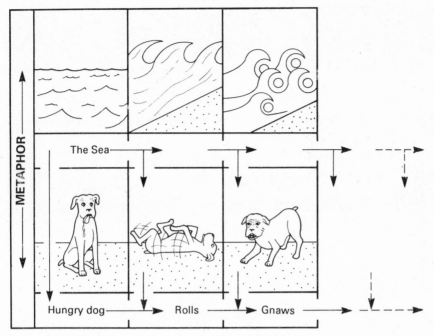

Figure 6A Tropes: horizontal and vertical relationships in James Reeves's *The Sea*

has a corresponding sea-frame. So even there, as in many a metaphorical statement with a story element, 'consistency' of metaphoring implies a sequencing, too, and one way students can help themselves to appreciate that is to make drawings like that in Figure 6A.

But the trope most characteristic of story is the trope of association: the metonym. Where the metaphor describes one thing by describing it as something else – for instance the sea as if it was a dog (or love as if it was a charm, or Helena's and Hermia's former amity as being two berries on one stem) – the metonym denotes one thing by means of representating something else normally associated with, or representing, the subject – for instance by representing the sea as a wave (or love as a sigh, or Helena's and Hermia's former amity as their sitting on one cushion sewing together). Brecht's *The Caucasian Chalk Circle* is full of metonyms: 'hired fists'; the spring glockenspiel of melting snow for the end of Grusha's term of refuge with her brother; the boots which she swears to Simon will not be by her door when he returns.

Literary theory has fostered a revival of interest in rhetorical tropes. In section 5.2 I distinguish between the functions of Spit Nolan's rose as index, icon and symbol: there I am using a typology from Peirce, but the metonym/metaphor duality is associated with Jakobson (see Hawkes 1977: 77–80, or Culler 1981: 216). However, I have no intention to argue for the re-introduction of the

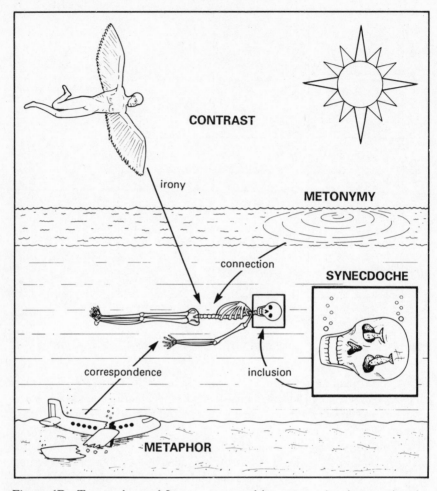

Figure 6B   Tropes: drowned Icarus represented by a connection (or a part) and a correspondence (or a contrast)

taxonomies I learned in school (all the illustrative phrases of Pope, Arnold and Tennyson I remember, but none of the Greek names for what they illustrated), nor to defend in stylistics what I could not defend in linguistics. But a distinction between tropes of association (which for stories are usually tropes of sequence) on the one hand and tropes of correspondence on the other is fundamental and worth making. Jakobson saw them as representing the two fundamental processes of sign-making – combining (to make sequences on what I've called a horizontal plane) and selecting (from vertically arranged items in one category). His interest partly came from distinguishing between a language disorder in which the sufferer substitutes an associated word for a forgotten word (e.g. 'bone' for 'dog') and one in which the sufferer substitutes a corresponding word (e.g. 'wolf') (see Hawkes 1977: 78).

Here the metonym, and metaphor will suffice, together with one other trope of association and one of correspondence. The other 'horizontal' trope is the synecdoche, which represents a subject by a part of it. Since a broad definition of metonym could cover this, and since some theorists make no distinction, I shall treat synecdoche as metonym (in fact my example of 'wave' for 'sea', above, was a synecdoche). The other 'vertical' trope worth mentioning here is contrast, a sort of anti-metaphor.

These are illustrated in Figure 6B. The drowned Icarus of *Business News* is represented by the ripple he's left on the surface, a metonym because it's significantly associated with him. He's also represented by his picked-clean skull with fishes swimming in it, a synecdoche-metonym because it's a significant part of him. Vertically, Icarus is represented by a crashed airliner, whose fate significantly corresponds to his, and anti-represented by his father, a contrastingly airborne and sun-kissed figure who provides a significant irony.

Rochester's dog Pilot, whose arrival heralds his master (e.g. p. 305, Chapter 25), can be seen as a metonym of Rochester, whereas a metaphor is the old chestnut of Rochester's comparison of himself to the old chestnut tree (p. 469, Chapter 37). However, it should be said that the same item in a story can act in both ways at once: Spit's rose has already been cited, and in *Jane Eyre* the sound of a distant storm (Chapter 12) is both a symptom of calm weather locally and a metaphor for Jane's future. Some may even wish to cite the cigar smell (Chapter 23) as all of a metonym of Mr Rochester's presence, a phallic comparison, and an appropriately smoking reminder of his Jamaican past and coming nemesis. Once an awareness of tropes is abroad, it can run riot. Ingenious readers can find a tropic significance in any old detail: what does it mean that Jane collects windfalls on the evening before her near-marriage (Chapter 25)? This propensity in readers could be useful to authors who have difficulty finishing off a tale so that a sense of ending is satisfied: describe a scene or the weather at the end and the reader will surely interpret it as a satisfying metonym or metaphor for all that has gone before – or for the new state of equilibrium to which the plot has brought its characters and motifs – or for the implied future on the threshold of which the characters stand . . . With literature, we are all superstitious.

There would be no harm if students recognized the function of metonyms and metaphors in guiding their meaning-making in literary reading and maybe in transferring it to their own writing. It may help to give the two techniques less forbidding titles. I have always called them 'symptoms' and 'comparisons' in my teaching. Technically, these are sloppy words but they are familiar, and 'symptom' has the advantage of suggesting, from its medical use, both an accompaniment (of a disease) – like a metonym – and a part (of a disease) – like a synecdoche-metonym. I don't want to introduce the systematic decontextualized learning of rhetorical devices such as I endured, but I am all for some 'hunting the metaphor'. If a class project had students (each sub-contracted for 20 pages) tooth-combing *Jane Eyre* for animal comparisons (animals include birds), they might produce lists which could be categorized to provide some useful collective talking-points, as well as producing incidental insights from individuals' scrutiny of their sections of text. Metaphor-hunting also has some pay-offs in language-awareness and some of the cultural and critical work I describe in Chapter 4 because it exposes historically-originating and value-loaded buried metaphors (including animal words). Bilingual students can make a valuable contribution to this: first, it is much easier to spot metaphors which are domesticated in a language if you are reading it as a second language; secondly, a comparison of metaphors between languages and cultures (e.g. which animal-comparisons are insulting or flattering) can reveal which tropes are culturally specific and which (like roses?) are apparently universal. With a historical text such as *Jane Eyre* there is an analogous opportunity to appreciate the historical specificity or continuity of tropic language.

Students recognize how authors signal characters with some symptomatic eccentric characteristic such as a trick of speech in Dickens, or Black Jack's slow speech. They also recognize the connotations of names. In *Black Beauty* a hot-tempered horse is called Ginger and a thoroughly good farmer is Thoroughgood (whereas villains include Skinner, Filcher and Smirk). *Jane Eyre* is subtler with names but the narrator (with a little help from a teacher?) makes sure that 'Eyre' and 'Reed' do their work as well as 'Temple' by referring to their connotations, and 'Burns' connotes both poles of the binary opposition of the comforting and the threatening – the healing and the hurting – in the text's recurrent metaphor of fire.

Moving from the tropic possibilities in the names of characters to the titles of books, Lodge (1981: 3–6) uses the metonym-metaphor distinction for an interesting piece of historico-literary interpretation. He characterizes the (carefully selected?) titles of novels of the 1920s as mostly metaphoric (*The Rainbow, Ulysses*) in line with their poetic form, whereas in the 1930s the titles are metonymic (*The Road to Wigan Pier, A Gun for Sale*) in accord with a documentary sensibility he claims for the literature of that period in England.

We could make more use of titles to encourage students to think about the books we introduce them to in class. It has become a common practice – implicitly drawing upon response-theory-validated anticipation – to ask pupils what they expect a book to be about from its title (and cover) before they read it. Maybe we could ask them to think about why the title was chosen after they have read the book. To what in the book does the title refer? What does the choice of title suggest that the author saw as particularly significant, and why, and do they agree? What difference would a change of title have made to the meaning they made of the book? And so on. If it's one of the animals discussed in section 4.6, is it because the animal is a character, a comparison with a human character, or a portmanteau symbol?

In an exercise which could be adapted for use with secondary pupils, post-graduate students brain-stormed all the novel-titles they could think of in five minutes, and then categorized them. They came up with long lists of: proper names (e.g. *Jane Eyre*); metonyms (*Train to Pakistan*); metaphors (*The Waves*). They came up with shorter lists of titles which were: references to places (*Watership Down*); quotations (*Far from the Madding Crowd*); self-quotations (*Come to Mecca*); abstract qualities (*Pride and Prejudice*); self-descriptions (*A Tale of Two Cities*).

Their discussions of these lists threw up three specially interesting topics. First, how to categorize titles which seemed to belong to more than one group because they had multiple significances some of which were only discovered during the discussion (e.g. *Swann's Way*). Secondly, could the categorizations of the titles be associated with some other features of the texts such as genre, period, or intended readers? (Yes: children's novels had titles which tended to cluster in certain categories more than adult novels.) Thirdly, what did the title suggest the author thought was the most important characteristic or element in the book, and how did the title predispose a reading? Equally interesting is the consideration that a title should be classified as partly metonymic or only metaphoric according to whether its referent is in the text or not. Interesting, but not of any importance for the classroom, so here, to compensate, is another unrelated practical suggestion for using titles.

Allocate titles to untitled short texts (poems, stories, or extracts) and discuss the reasons for the choice with other students. In the 'anthologizing' exercise that I suggested at the beginning of section 2.2, a study is worth while of how thematic categorization influences titling and how titles influence thematic categorization.

2.5   Prodding and padding

Roland Barthes's 1966 classic *Introduction to the Structural Analysis of Narratives* is easily available to English readers in Pugh *et al.* 1980 (it is also in the translation of his *Image–Music–Text*, 1977). I summarize part of it here because it uses distinctions on which I shall base a simpler binary distinction between items of signification in narrative texts which work, in my terms, horizontally and vertically.

Barthes makes a model of narrative to provide him with terms to analyse particular examples (many of them James Bond stories) and to construct a theory of how narrative texts work. This model, like those of the narratologists mentioned in Section 2.1, corresponds to that of a discourse's smallest unit – the sentence – and the correspondence runs through structures at different 'levels' as in a medieval model of the universe. In increasing degree of coarseness, Barthes's levels are those of: functions, actions and narration. At the second and third of these levels groups of items from a finer, nearer-the-surface, level become items which can be chained together in certain ways to make stories, in the same way that words are strung together to make sentences. To illustrate this from our *Spain, 1809*, I should take it that, at the level of functions, 'One filled a cup' is a function linked to other details such as the 'small mouth' swallowing to make a group which could be called 'The Baiting'. At the level of actions, The Baiting would then become a function, linked to other actions such as Hiding One Wineskin, to make a group which could be called 'The Trap'. The Trap would then become an item at the level of narration in the overall 'Revenge' tale.

Barthes ingeniously explains how every word in a text is forced to signify by being a unit or part of one, however carelessly or pointlessly planted by the author. At the finest level, Barthes's 'functions' relate to other functions on the same level – for instance actions which cause subsequent actions. Consequential functions are *nuclei* on which the course of subsequent action hinges, whereas *catalysers* (less misleadingly translated as *satellites*) are merely sequential functions which pass the (reading-)time, as it were, and space out the narration, without influencing subsequent events in history-time. All my examples above from *Spain, 1809* are intended to be nuclei at the level at which they are identified.

Barthes's other main category of narrative units at this level are *indices* which relate to units on a different level – for instance different sorts of indices characterize actors or give atmospheres to settings. Within 'The Baiting' above, 'small' is an index. Barthes himself relates his distinction between functions and indices to the distinction between metonyms and metaphors (and points out how one unit may belong to more than one category simultaneously).

Barthes suggests that the dominance of one sort of unit or the other can aid a first classification of genres (so that folk-tales would be rich in functions – as is *Spain, 1809* – while psychological novels would be rich in indices). I suggest that the model also helps with the sort of summarizing I recommended in section 2.1: those verbal 'storyshapes' are best obtained by preserving coarser-level equivalents of nuclei and deleting satellites and all but a few indices (critically and carefully chosen). Elsewhere in the essay, Barthes gives a hint that it is the summaries of narratives, their representations as sequences of functions, which are translatable between languages or between forms of discourse (such as book and film). The indices are not translatable.

Turning to the possibility of a grammar for combining functions and indices, Barthes suggests that whereas indices are freely distributed, functions are mutually implicating, and sequence themselves into groups such as 'having a drink' (in Bond) or 'seduction' (in Propp's tales). We can recognize and predict the functions of these groups from our previous storying. Such groups (Barthes calls them 'sequences') also constitute units (functions or indices or both at once) in an analysis of the narrative at a coarser level, and so on upwards, hierarchically. 'Having a drink' is a group of functions at a fine level; it may be one function in a 'seduction' group at a coarser level (or, in my example above, in a 'getting poisoned' group!). So groups which may seem independent at one level (e.g. from another of 'our' texts, the stories of Grusha and Azdak) are linked at a higher level.

To use Barthes's phrase, 'the structure of narrative is fugued' (Pugh *et al.* 1980: 257). Groups may overlap in a way which pulls the reader on, receiving the first items in a new sequence (such as Azdak's story) while still searching for the closure of an earlier one (Grusha's). This works if we have enough experience of narrative (and therefore knowledge of its codes) to recognize an unfinished sequence when we read it.

Adapting Barthes, I am going to call these contrasting sorts of narrational units *forks* and *descriptors*. My forks are the functions, or groups of them, at whatever level, and descriptors are the indices (with none of the subdivisions which Barthes makes in his indices). Forks are the parts of narrative which move it on. I call them 'forks' because they prod the narrative forward and also because they represent choices (to go one way or another, to do something or not to do it, for something to happen or not, and so on, thinking binarily!). On any level, forks relate to each other in sequences, horizontally. Forks are associated with events, with decisions and actions by characters, with confirmations or confoundings of reader's expectations. They are the 'verbs' of narrative grammar. Isolate them and list them in order and you have the fundamental sequences on which stories are based, as in the *birth*; *love*; *force*; *marry*; *escape*; *follow*; *believe*; *betray*; *give*; *meet*; *copulate* sequence of section 2.1.

Descriptors, on the other hand, are the padding and realization of the characters and settings of the action. They are associated with descriptions of characters, with creations of moods and atmospheres and with relating fictional items to readers' real worlds. They can include factual discussions, like how to make a trolley in 'Spit' or break in a horse in *Black Beauty*, or sermons exemplified in both these texts. Descriptors produce correspondences and they include metaphors. Descriptors are created by readers' visualizations or by their projecting fictional actions into their own real worlds or projecting their own experience into the fictional world. When, as in Beckett or Pinter, textual descriptors are in short supply and provide little material for the reader's visualizing or projecting, then the narrative can seem baffling.

Let us illustrate an analysis into forks and descriptors from our own recurrent texts, once using forks and descriptors in a gross sense, and once using them in a finer sense.

First, take forks and indices on a gross scale, and relate the concepts to whole sections of a whole story – 'Occurrence at Owk Creek Bridge'. In the first part of the story, in history-time, until the last sentence, almost nothing happens, and almost no time passes. The part merely describes the scene (though actually, of course, far more of the visual detail and assumed geography will be provided by the reader filling gaps and responding to clues and the active reader may also be providing forks by anticipating). On a macro-scale, the first part of the story is a descriptor. The first half of the second part is descriptor too (though to provide the information about Farquhar it uses some retrospective small-scale forks, too: Farquhar had sided with the Secessionists and been prevented from fighting so far, and so on). The second part is a fork: the scout's offering and Farquhar's implied receiving of the bait. The third part has a double nature. At a first reading it will seem a fork right up to its last paragraph: Farquhar escapes hanging. At a second reading it has more the nature of a descriptor (what is in the dying man's head at the fatal moment).

Either way, at a smaller scale, Part III is a rapid alternation of meso-forks and meso-descriptors – sentences and phrases of event and description (e.g. 'He heard a second report (*FORK*) and saw one of the sentinels (*FORK*) with his rifle at his shoulder, a light cloud of blue smoke rising from the muzzle (DESCRIPTOR))'. This ambiguity, this interweaving of action and texture – or this progression on a horizontal scale while moving on a vertical scale too – is a feature of the story's appeal.

Returning to the coarse analysis to remind ourselves of the grammatical analogy, and using italicized phrases for sections which, on the whole, are forks, and unitalicized phrases for sections which are descriptors.

I	D:	At a bridge /
	D:	a man /
II	F:	*who had been trapped into a failed raid/*
III	D:	thinking he was escaping /
	F:	*hung*

I	D:	adverbial /
	D:	nominal /
II	F:	*adjectival /*
III	D:	adjectival /
	F:	*verb*

Now, for a fine-grained analysis, look at the beginning of Egeus's big speech in the first scene of *A Midsummer Night's Dream*. At a meso-level it is a fork which could be called 'Egeus's complaint' and could be grouped to make another fork at a coarser level called, perhaps 'The Provocation'. I have divided it up, word-by-word, into micro-forks and micro-descriptors. The italicized words are those I judge, on the whole, to act as forks, and the unitalicized ones are those I judge to act as descriptors:

/ Full of vexation / *come I,* / *with complaint* /
against my child, my daughter Hermia. /
Stand forth, Demetrius! / My noble Lord, /
This man / *hath my consent* / *to marry her.* /

Some of these ascriptions are difficult and a matter of judgement and dispute. I have counted 'with complaint' as just as much a fork as 'come I' because I think it has the quality of a performative – by saying this, Egeus is making his complaint rather than describing himself; I have counted 'hath my consent' as a fork because its effect upon an audience (a responsive, meaning-making audience) is to provide them with information about an action in the past rather than a state of the present; similarly, 'to marry her' is an event in the genre-related sequence of events the audience is anticipating. I have counted 'against my child, my daughter Hermia' and 'My noble Lord' as descriptors because they fill in information about the nature of his fork-like complaint – the subject and the direction of his complaining, respectively.

Everything counts. In the terms of section 3.3 it either tells or purports to show. The determined reader can make the most ornamental passage ('I know a bank whereon the wild thyme blows . . .') a significant descriptor and therefore a significant part of the narrative – finding metonyms or metaphors in innocent passages is one common interpretative ploy. And by taking indices as omens they can be turned into forks, as I shall do with Spit's rose.

Applying this distinction, with whatever degree of focus, has the value, repeatedly cited above, of directing students to close interrogation of the text and into talking about it. It is a good basis for the segmenting and labelling of passages or summaries which Lunzer and Gardner (1984) recommend (Part 1A3). It would show how *Black Beauty*, for instance, is made into a novel by listing some of the things which can happen to horses, then ascribing some of them to the protagonist, putting others into the reminiscences of other horses, and separating and surrounding dramatic events like a stable fire with homiletic or descriptive padding like The Old Ostler or John Manly's Talk (Chapters 15, 16, 17).

The terminology is useful in explaining the effects of flashbacks and flashforwards (since these distort the expected sequences of forks intriguingly). Understanding the workings of indices can help to explain the relationship between narration and reading-time (because indices increase the duration of reading-time), and the notion of levels is useful for examining differences between history-time and narration (because a plot's compressing a sequence of events in history-time can be explained as increasing the coarseness with which the narration proceeds and a plot's stretching out a sequence of events in history-time can be explained as increasing the detail of the narration).

More playfully, forks have two prongs. What if Egeus had not come to the Duke, or not complained, or not presented Demetrius, or not consented to Demetrius's suit?

And suppose the descriptors were different – Egeus was full of joy, Theseus was an ignoble worker, and 'This man' was 'That man', and so on. In many cases the answer to 'what if these had been different?' is 'there would have been no story'. Finding this out, and asking why, seems to me a better way for students to begin to explicate their intuitive sense of the essential ingredients and structures of plots than does appealing to a linguistic paradigm. So does finding out that if the forks taken provide no surprises for expectant readers, then there is no point in reading on.

3　Ways of telling

Introduction: the phantom of the author

In Chapter 1 I claimed to have killed off the author in a bid to put the creative reader at the centre of the literary reading process. Chapter 2 sided with New Criticism and against the Intentionalist Fallacy by siting meaning in the text, and emphasizing the structural and maybe universal codes through which readers read text. But the author's ghost has kept appearing. To some extent, of course, it is just a verbal shorthand. It is easier to say 'Brecht suggests . . .' than 'in reading *The Caucasian Chalk Circle* we are guided by the hints in the text into thinking . . .'. In the next chapter the real author, as a living or once-living purposeful originator of the text, will appear. It is not that real author who is considered in this chapter. Rather, it is what Wayne Booth (1961) dubbed the 'implied author', whom the responsive reader constructs from hints in the text. To oversimplify, it is the voice which the reader gives to the narration. Booth deals comprehensively with different sorts of narration, as – with variations – do Genette (1980) and Chatman (1978). Here I want to deal with two aspects of narration which I think suggest useful classroom activities for promoting an understanding, and emulation, of narrative as literature: viewpoint and modality.

But I want to begin with a comparison between books and films, both because the comparison helps to foreground and clarify ways of telling stories in literary narratives and because it suggests comparative approaches to the study of texts in class.

3.1　(book is) Book as film (is film)

The first thing you have to understand is that a film is, essentially, the creation of a director and not of a writer . . . The biggest difficulty, from my point of view, was in trying to find a way of adapting a first person story into a visual third-person narrative . . .

(Janni Howker in Howker 1989)

So far this book has ignored some important differences. I've dropped some hints about the differences between the surface and structure of narratives (and these are neatly illustrated by Protherough's criticisms of a simplified *Jane Eyre* – Protherough 1983: 156–7). The differences between different forms of verbal art will be dealt with in section 3.4. The differences between art and life will be dealt with in Chapter 4. As for the differences between good art and bad art, the limits of space let me off the hook. There is no need to add to the evaluative critical tradition which has shaped most of our literary educations. Literary theory tends to prefer description of texts and blame value on psychoanalysis, interpretative communities or cultural capitalists.

Here I raise one example of the differences between different forms of narrative art, partly to defamiliarize literary narratives and partly because there are some classroom applications to studying literary narratives. It is the difference between two forms of story-telling which have to resort to different narrative tactics, but often to tell the same story.

In a book on this scale and with these purposes, it would be impossible and improper to deal with film as an art or with film studies in school. But it is worth looking at the ways filmed stories are like and unlike written stories – especially with respect to their narration – and how the insights arising from such a study in the classroom can be used to service study of a book, especially through comparing and rewriting.

The differences between film and book

More simply than will eventually be allowed, a book is an array of words with dialogue, descriptions, thoughts and comments. It tells, it offers variable sequences of events and variable durations of time, it includes selective descriptions that *stop* the action, and it makes you *see* what you *believe*. A film, on the other hand, is a succession of *pictures* with dialogue and music. It shows, it imposes a fixed sequence and duration of events, it includes total descriptions that accompany the action, and it makes you *believe* what you *see*.

Practising what I preached about using comparison as a method of directing attention, I now intend to examine some of these differences (and the points in common between book and film which survive), and imply ways in which we can use this difference to develop students' awarenesses of the workings of literature. Here I am using 'book' for 'literary narrative text', including stories, plays and narrative poems. When a film is made from a narrative text, of course, it is nearly always from a novel, because novels are the sequential and consequential forms of verbal literary works which suit film's sequentiality.

The social production of books, even best-selling novels, is more modest than that of films and involves no armies of best boys, gaffers, key grips, Mancinis or Streeps. For that reason, many more books are published than films are released and they are more various. Nevertheless, published books are artefacts of political, economic and ideological importance, subject to the constraints of cash, taste and in some cases, the whims of a few rich moguls, and this important point can be brought out by analogy with films (whose production students are aware of from gossip columns and the films' own credit sequences). The difference in degree can be raised by discussing why happy endings are sometimes tacked on when books are filmed or why beautiful actors play plain characters or why in Polanski's film pretty Persil-white-clad girls play Hardy's all sorts and conditions of off-white women in the club dance of *Tess* (Chapter 2). It is easy for students provided with texts and videos to find examples and discuss the explanations.

The popularity of films is also responsible for their differing from books in other ways. There is no equivalent in written stories to the use of stars, remakes with newer stars and more modern technology. Then there are the consequences of the differing social conditions under which books and films are consumed, such as the intriguing contrast that watching a film is usually a public spatial experience in time, whereas reading a book is a private temporal experience within a space.

There are correspondences as well as contrasts between films and books. Both depend on reader/viewer's imaginings and on their knowledge of narrative codes – in the film you infer that the grave by which Tess stands is that of her baby, just as you inferred that the Peyton Farquhar described in Part II of the text of 'Owl Creek' is the man being hung in Part I – using a filmic 'code' of 'montage', perhaps, to match a verbal code of consequence.

Then there are filmic equivalents of intertextuality: you need to have seen other films to know the significances of juxtapositions or dissolves or zooms or riding off into the sunset. Olivier's Agincourt in the film of *Henry V* used references to the Battle on the Ice in another film which hijacked a historical national victory for the purposes of contemporary war propaganda – Eisenstein's *Alexander Nevsky*, and references to famous films can be used in TV series or commercials. So long as some are familiar with the films 'quoted', students can share their appreciations of the effects of these references to old films in pop genres.

Turning to comparisons which are specifically related to narration, there are some things that film can do that words can't, some things that films can do that words can do differently and some things that words can do but films cannot do. To list some of these might help to establish some of the problems, terminology and repertory of narrational tactics for the next two sections.

Film uses many channels. It uses speech, music and sound effects (and writing too, sometimes, in captions, notices and so on). So when you see Polanski's film of *Tess* you also hear the characters' Dorset accents, you hear the spooky sounds of nature at night as Alec rides Tess into the forest, and when he rapes her the metaphoric clouds blow to lushly orgasmic music to make sure you know what is going on that the camera dare not show. Students can suggest appropriate music and sound effects for the silenced extracts (though the example I have given may not be the most suitable!) Films can show scenes more economically than words can tell them. Polanski's *Tess* tells you that the milkmaids are faced by a flooded stream on their Sunday morning jaunt simply by showing one image of them reflected in the flood. Hardy needs half a page (Chapter 23). The sensuality of Tess's lips is clearly shown in the film, but it may (or may not) only be inferred from Hardy's descriptions of her enunciation (Chapter 2), her strawberry-eating (Chapter 5) or her attempts to whistle (Chapter 9). Film can use visual metonyms and metaphors effectively, too. The *Tess* film zooms in on the marmalade jar for Tess's dead infant's flowers to exclude its distracting surroundings. In film, that seems forced: Hardy can more naturally select that detail (Chapter 14) because it is normal for writing to select and omit the 'semiotic noise' of irrelevant detail, whereas it is hard for film to present a 'pure' image devoid of its surroundings. Film can also evoke by alluding to other familiar images (like Millet's painting for the reapers in *Tess*) where words would have to make that allusion laboriously and inappropriately (and distractingly, if the image does not register). Some people complain that the visual power, economy and specificity of film has penalties, especially when it is the film of a book. In what McLuhan called a 'cool' medium, a viewer is deprived of the chance to do the imaginative work of visualization, which the responsive reader does in the 'hot' medium of print. So viewers may be disappointed to find that a filmic realization does not match their visualization from a reading (it never could, since a filmic realization is invariably one for all viewers whereas all its readers make their own unique visualizations of the same text). There are some students, however, who are helped to read difficult texts by having seen the film first. If students have read before they have viewed, on the other hand, to discuss how the appearances of characters of settings in films confound their expectations is a good way for them to become aware of how they have formed those expectations and therefore how they read narrative. However, film is not an entirely passive medium. A viewer is as active as a reader, though in different ways. A viewer must infer unspoken thoughts from faces, without the help which a reader would get from the words of an intrusive, omniscient, or subjective narrator.

Films and books both use tricks. Occasionally, films speed up action (usually for laughs) and sometimes slow it down for instance to emphasize the horror of Bonnie and Clyde's deaths or the dreaminess of the pillow fight in Vigo's *Zéro de Conduite*. Even more occasionally, films repeat shots, as when Farquhar's wife is seen rushing to his arms over and over again at the end of Enrico's *Incident at Owl Creek* film, or they reverse them as when a character bounces back off the surface of the river they've just fallen in (or on) as in Lester's *The Knack*. Speeding up, slowing down and iteration have their book equivalents (as discussed in section 1.6), but reversing is rare, though there is the beautiful reversal of a bombing raid in Vonnegut's *Slaughterhouse Five*. We tend not to experience the book-versions as tricks because in books we do not expect the naturalness we expect from films. Students can list the devices of films, starting with the tricks then moving on to the more taken-for-granted but still conventional narrational techniques, such as changes of scene or angle or viewpoint or scale or focus. Then they can discuss why the director has made those changes at those points. Thus they are helped to recognize the artefactual nature of that 'naturalistic' medium and maybe, by comparison, the corresponding taken-for-granted devices which the narrators of books use. Devices thus foregrounded become available for analysis, appreciation and emulation.

Films and books both use dialogue, but what is natural in books would be tedious in the films: the film-maker explains to the posh scriptwriter in Fitzgerald's *The Last Tycoon* that his rejected scene was '. . . just talk, back and forth . . . interesting talk but nothing more', whereas the one he, the film-maker, improvises is moving pictures (exemplarily full of enigmatic visual metonyms like the discarded nickel, the burnt black gloves and the unseen observer – pp. 39–40). Hardy includes an apparently digressive dialect story (Jack Dollop in the milk churn) in his uncongealing milk episode (Chapter 21) which Polanski omits (thus reducing the significance of Tess's fainting). On the other hand in the film Angel helps the viewer by greeting Mercy Chant on his visit home, where Hardy, with omniscient narration available to explain who Mercy is, can have Angel silently avoid her (Chapter 25).

Without resorting to devices such as voice-over, which seem unnatural for the medium, film cannot cope with such essentially verbal narrative devices as quoting characters' unspoken thoughts or making philosophical authorial intrusions. Where Enrico's film *Owl Creek* is superb at catching the early morning sylvan scene in which Farquhar is being hanged it has no way of incorporating Bierce's ironies about the military code. Flashback and flashforward are also effects which are difficult to use in film: flashbacks in films are usually signalled clumsily with dialogue, captions, or music of a type conventionally associated with flashback. There is no equivalent to Bierce's 'Owl Creek' Part II in Enrico's film and viewers watching a film are locked into one viewing-duration and sequence determined by the film-maker. It's therefore symptomatic that films are made from novels, short stories and even plays, but they are not made from poems. Film-viewers have neither readers' freedom to take or leave or skip or gobble the text, nor are they given much option to take in the events of a plot in any but the sequence they had in the story, in history-time. Chatman (in Mitchell 1980) makes the point that our reception of film is so naturalistic that its history-time keeps rolling for us even while it is providing the descriptions. So, at the start of the *Owl Creek* film, we assume something is going on on that bridge while the camera pans around 'describing' the setting for us. In books, or the 'Owl Creek' text, the equivalents are read as 'time-outs' which interrupt the action-in-history-time.

Finally, to home in on the two themes of the next section, books can handle viewpoint and voice more flexibly than can film. A film can have only one viewpoint at once (where the camera is). It cannot tell what's 'off-screen'. It cannot show its 'narrator' (the camera) within its own narration. So we are thrown (at least I am) at seeing the paranoid subject of Polanski's *Repulsion* in the same frame as the groping hands she hallucinates. Watching the film it is harder than it is reading the text to realize that Farquhar's 'escape' is what he imagines while hanging from the rope, because we see him swimming down river. That view of him seems to have the authority of objectivity (where his repeated vision of his welcoming wife, shot from his viewpoint, is easily interpreted as his unreliable illusion). Attempts like that last – directly to imitate a protagonist's vision – are rare in films. The voice of Dickens's old Pip gives us the church going 'head over heels before me' from young Pip's viewpoint as he is inverted by Magwitch at the opening of *Great Expectations*. The film director David Lean does not shoot an inverted church through young Pip's eyes but an inverted Pip through Magwitch's legs. We have seen what Pip sees – the menacing storm-tossed trees, for instance – but the mix with frames containing Pip shows that we see as if we are with Pip, rather than inside him. This seems to me an equivalent to that style of engaged reading where we seem to accompany (rather than identify with) characters, which I mentioned in section 1.2.

Books can use authorial intrusion to place the viewpoint of the narration. Hardy's 'voice-over' sentimentalizes on the marmalade jar and separates the narrator's from the protagonist's viewpoint: 'the eye of mere observation noted the words "Keelwell's Marmalade"', but not 'the eye of maternal affection' (Chapter 14), and at the end of Phase I (Chapter 11) the author can address the reader directly about Tess's future in a way that no camera could. Whereas a film narrates directly, a book can use many voices, embedded in each other or competing, and by comparison we can use this difference to develop students' awarenesses of the complexity of viewpoints and voices in texts.

To secure that term-by-term comparison of the two media, and perhaps provide an over-detailed model for students' comparings of works in the two genres, here is a short comparison of the two realizations of one story which is simpler than *Tess* or 'Owl Creek'. I have chosen *The Hound of the Baskervilles* for three reasons: it is a book which will be familiar to most teachers and which many students still read; it is an example of a very distinct genre, heavily loaded with many of the most characteristic narrative devices dealt with elsewhere in this book (and at first consideration difficult to transfer into film); it has an inherent ideology which I shall quarry in the next chapter. Sherlock Holmes stories have also already attracted the attention of literary theorists: I mentioned O'Toole's binary analyses in section 2.2 and Belsey (1980: 109–17) uses a Holmes story to illustrate a deconstructive reading which exposes unconscious contradictions in a work (in this case that 'bourgeois scientificity' claims to explain all, but has to stay coy about the female sexuality which plays an essential part in the crimes and plots).

Holmes stories combine standard characters (stupid policemen, distressed heiresses) and incidents (the initiating step on the stair, a hansom ride through

London streets) into a standard plot (with the victim's explanation of the problem as a second segment, Holmes's explanation of his deduction as a penultimate segment). With their flashbacks and embedded narration, they would seem unfilmable, but they have been filmed over and over again. An impeccable source (*The Sport*, 9 March 1990, p. 17) says there have already been 197 films with Sherlock Holmes in them. It is apt that the scientific inventions of film and TV should be used to enhance the popularity with superstitious and sensation-loving viewers (among whom I count myself) of a story in which men of science whose profession is covering up the scandals of the rich and powerful confront dark deeds and forces and explain them away as a greedy man of science's trick with a luminous dog.

Brian Mills's 1988 Granada TV film of *The Hound of the Baskervilles*, adapted by T. R. Bowen, is relatively faithful to Conan Doyle's 1902 novel. There are some simplifications: in the final chase Mortimer (with whom the viewer has become familiar) replaces the stupid policeman familiar to Holmes fans but otherwise unused in this story (actors cost money; characters don't). Much de-scriptor-detail (e.g. Stapleton's background) is omitted or reduced, but all the major forks are there. The film neglects some of the book's fuguing, though. The Selden mystery is solved before the Stapletons become suspect, and the second-man-on-the-moor mystery is solved before Laura Lyons appears: in the book there is more overlapping of the sub-plots. Perhaps this is a con-cession to viewers who cannot backtrack to recap, as is having Holmes reiterate 'Baskerville' on its first mention, or a voice-over re-reading of Holmes's in-structions to Watson. One would expect a transfer from a cult to a mass medium to involve some vulgarization, but little is needed with a plot already so sensational. Even the casting of pretty women in the two main female roles is justified by the gallant Watson's description of them as beauties in the book, though one could argue that this is an instance of the camera trying to film from Watson's viewpoint! In accordance with modern British taste for kindness to animals but cruelty to people, the film (which brings Stapleton's off-page grisly death on to the screen) discreetly keeps the pony's drowning unseen and omits the fate of the spaniel which gives the novel a nice symmetry. There's an inter-esting insertion in the film which probably reflects changes in values: in the book it is agreed to dispose of the murderer Selden by exporting him to South America, whereas in the modern film it's acceptable only because he's had a disabling brain operation first. In feasting the eye and cutting the cackle the film justifiably expands the scenic steam-train journeys and shrinks the speeches. Being openly sensational rather than pseudo-scientific, the film is able to shrink or re-allocate Holmes's egotistical post-mortem lecture and end almost as soon as the deaths of the hound and the murderer remove the film's main interest-bearers.

Filming a book like this presents problems of narration. The texture of the book is varied by studding dialogues and monologues and Watson's retrospective reports with the texts of imitation written documents such as the old manuscript of the legend, a cutting from *The Times*, a quotation from *The Medical Register* and Watson's letters and diaries. Some of the contents are nugatory – authenticating detail which count for little to us now or descriptions of landscape which the camera can do better. Some of the necessary contents are conveyed in the film by having extracts or summaries read aloud in dialogue, as when Holmes reads extracts from the manuscript of the legend of Sir Hugo and the original hound. The film does not attempt – as a more ambitious one might have done – to match Conan Doyle's literary pastiching with a filmic equivalent. For instance it would have been amusing and appropriate for the film to insert a short (jumpy, grainy, black-and-white?) swashbuckling film of the legend to tell the legend and, by its stylistic correspondences, underline the absurd romantic supermanly and sufferingwomanly nature of the 1902 plot. (A Schools Radio version in 'Secondary English' had embedded in it an over-the-top enactment of the legend, with screams, neighs and wurzelling rustics). Perhaps one reason Conan Doyle resorted to narrating some of the story through Watson's letters and diaries was for the prestige of seeming to be showing, by presenting unmediated quasi-realia, when he was really telling (see section 3.3), or perhaps he thought the immediacy of journal would be more engaging than the coolness of memoir. Anyway, it produces some virtuoso embedding, as when the reader will read what Conan Doyle writes that Watson wrote that Henry Baskerville has said that Stapleton had said to him (p. 102). Some of its information is ingeniously conveyed elsewhere in the film – for instance by inventing a dinner-party at which subsidiary characters described in Watson's writing can introduce themselves photogenically.

In handling the book's flashbacks, the film takes the opportunity to show something of Sir Charles's death, and introduce a hint of the hound (its feet) in a wordless credit sequence which neatly avoids the problem of reproducing the book's local newspaper report. More of this sub-story appears at a point in the film's plot which corresponds to its appearance in the book. The flashbacked nature of this telling is signalled by cutting to a sequence which shows the events in a setting, lighting and length of shot all contrasting to their Baker Street introduction but with the Baker Street telling of them continuing with music over.

The film gains from being less locked than the novel into Watson's viewpoint. The camera can show the tell-tale portrait before Watson knows its significance, or tell us (with mysterious shots of black gloves) that unknown to him someone is intercepting his letters, or suggest that people on the moor are being watched by filming them in long-shot past a nearby obstacle. But the film misses some of the subtleties of voice which Conan Doyle inserts into the text. The author has the narrator tell his tale in such a way that the reader can infer a third voice – that of the implied author – mocking the vanity, obtuseness, loyalty and admiration with which Watson reveals himself as Holmes's amanuensis, apprentice, hit man and butt. Having the banal Watson as narrator allows the book to introduce the hall with a romance and portentousness (counterpointed by the American's boyish enthusiasm) which an educated Edwardian writer would disdain in his own voice. Narrating from the viewpoint of the dim, self-congratulating and conclusion-jumping Watson, and narrating with Watson's comments, helps the plot more effectively to lay such rhetorically important false trails as the suspicion that the bearded Barrymore is the murderer ('I have tried to make a reader share those dark fears and vague surmises . . .' – pp. 172–3): the film attempts to do this by dwelling on Watson's stares at Barrymore.

These brief comparisons of the narrative devices of film and book are meant to begin to introduce some of the terms and concepts for discussing the teaching of the mechanisms of literary narrative – implied authors selecting detail, interrupting with description, alluding, intruding, showing and telling, knowing all, being ironic and authoritative, changing voices and viewpoints. Most students will recognize the filmic devices. Identifying them will help them find the literary ones.

Teaching the book through the film of the book

When I read *Black Jack* with the students who identified the speakers of its dialogue in section 1.3, I asked them to pick out parts of the plot which they thought would film well. Then I showed them the Loach/Garnett film of the book and asked them to comment on it, especially with respect to the filming of the parts they had selected. (The film is transferred to Yorkshire, with some re-naming, presumably to allow the use of a team of largely amateur actors such as were used in Barry Hines films. How it manages to make Garfield's melodramatic plot boring makes an interesting study of the quasi-visual but unfilmable tricks which written texts can play on us.) This is what one pupil wrote:

> Three parts of the book which would film well are the hanging of Blackjack as in the book it goes into detail about it and describes it well. In the film it completely cut out the part of the hanging and went straight onto the coffin. A second part of the book which would film well is when Dr Carmody is selling the so-called miricle medicine as in the book it also reads like you are there and gives the atmosphere, in the film it had sound but it wasn't very good and the crowd stood around and it sounded as if they had only been given there words ten minutes before hand. The third part of the book which would film well is near the end when they are looking for Belle in the madhouse. Blackjack was kicking down doors and it would give an atmosphere of a dome and gloomy madhouse. In the film everywhere was black and dark and you couldn't see what the people were doing and with all the screaming and screaching in the background you couldn't hear what they were saying either.
>
> (Elizabeth Elliot)

Jenny Burgoyne's class used both the video of the film and the exercise of screen-writing to help their study of *The Great Gatsby* for A level (more of what they did is in section 5.4). Having worked on the book they watched the video episodically, discussing before each extract how they expected it to have been filmed. Their scrutiny of the film was all the more attentive and critical for their having already devised their own solutions to the film-maker's problems. They had taken individual pages of the book and made screenplays of them. One pupil's efforts to make the film narrated by Nick (as is the book) led him to devise an ingenious opening. When the class discussed this they said that the flashing back was a good idea though it could be confusing in this particular instance, but it was preferable to the director's solution of using a voice-over to make Nick the narrator.

> Classical music over titles. 'Tick tock' of parlour clock fades in. Music fades out. Cut to interior. In the room we can hear rain drops drumming on a window. CU (*close up*) Clock face. 'Tick tock' still going – coming from this clock. Pan around a well ornamented and dimly lit room to a bottle of whisky – blurred background – focus shifts to show a blank piece of paper with a hand holding a pen to the paper writing nothing but a single dot.

> The hand throws the pen down and we see the figure stand up. The whisky disappears out of our view – it is lifted up. We hear a sign and the sound of whisky being poured into a glass.

> The camera moves up and across and we see Nick's face looking out of a shot but he has a beard (closely cropped), his hair brushed back with a few strands of grey. He has very slight laugh-lines round his eyes but he is not laughing now; he is despondent. He lifts his glass and swills the whisky round his mouth.

> As he puts his hand up to lean against the wall, the camera draws away so we see the back of his head and the window that he is looking out of . . .

> (Dan Swinton)

This pupil's script (there is much more of it) shows that he understands some story-telling codes which transpose from book to film and film techniques which solve functionally equivalent problems by different methods, such as establishing a personality (with a whisky bottle) and a time of retrospective narration (with the beard).

3.2   Viewpoints and voices

> . . . stories he had once written, cruel stories of the American Civil War in which men succumb and survive because they have been granted a fragmented consciousness: because a man can be at once dying – hanging from a bridge with a rope round his neck – and watching his death from the far side of the creek . . .
> (Fuentes 1988: 139, Chapter 17)

Interfering too much is a constant danger for literature teachers. The 'applications' of theory which I suggest are best used sparingly or not at all for most students' readings of most texts, and certainly, with the obvious exception of prediction, not until they have finished a first reading powered by the desire to know how the story ends. The skill is in suggesting the few supportive or follow-up activities which would be specially helpful to provoke and refine a particular student's attentive reading, interpretation and criticism of a particular text. Working out what Jane might have done if on her return to Thornfield she'd found Bertha alive or Rochester dead may be a way of scrutinizing the created Jane or of matching her against students' knowledge of life. However, on the whole I think writing alternative endings or 'what happened afterwards' are usually specially inappropriate, because they seem to deny that sense of an ending or the appropriateness of the storyshaping which good stories use and teach. In contrast, the efficacy of rewriting parts of stories from different viewpoints would be supported by theory.

A student who retells a story from within the secondary world created by reading the plot has to revisit, revise and redeploy the givens of the plot. At the lowest level that means they have to know about those 'events' communicated by a text which were posited as part of a naive model and 'comprehension' approach in the introduction to Chapter 1. But the rewriter also has to consider which components of the plot would be known or unknown, important or unimportant, welcome or unwelcome to a particular teller. Retelling from different viewpoints can change the emphases or enigmas in ways which show up those aspects of the original. This is very obvious when in 1966 Jean Rhys retold the events of *Jane Eyre* as part of telling the first Mrs Rochester's story in *The Wide Sargasso Sea* or when in *The Wild Wood* of 1981 Jan Needle published the bucolic proletariat's view of the furry squirearchy of *The Wind in the Willows*.

Sometimes it is apt to generate the alternative viewpoint simply by changing the person (in the grammatical sense) of the narration. For instance to have part of *Black Beauty* or *Jane Eyre* told in the third person, or 'Owl Creek' in the first. The use of second-person narration might be worth following up. It is rare in fiction for narrators to tell narratees their own – the narratees' – stories. Prospero does it, of course – tediously – to his fictional listeners but not to the audience. Michel Butor has written a nouveau roman in the second person and discussed second-person narration in an article (Butor 1965). It may present possibilities to students because they are familiar with discourses which use the second person: *This is Your Life* is a Prospero-type example, and many popular songs – though they are addressed to apostrophees and eavesdroppers rather than narratees – tell 'you' that you are 'a breathless kiss of springtime' or whatever.

In one of my classes Stephanie Thay rewrote the story of *Spain, 1809* from a Spanish point of view. First, corresponding to the poem's account of the French riding all day, she narrates how the Spaniards got news of the impending raid in the voice of a Spanish narrator who – like Lucas's teetotal French survivor-to-tell – had a reason for being there to provide a viewpoint on the martyrdom and revenge (he had been knocked unconscious in a family dispute just before the evacuation). When he comes round, he overhears a conversation in which the woman justifies her decision and implies how she has come to be given the chance of martyrdom. This extract begins towards the end of her conversation with a remonstrating friend:

'My life is worth nothing without my only husband, only love, Pedro. Can't you understand I only wish to be with him? Go now, before it is too late. Those pigs will waste no time,' pleaded Carmen . . .

'What of your child, Carmen? And your mother? Not only do you sacrifice your own life but your sons and mothers also!' Her voice grew more shrill with every word.

'My mother will not survive this month out. You know that! Can you see a crippled old woman fleeing from the warmth of her bed and still surviving? And my son is also sick. He coughs with such pain that I cry for him sometimes. What has he to loose? My mother and son will die for their country, I will die to be with Pedro,' sobbed Carmen.

'We will make him well!'

'But I cannot leave my mother. Go now. You know deep down it is the right thing to do. Thank you for being my friend and supporting me through everything. You even stuck by me through my marriage, that even my father forbade. I will never forget such a beautiful friendship. Farewell,' said Carmen hoarsely. She squeezed her friend's hands gently . . .

Stephanie's narrator, in hiding, also overhears the woman's confrontation with the French Captain, and narrates it from his viewpoint but ingeniously using the same dialogue as in the original poem. Without the shame of Lucas's French narrator, Stephanie's Spaniard reports the Captain's reaction to learning he has been poisoned:

The captain rose to his feet and slapped her hard across the face. I felt anger as I had never before but there was nothing I could do. He hit her again and she fell to the ground.

The poison started to work. I hardly dared to breathe as I watched the sight before my eyes. Great, burly soldiers screwed up their faces in agony and fell to the ground. But a couple had not drunk the wine and they ran off in horror.

Before half an hour was gone, every man was dead . . .

Like Lucas's narrator, Stephanie's adds an epilogue:

That beautiful woman showed bravery that I have never or ever will encounter or witness again. I am ageing now but I still hobble down to her grave once a month to lay flowers at her grave. The words engraved touch my heart every time:

> Lies here, one brave and so beautiful,
> Who gave her life to save the lives of others,
> A Godly heroine gone and never forgotten.

I made sure she had a proper burial and received the praise she deserved.

San Pedro is once again a thriving village. It has beautiful scenery. Do they know they owe so much to people like Carmen and her son and mother who lay beside her?

In her re-viewpointing, Stephanie has matched the original in setting the scene economically and in creating a narrator who is plausibly reflective. She has taken account of the 'facts' – even to the old-woman's being 'bedrid'. With good reason she has put into her text some of the material which the poem's narration had left out but the reader would supply (e.g. what the Captain did to the woman). She has seen that what is an enigma from the French viewpoint would be explicable from the Spanish viewpoint (e.g. the woman's wish to sacrifice herself and her child) and provided an explanation. She has neatly turned a central point of information from the French viewpoint (the survival of Lucas's narrator) into an enigma from the Spanish viewpoint (two escapees – who was the other?) She has exposed some of the poem's hidden values of using women as pawns in that invented reference to the woman's father opposing her marriage. (Her friend's husband is a bit of a brute, too, in parts of Stephanie's version not quoted here.)

In treating Lucas's text as only one surface narration of a story which can have other narrations such as hers and to which invented detail can be added, Stephanie has recognized the artefactual nature of the text in a way which I shall argue makes for empowering, rather than vulnerable, readings. But she has also used her imaginative knowledge of how people perceive, think, feel, behave and talk and evaluate each other in order to reconstruct the woman: she draws on the connections between art and life which constitute the humane argument for literature I sketch in section 5.1.

The word 'viewpoint' is unsatisfactory: its literal sense is too limitedly visual to convey its meaning when applied to book-narration (as distinct from film-narration). And its everyday metaphorical use for self-interested opinion is also too limited. Charlotte Brontë's choice of Jane Eyre's viewpoint ensures that we get not just what Jane sees (and hears) but also Jane's internal debates, thoughts, fantasies, dreams, evaluations and hindsights, none of which would be available to any differently situated narrator.

There are taxonomies of narrators: big mouths; sidekicks; spear-carriers; peeping Toms; puppet-movers. We could make one with our examples: the confessional protagonist (Jane); the reflectively or unreflectively remembering minor participant (the French soldier, or Bill in 'Spit Nolan'); the detached commentator (of *Business News*); the hybrid ('Owl Creek' – where the narrator changes from a behavioural observer to a mind-reader like Brecht's singer with 'Hear what he thought and did not say' – Section III). Within these taxonomies, the theorists, since Booth, all take care to distinguish between viewpoint and voice (e.g. Booth 1961; Chatman 1978; Genette 1980).

Voice

There is little danger of confusing viewpoint and voice in eighteenth-century novels where authors tell what characters do, see and feel, then make their own urbane comments on it, all directly to the reader. But, especially since the influence of Henry James's arguments that the novel should be told through one central consciousness, and the invention of stream-of-consciousness techniques, there has been a tendency to treat fictional texts as if they were merely running commentaries on events, in their own voices, by participants. This is a special temptation with much children's literature, often written in the first person. But most narrators are more complicated than that. Consider how some classics manage to convey more than their first-person protagonists notice and report, as Swift's political satire through Gulliver's innocent account. Or consider *The Adventures of Huckleberry Finn* (rightly not classed as a children's book now, but still one that young people should be helped to read, in my opinion): there not only the viewpoint but even the idiolect is that of the innocent and unlettered protagonist, but still the author gets into the voice sufficiently to make his irony register with the reader.

A very clear distinction between viewpoint and voice is provided by *Black Beauty* where the viewpoint is a horse's but the voice a human being's. This can produce some odd effects. The horse can talk freely to other horses, but not to human beings ('"Dumb beast?" Yes we are: but if I could have spoken, I could have told . . .' – Chapter 30). But the horse can speak to the reader or at least narratee, and in quite a self-consciously authorial manner ('I must not forget to mention' – Chapter 3). The logical conclusion of this is that the text is addressed by a writing horse to reading horses. And if you read it as human to human you're pulled up short by such details as the narrator's apparent pleasure that when his friend Merrylegs is past work 'he should be shot and buried' (Chapter 21).

Another clear distinction between viewpoint and voice is in *Jane Eyre* – superficially a running commentary on events, in her own voice, by a participant. But though the viewpoint and central consciousness are those of Jane the participant, the narrator is old Jane, whose voice is not that of the young Jane. The immature child's fears of the red-room at Gateshead are conveyed in mature language (Chapter 2) and Jane's first sight of Bertha, narrated entirely from her own viewpoint, is narrated in the objective language of a retrospector, not that of an amazed and horrified participant (Chapter 26). Vocabulary is one indicator and so is tense: the voice of the narrator usually uses the past tense to narrate that for which the participating viewpointer would use the present tense.

The second passage quoted from *Black Jack* in section 1.3 neatly illustrates the interaction of viewpoint and voice. The description of the moonlight and the coffin is from the trapped apprentice's viewpoint, but the voice ('intricately fashioned') is that of the narrator. At 'In the eyes?' the narration enters Tolly's head and adopts his voice ('Sure to God . . .') even while remaining in the third person ('They were staring at him!'). But the next sentence not only resumes the narrator's voice, but adopts a new, distant viewpoint ('Bartholomew Dorking, sent from Shoreham . . .'). In *Jane Eyre* the voice of the narrator is fairly consistent: it is that of the implied old Jane who bonds with the implied reader with her 'Dear Reader'. However, there are exceptions – it's Currer Bell who tells us she's skipping eight years at the beginning of Chapter 10 or screwing up the suspense at seeing burnt Thornfield by the delaying 'illustration' of the sleeping mistress comparison (Chapter 36), and it is Charlotte Brontë, the eldest surviving daughter of Haworth Parsonage, who butts in to commend her patron's *Marmion* as better than most modern poetry (Chapter 32 – and see Wilks 1975: 67). But even the main narrator's voice is complex: it quotes the voices of other characters (selecting and censoring in accordance with the narrator's soundpoint and sensibility?); it also expresses a great range of experience such as sense impressions, thoughts, memories, moral judgements and even dreams and inner voices of reason, romance and conscience. It would help students to get a grasp on that complexity by allocating the parts of a suitably chosen part to different categories (the first page of *Jane Eyre* would do well enough).

A teacher's problem with *Jane Eyre* might be to find a way to draw the student-reader's attention to the complexity of that voice by slowing down the reading at some point and making the narration strange enough to be inspected. In contrast, with 'Owl Creek' the problem may be to familiarize the narration enough for the reader to be undistracted enough to read the plot intelligibly through the inconsistencies of voice and the changing relationship between viewpoint and voice. It starts with the voice of an uninformed narrator and an objective 'camera-type' viewpoint which seems to be drawing back from close-up detail to wider setting but at the same time other narrative devices seem to focus in (such as changing from the distant 'a' man to the more familiar 'the' man). Then both viewpoint and voice seem to become Farquhar's. The implied author enters with a comment on the problems of writing ('these thoughts, which have here· to be set down in words . . .'). At the 'ticking watch' part we have the character's soundpoint and the author's voice. Part II appears to begin in the voice of a knowall narrator but the second sentence suggests an irony (especially if you know something of Bierce) which changes the voice to that of the author – the one who had intruded into Part I with non-fiction remarks about Death and liberals hanging gentlemen. The third sentence also introduces that curious tease of the implied author's refusing to disclose an explanation to the reader. The perplexingness of the fantasy-escape of the third part of the story is partly caused by its staying with Farquhar's viewpoint (disconcertingly destabilized by knowall-narrator phrases such as 'the power of thought was restored' and observer-narrator phrases such as 'The man in the water saw . . .' and summarizings like 'All that day he travelled'). But throughout that section the voice – with its third person and literary vocabulary – is that of a cool writer, even when it modulates into the present tense before its sudden Farquharesque 'Ah, how beautiful she is!' The discontinuities in viewpoint and voice, and the misalignment of the two, seem to me to add to the disturbingness of the story already created by its inclination to sadistic voyeurism, but also to make it worthy of close study. Collaborative marking of photocopied text with different coloured highlight pens according to viewpoint and voice is one possibility. With more conventional stories than 'Owl Creek', it can be worth while to add representations of viewpoint or voice, or both, to 3W diagrams. Fuentes' characterization of 'Owl Creek' at the start of this section, seems to me to make it proto-modernist, but even classics of realism like *Jane Eyre* or simple melodramas like *Spain, 1809* (with its 'They had to learn', 'men are brave', and 'I remember') have their fragmented consciousnesses. As well as the different voices of author, implied author, narrator and characters, there are – in a reader's reading – the repressed voices (Bertha Rochester's) or the voices the reader brings from other related reading (so that Hermia might begin to speak of Bertha; Grusha or Tess might begin to speak of the Spanish woman; Icarus or Black Jack might speak through Farquhar or Spit Nolan). Bakhtin (1981) argues that many-voicedness characterizes the novel, and claims it as the discursive form which disputes the languaged hegemony of Establishments.

Maybe a developed self-consciousness about narrational voice might have helped Caroline, Jackie, Sue and Dawn (see section 1.2) in a way which would have led them to do more justice to Borges's opaque narration of his objective characters' doings, Saki's superciliousness at his characters' expense, and Hughes's identification with his subject. In particular, understanding the differences between styles of narration and differentiating responses accordingly, might help students to appreciate underlying ideologies in a critical way – the subject of the next chapter.

3.3 Showing and telling

A last feature of ways of telling is worth discussing because it involves a distinction which could help students with their own writing as well as with an appreciation of narrative structure and rhetoric. It is the distinction between showing and telling, which since Aristotle has provided a long-running controversy – about aesthetic policy rather than literary description. Chatman (1978) calls it 'showing/telling'; Genette (1980), following Aristotle and Plato, calls it 'mimesis/diegesis'.

Proponents of some practitioners of the nineteenth-century novel – culminating in James and side-lining Dickens – have made a virtue of the novel's supposed ability to show its events and characters directly to the reader, without the author appearing to intervene and tell about them. Ideally, a novel would have only one viewpoint and voice. From one character's viewpoint and in that one character's voice everything they saw, did, felt and thought would be directly conveyed to the reader. All show; no tell. The model would appear as simple as that in Figure A because all the artfulness of Figure F would be concealed. Such elegant economy (as practised by James) contrasts with overtly narrated and many-voiced eighteenth-century novels.

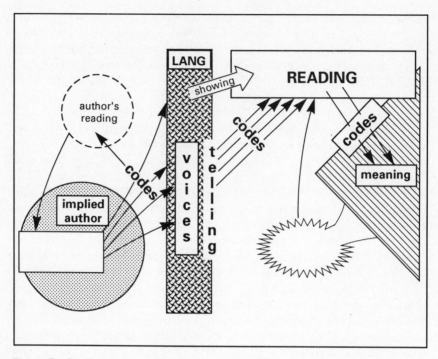

Figure F Reading the implied author's use of viewpoint, voices, and modality

Of course, pure showing is impossible in narrative art. A verbal medium is always a translation of 'real life', at best a metaphoric network of metonymic metaphors. All right, so how about using the more naturalistic medium of film with its untranslated images and sounds? But films, unlike life, have starts, finishes and cuts. Video, then – shooting real people and running non-stop in real time? Even that would be contaminated by tellingness – someone would have to choose the camera position, angle and focus. So suppose real people in real space. Then we have convention-ridden theatre. And even happenings are planned.

The contrast between the showing tendency and the telling tendency is discussed here in the context of narrative rhetoric, but it relates to section 5.1's distinction between realism and formalism in art and the tension between Dionysian life which should be fighting out of all art and experience, and the Appollonian art which should be shaping it.

The binarity of that is complicated by the reader's responsive role. What makes the reading is not so much what the author shows and tells so much as what the reader perceives and learns. Since much of that is carried out between the lines, we could project the reader's inference on to the narrator's plane and add implying to showing and telling. One function of the reader's inference can be to use clues in the author's telling to make the work show. With no naturalistic medium available to him, Shakespeare was honest about the need for the receiver of the work to play a part in turning telling into showing, a process which was cleverly paralleled by the way Olivier's film of *Henry V* changed from a record of a conventional staged telling to a naturalistically filmed showing:

> Suppose within the girdle of these walls
> Are now confin'd two mighty monarchies,
> . . .
> Piece out our imperfections with your thoughts:
> Into a thousand parts divide one man,
> And make imaginary puissance;
> Think, when we talk of horses, that you see them
> Printing their proud hoofs i' the receiving earth;
> For 'tis your thoughts that now must deck our kings,
> Carry them here and there, jumping o'er times,
> Turning the accomplishment of many years
> Into an hour-glass: . . .

The division of storying into showing and telling (and implying) is a matter of individual judgement and perhaps dispute between individual readers. Some parts of narrative texts might seem to fit both those modes of transmission, simultaneously. Others fit either mode, according to by what criteria, or at what points on some scale of degree, you make the distinction. I imply below that some whole works or even genres can be classed as either showings or tellings. But in practice the distinctions between showing and telling are blurred and different readers commit themselves to a story or recognize its artefactuality to different degrees. And in novels, especially, there may also be obvious distinctions between the rhetorical function of different parts of the text. In *Black Beauty* some parts of the story are obviously told: Ginger tells short versions of both her early and her later life (Chapters 7 and 40). (But notice how Anna Sewell is adopting a horsey persona through which to do her telling – in a sense she is *showing* us a horse *telling*.) Other parts of *Black Beauty* are more obviously shown. I, at least, feel I am taking part in Captain's Charge of the Light Brigade (Chapter 14) and share Black Beauty's view of Ginger's corpse, even though he says he 'can't speak' of parts of it (Chapter 40).

The emotional power of certain implied events can make us more involved and begin to visualize and infer quasi-real experience while we are reading. A novel can encompass these variations (and other forms of rhetoric: some chapters in *Black Beauty* are homilies). Writers of shorter pieces are more likely to keep them to one mode, as in a teller of a joke or a describer of the subject-matter of a descriptive prose poem.

When the text is showing, it tricks readers into forgetting that they are experiencing a verbal artefact: they feel as if they are directly experiencing what the story tells directly. Such tricky realism became the staple of the Victorian novel (and even drama) and remains the staple of the popular novel, including the children's novel. *Jane Eyre* is an example. Its ambition has influenced the popular vocabulary of engagement with books. We talk as if we become 'lost in the world of the book' or 'feel as if we are there' and can easily be misled into thinking that reading is a form of vicarious experience or even identification. In the next chapter I argue that students, by recognizing that they are being told what novelists would like them to think they are being shown, should learn to resist an uncritical commitment to worlds which authors try to create and which are insidiously and often unintentionally loaded with ideology. Texts which are read as if they were showing domesticate their values in their readers; texts which are read as if they were tellings estrange those values, and make them available for inspection and criticism.

Many realistic authors play on this susceptibility to treat art as if it is life by writing in a style of extreme showingness. They use documentary information, detailed description with little comment or selection, and apparently realistic speech and pacing of the language. The commonest of those features of literary narrative discourse which tend to showing must be the 'reproduction' of dialogue and monologue. We have seen how important and how various it is in *Jane Eyre*. But would a work consisting entirely of speeches have a plot? Only if some of them told the reader about events, like the old butler's description of the Thornfield fire (*Jane Eyre*, Chapter 36). Another narrative technique which makes for showingness is including or reproducing written documents (e.g. Rivers's self-righteous note to Jane at the start of the same chapter, or the 'Baskervilles-legend' document). But not even that can achieve pure 'mimesis': even if letters, diary entries or public notices are in facsimile rather than print they are still ditto objects in books aimed to entertain a fiction-reading public rather than one-off realia with historically specific sites, purposes and intended readers. There's nothing like coming across a reproduced press-cutting for reminding us that we're reading a book rather than looking through a window on the world. So a second problem with reproducing quasi-realia is that in most reader's experience it defeats any naturalistic object by drawing attention to the textuality of the would-be transparent text: it is a more effective device in a book about being a book than in a realist text: all a literary work can really imitate is itself.

A characteristic of telling is compression. Flashbacks like Part II of 'Owl Creek' are tellings. However, though 'telling' is often much more direct than detailed *trompe-l'oeil* and *trompe-l'oreille* 'showing', that need not necessarily be the case. Authorial intrusion is a feature of telling and such intrusions can be digressive: in the famous case of Sterne his intrusions not only manage to hold up the action but actually make time go backwards.

There is clearly a connection between this show/tell distinction and the previous chapter's distinction between forks and descriptors. The first section of

'Occurrence at Owl Creek Bridge', strongly descriptive, is a showing; the second section, a mixture of forks and descriptors, is also a mixture of tellings and showings. After the implication of the bridge raid in the gap between the second and third parts, the ambiguous third section mixes telling and showing, at a first reading at least, just as it mixes forks and descriptors.

A more detailed exposition of showing/telling would link it with earlier insights from theory about such features of individuals' responsive readings as reading-time and gap-filling and about such features of the structures of literary narrative texts as flashes, tropes, forks and voices. Take the opening of *Spain, 1809*. 'All day we had ridden through scarred, tawny hills' is a piece of *telling* in anyone's common-sense meaning of the word; one fork and two descriptors to narrate the events of a whole day in a reading-time of a second or so. 'At last the cool/Of splashing water' is more of a problem. I'd say this is a *showing*, because, for me at any rate, the words create a feeling and a sound which strongly suggests relief and comfort (it doesn't matter that the recreation of the implied experience is through touch and sound, rather than through sight, for it to be called *showing*). The next two phrases – 'Then two blackened mills,/A slaughtered mule' – are tellings, for me, because they do not evoke visual images so much as they make my mind work to inform myself of the implied situation and past actions for which they act as metonyms: my sense as I read them is of working out what has happened, not of sharing the narrator's sense-impression. The same applies to the next stanza – 'And there, crag-perched, the village – San Pedro – /We came to burn./ (Two convoys ambushed in the gorge below./They had to learn.) For me at least 'crag-perched' does not immediately provide a ready-made image of a comparable village in my own ill-travelled experience through which to show itself. Furthermore, the 'We came to burn', following so quickly on it, immediately subsumes it into a piece of anticipative telling. That powerful line 'We came to burn' – 'telling' in both senses – combines with the next two, the telling of 'Two convoys ambushed in the gorge below' and the implicatory 'They had to learn', to provide our second example in this poem of telling and showing by *implying*. (The first example is the heat and discomfort of the all-day ride, and another – whenever it happens for any particular reader – will be who are the 'we' and whose is the narrative voice.) The responsive reader, inferring what 'they' 'had to learn' now sees the purpose of the all-day riding, forsees the fate of the vulnerably 'crag-perched' village, and – in smaller focus – infers the significance of 'They had to learn'. Reverting briefly to the voice, narrating a story in the first person, as here, in one sense creates its mimetic force by appearing to authenticate what's narrated. On the other hand, by foregrounding the narrator, it exposes the work as an artefact rather than a slice of life.

This analysis shows how the categorization of parts of a narrative text into showing and telling is a fluid business. A section of text cannot be categorized on purely internal evidence – it needs a context – and it may have its categorization changed by changes in the reading-time (when more context becomes available to bear upon it). Furthermore, a section of text on a middle scale (here, the few lines which *imply* that the village is to be burned in a retaliatory raid) may contain elements differently classified on a small scale (here, the *telling* of the ambush and the potential *showing* of the crag-perching).

Moving on in less exhaustive detail, the next few stanzas show the state of the deserted village. Except for the telling implications of past forks in 'left behind', 'slashed and hacked' and 'fed', it is all showing. Some parts are metonyms selected from the whole connected scene (the gutter, the smoke, the absence of a goat) and some are correspondence-tropes ('death's-head hovels' – an extended metaphor in conventional terminology – and like 'human dead' – a simile in conventional, terminology). In verbal texts, all such description must be metonymic or metaphoric because it is simply impossible for words to show an experience as completely as film, say, can show visual experience. But film has more difficulty than verbal text in selecting detail so suggestively as the poet has done with his metonyms here, or making such obviously pointed correspondences as the comparisons here to 'blood', 'human dead' and 'funeral-pyre'.

Skipping the sixth and seventh stanzas, the conversation I take to be showing, even though we don't hear it. My criterion is that the author tries, through a convention we now accept as realistic, to reproduce exactly what was said, in the order it was said. Stephanie's word-for-word reproduction of these fragments of transcript in her re-viewpointing of the last section would reinforce my argument, as would the fact that in the reading-aloud which a poem should receive, the history-time and reading-time are the same. But many qualifications remain: did the Spanish woman and the French captain converse in the English language reproduced in the poem's text?

And so on. The rest of the poem provides some obvious, and some problematical, examples of the categories. Sometimes there are words that even state their own categorization ('that grim surmise' tells of an inference the reader is thus invited to share) and there are some interesting examples of phrases which have a double function ('Ashen-grey' seems to me both to show the woman and to tell that she is dying). The striking 'I will not tell' obviously implies, but also, because it perversely urges us to imagine the atrocities it refrains from listing, may have the effect of telling us what it will not tell and even – if we have a strong visual imagination – of showing us it too – a paradoxical performative.

Any analysis like this, even a coarse or partial one, entails close examination of the text and discussion. That alone is an argument for encouraging students to look for the show/tell distinctions, providing they understand what they are. The distinction is a useful one for discussing differences between stories in different discursive forms (e.g. book and film; radio and TV adaptation; photo- and prose-record) or indeed between the forms themselves. It is also useful in studying the differences between history-time, narrative-time and reading-time. One way in which the showing and telling in a work can be mapped is for the plot (or story) to be segmented and then the segments marked on a time-line but above or below the line according to whether they are showing segments or telling segments. Such a mapping can sometimes reveal general structural or rhetorical features of literary narrative – for instance the frequency and advisability of alternating showings and tellings, as manifested by switching between dialogue and description and flashback and authorial comment in novels.

But probably the most important argument for thinking about this rhetorical concept is that it helps readers to recognize that texts are still telling even what they seem to be showing, and they are thereby more easily understood by keen readers to be ideologically loaded and deserving of caution.

3.4   Realism and convention

The operation of the rhetorical functions of showing, telling and implying, and the interactions between them, differ in particular forms of narrative text – poems, short stories, novels, plays, films or whatever. The differences between these different discursive vehicles, especially in the ways in which they seem to show or tell, raises some issues for the next chapter about appropriate texts for developing critical and resistant readers.

Dramatic works might seem the best examples of texts which show: plays have real talking people (even if they are in a room with a missing wall). Films can improve on that: they can replace their book-source's verbal descriptions of scenery with real woods and fields and if they are films of plays they can 'ventilate' them by taking Puck round the world in forty minutes or Albee's George and Martha down to a car-park for one of their rows. But are films all that realistic? When they change the details of a stage convention they may substitute an equally unrealistic film convention (the hero standing tall through falling masonry for the melodramatic ending of the film of Shaw's *The Devil's Disciple*). And what is film but illuminated images cast on whitened walls? Some of its actors are dead. The importance of spotting the narrative devices (less obvious but just as powerful as the narrative devices of stage-plays) was urged in section 3.1, based on the assumption that any recognition of narrative device in any discursive medium would transfer to an appreciation of, and wariness about, text.

Consider the possibilities of a student's first encounter with *A Midsummer Night's Dream* on page, stage or screen. (It would be unfortunate, as I said in section 2.1, if schoolchildren's first encounter with the play was with the text – the text which may tell not so much what the dramatic realization tells as what its dramatic realization is to show.) Despite my qualifications above, film and TV are media relatively well suited to showing events realistically. They have inspired a genre – the documentary – with realism as its essence. The production of *A Midsummer Night's Dream* in the BBC TV series had lots of real water and mud. At times one could imagine that one was being shown – on television – events in a real wood rather than on a screen or in a TV studio. One could imagine that, but most viewers would not believe that. The young children with whom I watched it made remarks which showed they knew it was a TV production with actors in a studio, not Athenians in a wood, and they were not, unfortunately, likely to get spattered with mud.

> They'll be playing a record for that noise.
>
> Those kids won't be singing that . . . They don't have to do anything: they just sit there.

They also made remarks which showed they knew they were watching TV in a house, not eavesdroppers in a wood:

> (*picking up the dog*) It's fair Helena, my own true love.
> Oh, I've to kiss you. I don't fancy that.
> Do you like my furry Helena?

Peter Hall's 1969 film of *A Midsummer Night's Dream* had more potential for illusory realism. A film budget usually allows more cash to be spent on locations, and the experience of watching a large screen in a crowd in a dark cinema is more enveloping than watching a small screen, perhaps in an illuminated room of a house in which other activities such as playing with the dog are also going on. But in some respects even Hall's film made no pretensions about its nature as a telling, rather than a showing. The lovers wore modern clothes and the setting included what was clearly an English country house, not an Athenian dwelling of any period. (But then, of course, in Shakespeare, Athenians were like his English contemporaries – at least they spoke English and referred to English flora and fauna.) The film-watchers were in the same position as the audience of *A tedious brief scene of young Pyramus and his love Thisbe*: needing 'imagination' to 'amend' the signs presented. For instance the use of jump-cuts proved there was no intention of hiding the fact that we were seeing a selection of events, or rather a selection of recordings of simulated events, through the eye of a camera, not our own eye. When the techniques characteristic of cinema are foregrounded we are reminded that we are being told, not being shown. In *A Midsummer Night's Dream*, story-telling is complicated by the importance of illusion and delusion as themes of the story. As well as being realistic media, film and TV are also media in which technical tricks are possible. Oberon, for instance, could become 'invisible' literally and instantly. But because we are aware of how this is done, we are also aware that we are being told, in cinematic language, that he becomes invisible, rather than that we are being shown an instant invisibility which we do not believe could happen in 'real life'. (There is also the difficulty that the presence of a genuinely invisible eavesdropping Oberon is not perceived whereas the presence of a conventionally invisible eavesdropping Oberon is obvious!)

In Peter Brook's 1970 stage production of *A Midsummer Night's Dream* the magic elements in the story were emphasized by having the actors dress, play and juggle like magicians. The setting and costumes were quite unrealistic and the use of conventions from familiar but non-narrative forms of entertainment (circus, music-hall) emphasized that here were entertainers telling us a story rather than showing us events. In John Caird's 1989 production there were 'quotations' from cinematic special effects, with Puck magically reversing his victims' movements, for instance.

The high points of would-be naturalism in the theatre were the great Victorian actor-managers' productions on large stages. Herbert Tree's production of *A Midsummer Night's Dream* had real trees and rabbits on stage presumably to have the audience feel they were being shown the Athenian wood. In Shakespeare's own day, in contrast, there could be little chance to pretend. The audience were present at what was a telling of the tale of the Athenian lovers as unrealistic as the workmen's presentation of *A tedious brief scene of young Pyramus and his love Thisbe*. The women would be played by boys. The scenery would be minimal, except what was planted in the audience's perception by deliberately scene-setting speeches. The actors would perform on a stage surrounded by people, visible to each other, on three sides. They would perform in whatever light and weather was overhead. The action would be seen from as many viewpoints as there were viewers, not one dictated by a camera or proscenium arch, and, because no one believed that the Queen of the Fairies looked like a London boy who played her, the viewer's visualization of Titania would not be forever associated with the appearance of Judi Dench.

In one sense, obvious artificiality can make for 'realism': when the lovers are clearly actors, you can recognize whom you like in them – including yourself. The 'openness' of an authentic Elizabethan production would produce an experience nearer to that of reading a text than would a modern filmed production, even though the text would have been an unimportant or unintelligible manifestation of the work to most of Shakespeare's contemporary appreciators.

Brecht wanted to draw his audience's attentions to aspects of their own situations by their watching his unrealistic plays. He intended his plays to show, not quasi-real events, but moral and political truths which audiences were provoked to recognize by the manner in which the actors *told* their tales. The plays contain many unnaturalistic, non-mimetic strategies, such as characters speaking thoughts aloud, or directly to the audience, or commenting on their own actions, or singing or using captions. *The Caucasian Chalk Circle* opens with an actor playing Story-teller and beginning with the words 'In an olden time . . .' The Thames TV schools version of it kept some of the deliberately unrealistic formalized aspects of epic theatre (such as masks for the high-ups) which helped the pupils with whom I watched it to recognize their functions – to recognize, through these visual signs, abstract, rather than real-life visual, features of characters. Brecht objected to the bourgeois theatre of illusion because it encouraged audiences to accept the (to him) objectionable conditions of their lives as natural and unchangeable. His method aimed to estrange the taken-for-granted and make those objectionable conditions of their lives seem unnatural and in need of change. His intention and method are captured in these two extracts from the 'chorus' of all the actors in his short play *The Exception and the Rule*, the one which Graham differentiated from Brecht's *The Children's Crusade* in section 2.2.

> Examine carefully the behaviour of these people:
> Find it surprising though not unusual
> Inexplicable though normal
> Incomprehensible though it is the rule.
> Consider even the most insignificant, seemingly simple
> Action with distrust. Ask yourselves whether it is necessary
> Especially if it is usual.
> We ask you expressly to discover
> That what happens all the time is not natural.
> For to say that something is natural
> . . .
> . . . is to
> Regard it as unchangeable.
> . . . .
> What is customary, let it astound you.
> What is the rule, recognize it to be an abuse
> And where you have recognized abuse
> Do something about it!
>
> (Brecht 1977: 37, 60)

Histories of modern literary theory as often as not begin with Russian formalism, one of whose concepts was 'estrangement'. Shklovski believed the value of poetry is that it defamiliarizes the familiar (Hawkes 1977: 62), and crystallizes our perception of experience so that we can see its structure and nature. Brecht wants to bring the taken-for-grantedness of life into focus through the medium of his estranging literature. Among the too-easily-accepted elements of life he would expose are ideologies. Ideologies are domesticated by naturalistic literature which tells the ideological in the guise of showing the natural. Importantly for Chapter 5, non-naturalistic literature, which does not seem like life, may have more to *do* (literally) with life than naturalistic literature.

To explore theories which examine the ideological in literature we need to move out from text and its ways of telling into the context of literary reading and writing. In the next chapter we move into the culture which makes, sustains and shapes readers, texts and writers.

4   Culture and criticism

Introduction: authors in history

Step aside the text-creating or identifying reader; step aside *Jane Eyre* the text,
young Jane the protagonist and old Jane the narrator. Enter Currer Bell the
author and Charlotte Brontë, the daughter of the parsonage, the pupil at Cowan
Bridge, the governess, the good woman of Haworth, the curate's wife and the
polymath and literary figure. And follow her *The Halifax Chronicle*, Mrs Gaskell
and John Calvin. I find it interesting and helpful to understand texts as a
reflection of their writers' lives, times and beliefs. In interpreting their texts and
forming our responses to them it helps to know that Charlotte went to a school
like Lowood, that Anna Sewell was disabled and of Quaker background, that
Brecht was a communist, and that Ambrose Bierce was a restless romantic
adventurer who disappeared during Pancho Villa's Mexican war of independence and features in the Fuentes novel on which the film *The Old Gringo* is
based. (In Fuentes's novel, Bierce carries *Don Quixote* with him, seeks death by
crossing borders and bridges, and 'dies twice'.) And wouldn't we all like to know
if Shakespeare really existed? In the meantime we can infer – from the 3W
diagrams of his *Dream* or *As You Like It* perhaps – that he was a provincial gent
who preferred the humane aristocratic polity and politics of the usurped duke's
Stratford to either the machiavellian excitement of the court at the capital or the
Edenic simplicities of the Arden foresters, peasants and vagabonds.

This chapter will be more concerned with the cultures in which authors write
and readers read than with literary biography. Although I can't do equal justice to
all the influences of culture on reading represented by the questions in Figure G,
I shall suggest that both authors' texts and students' readings may deploy values,
attitudes and beliefs of which either party may remain unaware and which come
from dominant ideologies of the societies which produce the texts and the
readers. This is so even if the authors are unaware of them or are rebelling against
them: they are defined by absences and oppositions as well as presences and

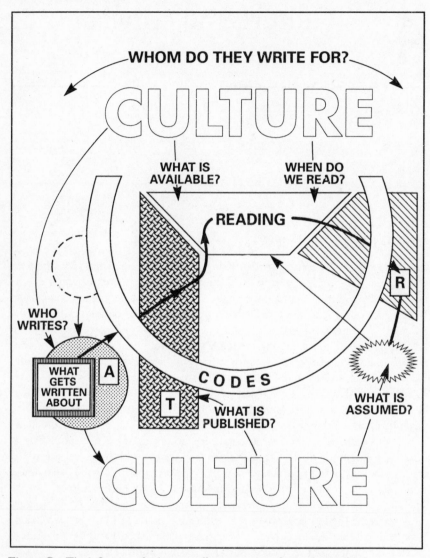

Figure G   The influence of culture on all components of narrative reading

allegiances. Nevertheless, just as I indicated the value of response theory for reminding us of the individuality of readings, I should like to assert now that the production of texts is the exercise of individual imaginations within, or even against, a framework of culture. *Jane Eyre* may say more and less than Charlotte intended, but it was not written by a spirit of the nineteenth-century mind, nor a spokesperson for the Church of England, nor a governesses' collective, nor

Engels, Darwin or Flaubert. And nor was it written by Emily Brontë, nor any old governess, nor Bessie Bronte a machine-minder in Haworth Mill.

Students are interested in authors' lives and circumstances of composition. For instance, reading Owen's letters to his mother and guessing which incidents described in them he might turn into poems illuminates a poem like *The Sentry*. To make such comparisons with life – for instance by working the other way round and using the text as a basis for guessing what might be the author's period, life-style, politics or whatever – seems to me more than a trivial party-game and to have a part to play in the more critical approaches which teach texts as contexted in culture.

So much for authors. But I said cultures also make readings by creating readers. West (1986) shows how such factors in schools as the provision of resources and the distribution of power in classrooms make differences (which presumably last for life) to students' reading tastes, styles and commitments.

In this chapter I start by describing an instance of how the period in which you read can influence what you make of a reading, and move on to how other readers – namely theorists and critics – influence readings of literary narrative and what implications that has for students. In the central section I return to authors and their cultures, and exemplify how the ideologies of their times are consciously or unconsciously infiltrated into their works. This gives a first chance to raise the question of what should be the canon of literature formally taught and recommended in education (the second is in Chapter 5). Finally I look at two vehicles of ideology in literary narrative and ways of helping students to recognize how they work: language and references to animals.

4.1 Readers in history: different generations read *Bleak House*

In 1818, *Frankenstein* appealed to readers' fear of Chartists and Luddites. In 1931 a version of the story appealed to insecure and potentially racist American film-goers' fear of violence from discontented 'degenerates'. In 1957 another film version was a Cold War parable. O'Flinn (in Humm *et al.* 1986) shows how contemporary history of different times of the production and reception of versions of the story explain its continuing popularity and the changes that were made in the different versions. (As a footnote to the last chapter, he also shows how important is film's inability to use Mary Shelley's three different narrators to influence the interpretation and effect.) The dog on the moor in Janni Howker's *The Nature of the Beast* (1985) does not symbolize what Conan Doyle's hound did.

Response theory makes clear that it isn't just the authors who influence readings, and it isn't just authors who change with time. Critics' views will influence our readings of stories, and critics change their readings with the changes in the values of the different times they live in. But few of us read criticisms of the narratives we read, especially before we read or re-read the works, and for most of us the more general climate of values in which we live is a more important influence. So we read with such contemporary values as self-development, public spirit or respect for the environment.

Literary education will influence our readings. Changes over time in the main emphases of semi-professional (i.e. teachers') readers' ways of reading was illustrated for me last year when I read Dickens's *Bleak House* for the first time. I owned an Everyman edition of 1907 which, as it turned out, had been the one which my late mother had used and annotated at teacher training college in the early 1930s. I enjoyed the irony of reading her copy of this mother-discovering novel and discovering something about her from it.

My mother's 1930s annotations were almost all concerned with characters in the plot – about whom she writes as if they were real people – or with Dickens's own biography in relation to the biographies of quasi-people in the plot. Thus, on the characters, she pencils in by one of Richard's remarks that he is 'the life and soul of the party' and 'R who gives all jokes, full of repartee and laughter'. She notes that 'we have to love Caddy' and the 'effect of Mrs J on Mr J shows effect on Caddy. She has not had support of father. Has had to grow up alone.' Of Dickens's relation to the characters in the book she writes 'Dickens' children' by a description of the neglected little Jellybys and, inside the front cover, 'Fully qualified to talk of all lower classes. But knew nothing of the Dedlocks.'

I do not know whether these, and many similar, notes were made under direct instruction or spontaneously. And if the latter is the case I don't know whether they were made as a result of my mother's natural style of engagement with the text or at the prompting of some essay-preparation task such as tracing the destruction of Richard or the salvation of Caddy. However, whatever the explanation, I think they show that sixty years ago the fashion which was taught and learnt was to treat novels as fictional biographies.

My own interest in the text, of which I have some evidence from the notes I took, show different but equally modish and culturally determined emphases. I don't know much about Dickens the man and I have no inclination to regard the characters as real people. Where their speech or behaviour arouses my emotion – as my embarrassment at the way Jo dies or Esther talks about her 'darling' Ada – the emotion is directed against Dickens the author for writing such stuff rather than against his quasi-human creations for doing or saying such things.

As my mother was, I am aware of the author behind the text, but my interest seems to be much more in Dickens as a crafty writer rather than as a father/husband/knower-of-the-lower-orders. I am interested in his repertory of styles: his clever phoneticizing of the decadent speech of the aristocratic cousins; his use of rhetorical repetition; his broad sarcasm against the parliamentary system or do-gooders. I admire, in my notes, his use of natural detail to create such suspense as that in Dedlock's wait for news of his errant wife or to act symbolically as in his famous foggy opening. And the first thing I noted was that the book has at least three narrators: Dickens as Esther; Dickens the knowall; Dickens the social satirist. And I was interested in parallels and contrasts with *Jane Eyre*.

My interest in the plotting is different from that of my mother (on the evidence of her notes) and of G. K. Chesterton who wrote the introduction to this edition. Where she seems to imply that the centre of the plot is the decay or development of character, and Chesterton that it is a comprehensive illustration of the maleficence of Chancery, what I noted were the parallels and contrasts of motifs (e.g. mothers and children lost and found), the foreshadowings (of Richard's ruin and Esther's marriage), the explicit overlappings of time and the judicious introductions of flashbacks, and the economy with which such early threads as the brickmakers' wives were picked up and woven in to fulfil some function in the story later (often implausibly coincidentally in naturalistic terms). I also noted – in another awareness of the author as craftsman – how some foundations appeared to have been laid for later buildings which did not materialize, e.g. Caddy.

Comparative cultural interests reflect my own historically situated and intertextually determined interests and prejudices. I saw (with crossed fingers) the novel as a reflection of the insecurity of even privileged lives in the high capitalist Victorian Britain we are now supposed to emulate, and was angry (with Dickens) for the complacency with which the Rouncewells co-existed with the Dedlocks and with which the Jarndyces and Boythorns were endorsed. Possibly because of my interest in Richard Sennett's *The Fall of Public Man* I saw *Bleak House* as a fascinating instance of Victorian belief in, and fear of, self-exposure by physical clues, which for me suggests comparison with *Jane Eyre* and, of course, the detective genre which culminates with Sherlock Holmes (see Sennett 1974: 161–74). This obsession is also reflected by the importance of incriminating letters and physical resemblances in the plot. The most interesting parts of the book for me were dominated by the work and speech of Inspector Bucket, who selects telling little objects, incidents and remarks (like a writer of novels), and then infers a significant story from them (like a reader of novels).

4.2   The influence of critics

A reading is influenced by the reader's having read other texts which bear on a particular reading by suggesting correspondences, or defining a genre, and so on. So, I argued in section 1.5, teaching can recognize, exploit and develop the influence on individual students' readings of their readings of other texts. Intertextuality is a function of the culture that creates the reader as well as of the reader's psychological processes while reading one particular text. Another possibility is that our reading of any one text may be influenced by other people's readings of the same text, which is good news for teachers. Even Holland (1968: 246) says he finds works more resonant when myth-critics show him the myths in them. This exerts a powerful influence in school where pupils (at least in my experience and on the evidence of small-scale surveys I have done) are as much if not more influenced by their friends' recommendations in their choice of novels from libraries, for instance, as they are by other factors such as teachers' recommendations and – intertextually – their own readings of other, related, texts. As for the use in school literature teaching of critical readings of the classics, Protherough (1983: 144–5 and 1986: 45) has some neat approaches to using critics in ways which discourage slavish imitation, and Brown and Gifford (1989) show the use of critics in A-level work which, by being comparative and related to creative and personal responses, serves to provoke the students into making their own criticisms rather than assimilating those of others (e.g. on Shakespeare, pp. 65–71).

If we take 'other people's reading of the same text' to include our experiencing of different productions of a play text, then an example would be the different interpretations of *A Midsummer Night's Dream* referred to above in section 3.4 – the TV mudbathers, Brook's acrobats and so on. Directors are readers whose readings are passed on to us by their productions. Seeing those productions influences our own readings (including visualizations) of the play texts.

More to the point, seeing different productions influences our students' readings of play texts. If they have seen only Hall's film they may think Hermia and Helena are miniskirted, but if they have seen other productions they could visualize them as Grecian, in Oxford bags (Bill Alexander's mid-1980s direction) or Victorian nighties (John Caird's 1989 RSC production). If they've seen many productions they are reminded that 'characters' in narrative literary texts are clad only in what readers clad them in – they are just signs available to be invested with whatever meanings and appearances a reader chooses. Here, of course, 'readers' include directors.

For instance, directors often set Shakespeare's plays in historically recognizable but non-Elizabethan periods and places – the Raj, Ruritania, Tombstone, Capone's Chicago or pre-war Germany. Though this may sometimes seem to be done for perverse novelty it can often be justified as finding a way of making both a comment on the society used for the setting or of finding new possibilities and cultural analogies within the text.

Directors who find such novel ways of staging classics are acting as critics, and sometimes they are influenced by critics. Critics are also alternative readers who influence our reading of a text. Let me illustrate the variety of different, ideological readings of *A Midsummer Night's Dream* by summarizing what three critics have said about it. One temptation to do so in this context is that I can give what may seem partial and biased accounts of what the critics say and excuse my idiosyncratic readings of their readings as examples of the personal response which has been argued for throughout!

Three 'readings' of A Midsummer Night's Dream

In *Shakespeare Our Contemporary*, the Polish critic Jan Kott has an essay called *Titania and the Ass's Head*, which influenced Hall's film. Kott assumes that the play was written for a first performance at a drunken teenage mate-swapping party at a wedding in a stately home – and included in-jokes about personal references and such fashionable neo-Platonic ideas as that Eros is blind. Such an aristocratic origin would explain the contempt for the workers inscribed in the text – at odds with the inclusive humanity for which Shakespeare's work is often praised. That's an example of the culture of a writer's intended audience influencing readings.

Kott draws our attention to the frightening aspect of the wood into which the lovers are plunged. The animals in this wood – snakes, hedgehogs, newts, blind-worms, spiders, beetles, bats – are far from the Disney-like accoutrements to a pleasant sylvan setting such as many depictions or productions of the play (or settings of its songs) would suggest. Using knowledge of contemporary beliefs and the imagery of the text, Kott brings out for his readers some of the suggestions of the text which would be more available for Shakespeare's contemporaries than they are for us. For instance, he tells us that the donkey was regarded not so much as an amiable pet but as a byword for rampant sexuality, and Puck not as a mischievous fairy but as an evil force of nature.

To read Kott and receive such information will colour our reading (or visualization, or reading-aloud, or watching, or performing or directing or writing about) *A Midsummer Night's Dream*. In the essay he also describes orgiastic images from Bosch and Goya which he suggests as apt guides for directors. I confess to having been influenced by this essay when I directed a travesty of *A Midsummer Night's Dream* involving the whole fourth year of a secondary modern school when I was a young teacher. The audience were bombarded with concrete music, flashing lights, aerosol scents, four identical Pucks each with four identical faces, and infiltrated and teased by ill-clad dirt-streaked fairies who'd been chosen for their emaciation and deprived of their wings to the despair of the needlework teacher. (A similarly monomaniac friend of mine designed a school production of the play to be a sacrificial nature-cult in a Stonehenge setting.) Kott's historical knowledge of the circumstances of the text's first realization suggests a contemporary introjection – I 'sold' the story to my fourth-years by appealing to their experiences of blind infatuation with its attendant jealousies, self-disgusts, deceptions and so on. Further, Kott's cultural knowledge of the references in the play suggests a significance which it would have for its first audience and can lead us to see it as a more natural and erotic play than we may have been led to believe by the fairy-like or Wordsworthian connotations of the cultural codes and intertextualities with which we approach a fairy-play nowadays.

Another suggestive reading from a critic is René Girard's *Myth and Ritual in Shakespeare: A Midsummer Night's Dream* in Harari (1980: 189–212). Girard, like Kott, hangs his interpretation on some clues in the text to which he draws his readers' attention. For instance Helena complains that Hermia's eyes are 'lodestars' and Hermia deplores love chosen 'by another's eyes'. Girard takes these as justification for interpreting the play as a demonstration less of the follies, dangers and horrors of being given away in marriage (as Hermia would be or, in the next chapter, Hir), so much as the hell of giving way to a form of desire which is based on envy. Lovers desire the things or people which others desire because other people desire those same things or people. So Demetrius is attracted to Hermia just because his rival Lysander wants Hermia. Hermia provides a focus for his rivalry to Lysander (and when Demetrius, in the wood, switches his lust to Helena, Lysander follows suit). Similarly, Helena envies Hermia and her lodestar eyes for attracting what she herself desires. Is Helena's lust for Demetrius any more than a projection of her envy of Hermia?

Such a machinery of desire – which essentially projects itself on to love-objects already spoken for and despises and ignores the available ones – inevitably leads to envies, jealousies, rivalries, acrimonies, enmities and conflicts. It leads to the accelerating oscillations of acceptance and rejection, idolizations and self-abasements (again signalled by imagery), and alternations of fulfilment and frustration which provide the comedy.

By using a quasi-structural analysis of the processes of desire, Girard is reinterpretating the romantic love which we are tempted to see at the centre of the play as rather a legitimization of more hostile and self-regarding psychic forces in us. The external troubles in the play (nature-reversals, family strife, lovers' tiffs, and unfeeling exercise of paternal and ducal power) are caused by these human failings. They are not natural phenomena against which the lovers' good old love is pitted. The course of true love never did run smooth just because it is the nature of love – according to Girard's *Dream* – to cause unsmoothness and look for trouble.

The play is not really a myth about humans being victims of the squabble of a god and goddess, but an external projection of the basic mental and moral unhealthiness of sexual passion, projected in this instance as a haunted wood inhabited by competing anthropomorphized psychic forces. A psychic myth rather than a nature myth. (Myths, of course, are dismissed by the prestigious figure of Theseus at the opening of Act V. But then, as Girard points out, Theseus is himself a mythical figure, so where's the authority in his scepticism? The same could be said for Sherlock Holmes.)

'Lovers desire the things or people which others desire because other people desire those same things or people. So Demetrius is attracted to Hermia just because his rival Lysander wants Hermia.' If Girard had been more interested in money than in myth he could have used that characterization of Shakespeare's lovers' loving to find in the play an anticipation of the behaviour of the acquisitive and advertising-influenced capitalist consumer. Terry Eagleton, in his *William Shakespeare* (1986: 18–26) does it for him.

Again, usually neglected words in the text are taken as significant hints towards a reinterpretation. Eagleton points out the mercenary metaphor in Theseus's opening speech:

> . . . how slow
> This old moon wanes! She lingers my desires,
> Like to a step-dame or a dowager
> Long withering out a young man's revenue.

He could equally have found a clue in Lysander's promising Hermia that they could elope to an aunt who was 'a dowager/Of great revenue'.

Like many a naive reader/viewer who has feared for the happy-ever-afterness of the marriages with which the play is consummated, Eagleton is sceptical about the naturalness and permanence of the unions: Theseus and Hippolyta were once rivals in war (and lovers of Titania and Oberon); Oberon and Titania have quarrelled over an illicit love-object; Demetrius and Helena were joined once before and it didn't last; Lysander and Hermia were separated in the wood and exchanged some unforgettable insults.

The eventual marriages are presented as a social control which provides a solution to the sexual chaos of the events before and during the narrated time, and retrospectively designates previous desires as illusory. Eagleton suggests all this is a con: why should the final desires on which the four pairs of lovers' marriages are based be any more reliable than the volatile infatuations and obsessions which have manoeuvred them up to then? Aren't the actions of 'real' people as controlled by illusions and absences as those of the lovers in their nightmare were controlled by the elusive Puck? (Puck's last word, like Theseus's dismissal of myths, is undermining: in his last speech of the play Puck promises 'all is mended' – as he is 'an honest Puck'!) So a 3W diagram, or a pattern of forks, may merely circle round on itself and repeat, filling in the interchangeable names. Another critic (Greer 1986: 119–24) tells us that Shakespeare's endorsement of marriage in his comedies was unusual and original.

In his striking opening remarks on the play Eagleton points out the paradox that love – of all momentous experiences – is the one for the expression of which we are most dependent on secondhand, clichéd, quoted, soiled, insincere-sounding wordings. Love-talk is inescapably intertextual. In our culture and *A Midsummer Night's Dream*, love is the quintessence and defining quality of the individual; but, paradoxically, love can only be realized in standard, interchangeable units, handled and soiled by many other users in the past. Love can be used, and attaches itself indiscriminately. The worth of your love, for other people, can change dramatically.

Of what else is that characterization true? In our culture money is the quintessence and defining quality of the individual, but, paradoxically, money can only be realized in standard, interchangeable units, handled and soiled by many other users in the past. Money can be used, and attaches itself indiscriminately. The worth of your money, for other people, can change dramatically.

So Eagleton finds in the play a critique of the capitalist values which were beginning to replace medieval and religious values in economic and moral life in

Shakespeare's time. In medieval society, a sense of mutuality put *use value* into people's entitlements and deployed absolute values as a guide to economic behaviour (such as – Eagleton does not say, but I would – the doctrine of 'fair price'). But in capitalist society, bourgeois individualism puts *exchange value* into commodities. People, like things (and the difference has diminished), have no intrinsic worth or worth which comes from their needs or their histories; their worth is defined by how much they are wanted, because such desirability determines what they can be sold or exchanged for.

Three readings of a work which, if we read them, will influence our own responses to seeing or reading the work. If we encounter more than one of these critiques, then we cannot believe that the characters and events of the *Dream* are real, nor that any one interpretation is unproblematical. But these three readings also illustrate that the components of literary – and more specifically narrative – reading are not just arbitrary signs, formal items to be disposed in pretty patterns. I said texts were signs available to be invested with whatever meanings and appearances a reader chooses. But when we readers, or their inventors, or other readers, invest them with meanings, we choose meanings about which we care about, loaded with erotic, psychic or economic significances.

4.3   Culture and meaning: insidious values in Victorian novels

> . . . reading is not an innocent activity. Readers are situated in culturally determined discursive traditions, and the effects of these traditions determine the nature of the reading a text will be given and the meaning assigned to it.
>
> (Gilbert in Corcoran and Evans 1987: 245)

'Black Beauty': *kindness to animals and rural idylls*

Black Beauty was written in 1877, when movements against cruelty to animals (and people) were not uncommon, but exploiting horses was central to both the rural and urban economies of England. Anna Sewell wrote it from within the culture of the time, culture being defined (as in my introduction to this chapter) as a social group's values, attitudes and beliefs. Anna Sewell was from a Quaker background and not entirely typical of her times and class. She was a leading critic of animal cruelty and in some respects her views were exceptional – cranky by the standards of her time and still progressive by those of our time (she was against fox-hunting, for instance). She was also disabled and relied on horses to get about even more than most of her contemporaries. So the attitudes to animals she embodies in her children's novel, though not revolutionary, are abnormal but well informed, and may have contributed to humane attitudes to animals and people's subsequent use of them. The episodic plot of *Black Beauty* systematically exposes such particular evils as tail-docking and the unnecessary use of blinkers and bearing-reins, and it also incidentally presents information about living conditions in its time, especially in the countryside. It depicts the big estates, many created by merchants newly wealthy from investment in slave-grown sugar or new industries supplied by raw material from mining or colonial conquest, the inns for stage-coach travellers, horse fairs, and the Poor Houses built for those who had become unemployed and homeless as a result of the creation of new estates and agricultural 'improvements'.

So much is history and obvious. But our concern is the work – the text and our reading of it – and there are pervasive moral qualities in the text less emphasized than kindness to animals. In general Anna Sewell is on the side of modesty, kindness and common sense. Some of her personal and group morality is openly expressed, especially in a plot which includes many inserted homilies by people and horses. For instance, she is against the vanity of the aristocrats and has a pragmatic Protestant disdain for those who preach their religion more than they practise it (Chapter 36). The embedded cultural values reflect aspects of the author's mid-Victorian bourgeois culture more typical than her causes, and, because of the continuing popularity of the book with children, continue to influence contemporary culture by forming attitudes in young readers, over a century later. As well as informing the readers about socio-economic conditions, the text, less openly, exhibits pervasive political and sociological ideas about people. In her time, the life of the genteel, rural middle-classes was being threatened by the energy and revolutionary potential of the new, brutal, industrial towns and the activities that went on there. With the threatened way of life went threatened values (which include rearing children into a passive, complacent docility, about which I shall say more in section 4.6). To expose this I have delayed until now some of my advocacy of the laudable fashion of using standard forms of game-making in literature teaching which I could well have put in Chapter 2.

The most easily used form of games is board games. Many popular children's books are quests, providing the journey element and the hazards and good fortunes which characterize Snakes and Ladders and its more complex and contextualized developments. Novels, as we have seen, even when they are not progressions through space, are progressions in time and often progressions in some more metaphorical sense, as from innocence to experience or from insecurity to security or from one apparently stable state to another. (These shapes themselves, like the comparative emphases in stories of character, event, or setting, or the strength of connection between causes and consequences, are ideologically telling. They are weak in *Black Beauty*: there's a lot of luck.) Black Beauty goes from a stable foalhood in a rural stable through a troubled adolescence among the aristocracy and an unstable maturity in the town, to return to a stable retirement in another rural stable. Such plots lend themselves to representations as a series of stages over which the players propel themselves by the luck of the dice and also the salvations and legs-up or disasters and set-backs provided by fortune, favour, wisdom (or their opposites). Furthermore, some versions of the basic Snakes and Ladders format involve acquiring cards or talismans for later use – like Perseus's helmet or knowledge of the world. Deciding that a board game is an apt representation of the progress of a plot, and deciding what spatial and visual form that progress should take, is an instructive decision for students to make. So is what sorts of events or characteristics should constitute advancers and retarders.

Now suppose our students are to construct a board game from the events and material of *Black Beauty*. How are we to represent the goal and the sorts of typical along-the-way vicissitudes which would represent advantages and disadvantages in the spirit of the text? What would a player acquire to his/her advantage? First, avoid men: they are the violent ones, the hunters, the soldiers and the overloaders of carts. Their anti-equine activities are often provoked by alcohol, exclusively used by men in the book. Tobacco comes off little better and starts a fire. When horses are saved from cruelty it is usually by women, especially ladies whose sweet reasonableness dissuades and converts ignorant male townees. Old is better than young (Mr Ryder than his cruel son or the Old Ostler than his careless assistant – Chapters 6 and 15) and that goes for the old ways too – the ways of the old countryside and its order are better than those of the new towns. (This has to be qualified by saying that in the plot the solid squirearchy are favourably distinguished from the irresponsible aristocracy, a distinction which I shall mention in the next section.) As one might expect from the circumstances of Anna Sewell's early life, her book shows the town as the site of most cruelty and drunkenness: it is where Black Beauty suffers most and it kills Ginger. It is also where there is politicking: the good grooms, ostlers and coachmen in the book are dutiful and deferent (the saintly cabman Jerry redeems his low urban origins by sabbatarianism, born-again abstention, love of the countryside and despising the activities of 'An Election') and the women didn't have the vote then. Breeding, not the vote, confers dignity, wisdom and grace. Although a rural paradise is set against an urban hell, the countryside to which Black Beauty returns is only an Arcadia because any who do not accord with its old order are ruthlessly expelled and disappear from a would-be critical consciousness – the boys and men sacked or left in a thorn hedge (Chapters 1 and 13), imprisoned or killed (Chapters 20 and 25), and in one case the dead boozer's family is banished to the Poor House (Chapter 26). Modesty, kindness and common sense is very much the preserve of the landowners (their retainers being at best obedient puppets) but it is exercised only with (*nouvelle*) *noblesse oblige*: one wonders if, were the roles reversed (as a classroom exercise might attempt) Lady Anne's kin would risk their lives for a turf-cutter (Chapter 24). Because her vanity makes horses suffer (Chapters 22, 23), the Duchess of W might seem a counter-example to this binarily structured economy of value, but she is a frivolous aristocrat and by disobeying her husband she proves another rule: obedience is better than disobedience. (The one disobedient mare in the story, Ginger, comes to a ghastly end.)

The dualities implicit in this analysis can be used to provide the snakes and

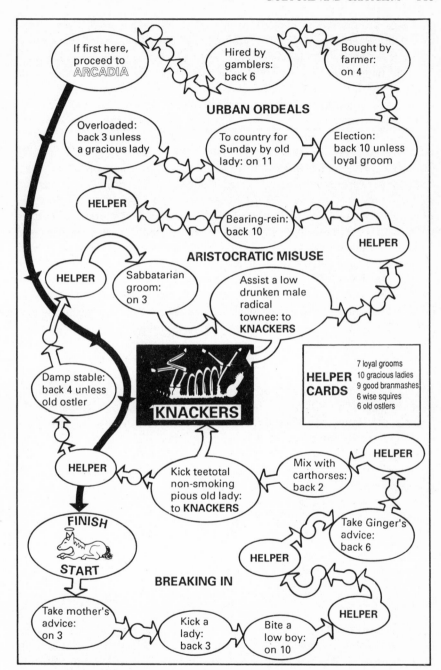

Figure 7   Binary values in *Black Beauty*: 'Return to Arcadia'

ladders of a Return to Arcadia for Black Beauty in a board game which might lead players or designers of the game to discover and question, rather than swallow, the values which it illustrates (see Figure 7). Obedience or positive involvements with the female, teetotal, smoking, old, rural and the high-born or deferent advance you. Disobedience or association with men, booze, tobacco, youth or towns, of the undeferent low-born on the whole retards you. So falling into the hands of a drunken young prole would be hell, whereas transporting a country lady would be heaven. Kicking ladies is wrong but kicking men might be excusable, especially if they were low-born or smoking. Figure 7 tries to incorporate these values in its vicissitudes, together with some other particular contemporary concerns of the author which find their way into the text, such as sabbatarianism and niceties of tack. For talismans, the game uses some of the stock goodies of the story who intercede on horses' behalf or deliver the homilies which are a feature of the plot, and the recurrent good bran mashes which are one of the health hints I take for arguing (in section 4.6) that the book is a disguised tract on the breaking in of the docile child.

Whereas the need to be more considerate to horses (like the need for temperance) is overt in *Black Beauty*, Arcadian conservatism is inherent, and childish tractability – I will claim – is a hidden message. Texts come from authors with purposes. Texts belong in historical contexts and thereby tell values, ideas and contradictions which come from the authors' times. Sometimes the overt message goes against the grain while the cultural assumptions are conventional, as I suggest is the case in *Black Beauty*. (Readers need to know if authors went against the grain of their times: you'll learn a lot about the treatment of animals, chimney-sweepers, slaves or contemporary urban workers from Sewell, Kingsley, Beecher Stowe or Dickens, respectively, but you won't learn about contemporary attitudes towards that treatment. To take a trivial but obvious example, you'd need to read Sherlock Holmes to realize that Anna Sewell's objections to tobacco were more exceptional then than they would be now. The pedagogical indication is, again, wide reading.)

Jane Eyre': sexy self-concealment and the rise of the detective novel

'Literary critics make natural detectives,' said Maud. 'You know the theory that the classic detective story arose with the classic adultery novel – everyone wanted to know who was the father, what was the origin, what is the secret.'

(Byatt 1990: 237–8)

We could move back a generation to glean or use information about governesses, mercenary marriages, missionary activities, land inheritance, plantations and private patronage of peasant schooling from *Jane Eyre*. We could more profitably see how that novel subtly embodies a general Victorian behavioural value while at the same time challenging it.

It is a commonplace that the success of the Victorian bourgeoisie and artisan classes was partly built on a self-discipline which was associated with making a virtue of suppressing self-expression. Silence, abstinence and patience were elevated to a virtuous status which they had not had a century before. If such self-control bottles up psychic energy rather than destroys it – as it would according to conventional post-Freudian hydraulic psychology – then the passion with which the disciplined Jane Eyre conducts her internal debates or occasional outbursts is explained. Furthermore, Sennett (1974: 161–74) argues that in the 1840s a fear of self-disclosure became paramount, as evidenced, for instance, by clothing which totally concealed the corsetted body and eschewed ornament. In terms of our section 2.4, clothing removed every metonym and became a complete metaphor for uniformity, control and unfeeling. This was not because bodily signs were unimportant but because they were perceived as so powerful that it was too risky to let them out. The implication of such modesty was not that the non-exhibitor had nothing to disclose but that beneath the unexpressive uniform of clothing and gesture lay signals and passions so powerful that every effort had to be made to guard against their escape or betrayal. Jane's silence, reticence, plainness and reluctance to dress up even for her marriage would thus seem, to Rochester paradoxical signs of her energy and make her powerful and tantalizingly sexy. This may be hard to understand for contemporary student readers to whom Jane may seem unattractive and boring.

Sennett links this fear of self-disclosure in Victorian bourgeois culture to the rise of the detective story as a genre. Sleuths like Bucket in *Bleak House* are needed to pick up the few tiny clues which careful and secretive people still leave inadvertently, and Sherlock Holmes is their late greatest practitioner. (Gillian Beer – in Yeazell 1986 – has a different but equally 'cultural' explanation for the rise of the detective story in the Victorian period: the influence of a prestigious and momentous need to select explanatory clues from a plethora of geological evidence about the origin of humankind.) It is Jane's Black-Beauty-like stoicism and preparedness to carry self-concealment to almost suicidal lengths (including lying and acting) but also at critical moments to let herself go, Ginger-fashion, in a way that is unbourgeois, unladylike and anachronistic which makes her so heroic and fascinating. The text makes it clear that her self-control makes her acceptable in situations above her social station (e.g. Chapter 29) (and she certainly regards herself as superior to the other servants at Thornfield) and one could argue that Rochester's blindness gives her special power over him by helping her to conceal from him any bodily clues to her feelings.

Sherlock Holmes as racist, snob and MCP

In all the Victorian novels I have mentioned (stretching two definitions to include the *Hound*) a sexual or kinship secret plays an important part. Such common themes, discernible to the wide and comparing readers we try to educate, tell something about what was important (inheritance) and suppressed (sexuality) in the cultures within which these works were written and read. Others recur which are literary symptoms of features of their culture. Some are often present and others significantly absent. From where, for instance, do many of the characters get their money? A curious reader may guess the bee-box of slavery is buzzing behind Rochester's connections or Sir Charles Baskerville's wealth. Who does the housework?

The Hound of the Baskervilles and similar Sherlock Holmes novels and stories, for all their high development of an original genre, are not as original or complex as *Jane Eyre*. Because they do not question contemporary values in the way that *Black Beauty* questions the use of horses or *Jane Eyre* questions the inequalities of marital partnership, Holmes stories are probably better quarries for examples of the way texts provide signs of the life of the cultures in which they are written, signs which can be perplexing or misleading to inexperienced contemporary readers. In Holmes stories these cultural contaminations appear explicitly, symbolically, and in significant absences.

Obviously women, from the long-suffering Mrs Hudson to the fluttering heiresses, are patronized throughout the stories by the clubbable and gallant narrator and his contemptuous hero, and Holmes makes unscrupulous use of urchins, cabbies, butlers, policemen and – of course – Watson. Rewriting from a changed viewpoint as advocated in section 3.2 would help to expose this, with a student trying to adopt Holmes's voice and revealing his values and attitudes to others, or Mrs Hudson writing a reverse-reference for her employer, or the New Worlder Henry Baskerville's views of England and its ways and people, or Mrs Barrymore's experience of her employers and the fate of her 'degenerate' brother. The aim is to expose how values naturalized in the text and made to seem universal are in fact partial, sectional and interested.

As an example of a more perplexing sign of the late Victorian gentleman's culture, consider the baffling references in the first chapter of *Hound* to skull sizes and Bertillon. The phrenological and comparative anatomical obsessions of Conan Doyle's times and class reflect attempts to put on a scientific basis the ideological racism which so benefited the lords of empire. Measuring different people's skull sizes could be used to argue that different groups of people were categorically distinct (i.e. 'races'), that some were intellectually (and by extension morally) better than others because they had bigger brains, and that therefore (in accord with a vulgar Darwinism) they had a destiny to rule the others. Conveniently, measurements could be made to show that white men like Holmes had big skulls. (In *Black Beauty* intelligence, like the moral fibre to resist drink, goes with class: the ladies seem to know more about horse-care than the grooms.) The racism upheld by late Victorian pseudo-science is more overt in other Holmes stories. (In *The Sign of Four* Holmes claims to be able to distinguish between the feet of Hindus and Muslims, an Andaman 'cannibal' is described as 'mis-shapen', 'distorted', 'bestial', 'cruel', 'half-animal' and 'hideous' though a 'faithful mate' to one of the less educated white villains (Chapters 10 and 11), and a Sikh – two Sikhs are implausibly named 'Mahomet Singh' and 'Abdullah Khan' – is described as 'jabbering'. Any contemporary reader who does not find this offensive needs to understand why it is offensive, what political project was advanced by such attitudes a century ago, and why the continuing popularity of the books represents a success for that project and may still blunt readers' sensitivity to its offensiveness: a new and unabridged edition of *The Sign of Four* was advertised in *The Use of English* as late as winter 1960, presumably for schools.)

Some cultural differences between our readers' culture and Holmes's original readers' culture are obvious (such as Holmes's open use of cocaine in *The Sign of Four*), and others shocking when they are explicated (such as the easy targets above). They need exposing to readers who would otherwise be seduced by the narrative power of the stories. Attitudes like racism may not be foregrounded in readings because they are taken for granted in the texts and form the 'common sense' of other, contemporary, texts which students also read (popular newspapers or war comics – see Carrington and Short 1984).

Powerful themes from their originating culture can be read as speaking through all the texts I've chosen. Women, for instance, are almost invariably victims: Tess and Grusha left holding the baby; Helena jilted and Hermia chattelized; the Spanish woman turned with her baby into a pawn of war; Mrs Farquhar (and maybe Mrs Icarus?) widowed to romantic ideals, and Lady Anne in *Black Beauty* punished for not knowing her sexual place. Such passivity or absence seems natural to readers of my generation brought up on this canon, and no doubt it has influenced our attitudes, both male and female readers, in ways we go on being shocked and ashamed to recognize. To ensure that younger readers are not so influenced it is essential to put counter examples in their way and to expose the strangeness of the inequalities in these domesticated texts. One time-honoured way is to reverse the genders in the stories and ask what differences that makes and if the altered plots seem thereby stranger. Another is to try re-telling from the point of view of underclass characters.

Racism, sexism and classism are specially naturalized in popular texts like *Hound*, which are intended less as axes to break the frozen sea of the mind than as protectives against new disturbing realities. But authors who unthinkingly incorporate the cultures of their groups and times may also unwittingly expose the instabilities in them. Take the three mysteries on the moor in *Hound*. Is it too fanciful for historical hindsighters to read in each of them a cultural message which Conan Doyle did not intend? In the escaped convict, the potential violence of an exploited underclass; in the hiding Holmes, the potential penetration of a hypocritical class's secrets; in the hound (whose legend arose with rape and whose continuing use is for murder), the violent appetites which would soon destroy the self-deemed civilization of a privileged class.

Such fanciful interpretations of plot-functions in psychological, political or other cultural terms are easy to make but no less worth while for that – the attic room of the madwoman with her 'propensities' is only the most famous. But to make the interpretations, the readers need to know the universal secrets which speak indirectly through the classic texts – slavery (why was Rochester rich?), syphilis (why was Bertha mad?), and mortality (why did Mrs Reed think she could get away with concealing Jane's legacy?). They need to be able to make those interpretations so that they can detect the values and read the texts in historical context and not as if they were authoritative contemporary documents which might seem to legitimate the racism, sexism, elitism or necromania to which they bear witness. It is easier to spot the ideologies which have been made to seem commonsensical in old books, where the ideologies are not ours, than in contemporary ones. Again, the hope is that ideology-spotting will transfer from the old to the new, so that readers 'playing the Martian' will in the spirit of the next section 'Find it surprising though not unusual'.

Maps, when you've learned to read their conventional signs, are intended to tell you how to find your way. But they can also be used to find out about history, climate, language and economic development. One way to expose the ideologies and break the text's power to impose them on readers is to invite students to summarize works in real or assumed roles with specific ideological viewpoints or special interests. What, for instance, would the following people identify as the six most important happenings in *A Midsummer Night's Dream*: a feminist; a botanist; a folklorist; a marriage guidance counsellor; a theatre historian; a narratologist; a romantic novelist? Maybe in the last case the main forks are: the love of two former rival warriors; the jilting of Helena; the father's thwarting; the moonlight elopement; the reconciliations; the eventual marriages. A reader with other priorities might find a place for the workmen or the supernaturals. To show that different saliences would appear to different readers, just as showing that different critics make different interpretations, demonstrates to students that they can make their own interpretations too, and need not be trapped by the absences and assumptions of the author's culturally situated ideologies.

4.4   Culture and meaning: critical reading of competing values

It is scarcely possible to conceive of the laws of motion if one looks at them from a tennis ball's point of view.

(Brecht in Willett 1964: 275)

Black Beauty makes propaganda for two minority causes of its time – kindness to horses and temperance – and at the same time incidentally and inherently exhibits some characteristic mid-Victorian conservative values. *Jane Eyre* uses features of Romantic and early Victorian psychology and morality to challenge stereotypes of behaviour within stock literary relationships. *The Hound of the Baskervilles* may only set out to tell a sensational tale, but in the process it exhibits a range of sectional values characteristic of the imperial late-Victorian provenance of its production and reception. *The Caucasian Chalk Circle* contrasts with all these – partly because it is a mid-twentieth-century play but also partly because of its author's theoretical position. It is an ideologically open work.

Whereas the Victorian novels innocently tell stories (with some open propaganda for limited causes in the case of *Black Beauty*), but insidiously invite readers' complicity in the ideologies of their authors' worlds, Brecht has no pretence about the ideological intent of his plays: the ideology is 'open' in that sense. 'Take note', his Singer tells us at the end of *The Caucasian Chalk Circle*, 'what men of old concluded,/ That what there is shall go to those who are good for it . . ./ Carts to good drivers . . .'

But his rhetorical practice is also such that his intended audience will construct their own ideological decisions in the face of his story-telling, rather than having no choice but to take over the positions of the characters, including the implied author. They are put in a position analogous to that of the active reader described in my first chapter. The ideology is 'open' in that sense, too.

Brecht is not principally a literary theorist, but he wrote extensively on theatre (Willett 1964), and his ideas are exemplified and sometimes expounded in his plays. *The Exception and the Rule*, the play which was compared to his poem *The Children's Crusade* in section 2.2, is a short 'teaching play' from 1929–30. As the part of its epilogue which I quoted in section 3.4 makes clear, the action has presented relationships between people which Brecht – from his own Marxist position – thinks we should find strange. As a rule, it would be right for the coolie to offer help to a dying man: he has a culture of mutual help which his class has constructed for its own benefit. But in this case the dying man is a merchant whose rule is competition and exploitation. The coolie offers the bottle because he is in a double-bind: if he offers the merchant his water bottle, he – the coolie – might die; but if he keeps it and is found alive when the merchant is dead, then a society run by merchants will certainly blame and kill him. It is also right for the merchant to assume any gesture towards him by a coolie he has beaten and exploited should be one of aggressive and vengeful intent, so, as the judge encourages him to argue, an act of comradeship between them would be an exception to their class enmity. So the merchant was justified in shooting the coolie in self-defence. Our natural temptation to empathize with the coolie is frustrated by his early death and the forceful arguments put forward for the merchant; Brecht exposes the contradictions in the economically determined values of different sections of a competitive society and the contradictions within our ostensible morality and the behaviour we condone: you can't have both peace and justice. Whereas in bourgeois theatre (which Brecht saw as still following Aristotle's model of cathartic showing), audiences have their complacent myths confirmed, in Brecht's 'epic' theatre, we are shown shocking truths such as our hypocritical assumption of altruism.

Like *The Caucasian Chalk Circle* and almost all Brecht's plays, *The Exception and the Rule* is set in a vague or distant time and a vague or distant place. Brecht would argue that this distancing makes the characters' relationships and the plots which involve them more relevant. There are two reasons for this paradox. First, events made strange by distance are more available for our rational consideration than ones which we feel are directly relevant to our own situations, situations in which we have a stake and take sides:

> . . . if we play works dealing with our own time as though they were historical, then perhaps the circumstances under which he himself acts will strike him as equally odd. . .
>
> (from Brecht's *Organum*, in Willett 1964: 190)

I accept this, but I think 'distanced' textual moralities may be less obvious to inexperienced readers even though they become easier to accept, analyse and critique once they are exposed (for instance by a teacher). So, in Section 4.6, I argue that texts which distance their ideologies by being quasi-animal stories are insidious.

The second reason for Brecht's arguing that distance can make for relevance is that we can see that the strange moralities instantiated in Martian, Mongolian or Grusinian plots are, in accordance with Brecht's Marxist philosophy, determined by the particular economic and political circumstances of the fictional societies he depicts. That is why they are 'ideological' and why it makes sense to talk about a 'contradiction' between the coolie's and Grusha's morality and the socio-economic relationships they are involved in. There is a contradiction in *Black Beauty*: the squirearchs – who presumably have recently earned the wealth that gives them their land and privilege – are the goodies, whereas the aristocrats – who have presumably inherited theirs – are baddies. But breeding, in horses and humans, conveys virtue. As in *Bleak House*, the author's class is aspiring to legitimize its new 'breeding' as against an old class which it sees as decadent. The connection between moral values and economic interests is harder to spot in our own cultures (which we tend to accept as 'givens' rather than as products of history) where morality is naturalized and where contradiction – the motor of change – is suppressed. (The singer in *The Caucasian Chalk Circle* apostrophizes 'change from age to age' as 'Thou hope of the people' – Section 1).

To see that changing circumstances change morality exposes the connection of circumstances and morality in our culture and makes us aware that the morality is as easily changed as the power structure. Brecht has fun with these reversals in Section 4 of *The Caucasian Chalk Circle* where, for instance, Azdak, the play's Lord of Misrule, objects to being told he has a 'good heart' when actually he's a 'man of intellect' and Shauwa equates being a Christian with being an ignoramus. As rogue judge in Section 4, Azdak takes the lid off economic injustices which are normally silenced (he 'peeped into the rich man's pocket, which is bad taste') and treats the bandit's robbing the rich to feed the poor as the miracles of a Christian saint. In accordance with the contradictions of the unstable, contested, polity, Azdak has to be both a good judge and a bad judge by our standards, just as Grusha has to be both a good mother and a bad mother.

Some of my previous arguments for 'defamiliarizing' literary works in education are based on assumptions analogous to this one I'm ascribing to Brecht – namely that to see the contradictions of culture and the materialist base of morality in distant societies is easier than doing the same for our own, but that once having done it for Mongolia or Grusinia we are in a better position to do it for our own society. The epilogue to *The Exception and the Rule* tells the audience to recognize a contemporary situation and act on their decisions; in *The Caucasian Chalk Circle*, the possibility of transferring to a contemporary setting the action's strangeness, the conclusions of 'men of old', and the audience's decisions is made obvious by the device of making the play a play-within-a-play, performed by travelling players as an item on the agenda of a meeting of two communities competing for the post-war use of a Caucasian valley – one using the argument of tradition and one using a 'best-use' argument.

The last component of this simple version of Brecht's 'estranging' theory is the often-called 'alienation effect'. Brecht virtually invented the word for this (*Verfremdungseffekt*), and it is variously translated, but I shall continue to call it 'estranging', in line with the usual translation of Shklovski's 'estranging' which Brecht knew about (see section 3.4, above, and Willett 1964: 99). Estranging makes you see the familiar in a new way, as when you enter a familiar situation in a new role or read 'Martian' poetry. The essence of this effect – important for my argument in the next chapter about the relationship we should teach between art and life – is that it should make an audience feel, but also think, and, as a result of that feeling and thinking, act. (Although not in a position to do much about it, one of my teenage students wrote about 'having seriously thought that hanging should be brought back' after an IRA bombing, but changed her mind after seeing the *Owl Creek* film.) The end is decision, not sensation. Their incitement to act is what gives Brecht's plays their potentiality as propaganda. The big theoretical difference between Brecht's plays and those of realistic theatre comes in the sort of feeling entailed by the estranging effect. Brecht did want his audiences to feel as well as think about what they saw on the stage, but not necessarily to feel in the same way as the characters. If you feel the merchant's fear of the coolie, or the coolie's despairing pity for the parched merchant to whom he offers his bottle, then you are trapped within their point of view and the moral system which creates their unjust relationship. But find it strange, as the epilogue instructs you, and you will feel angry about it, and want to change it – or rather change any situation like it in which you may have decided you are involved.

The practical means for achieving Brecht's estranging are his techniques for preventing the audience from being involved in the action as if it is real, and preventing them being trapped into the characters' attitudes. He constructs his plays, and instructs his actors, so that it is clear that the audience is watching an artefact. They are being told, not shown – or rather being shown actors who are telling. Actors face the audience and break off to sing, and the songs are demarcated by titles. There are dumb-shows like the Governor's execution and narrators like the singer of *The Caucasian Chalk Circle*. In *The Caucasian Chalk Circle*, as well as text which can be realized as naturalistic dialogue there is also a variety of other forms of speaking, many of them normally public, which emphasize the formal, performing and performative nature of the play – Grusha's beautiful promise-poem to Simon (in Section 1 of the play), Azdak's sentence (in Section 5), jokes, the beggars' antiphony (in Section 1), Simon's exchanges of proverbs with Grusha (Section 3) and with Azdak (Section 5). Then a production might follow Brecht's example and use non-naturalistic features of production such as back-projection, caption and title boards. If we filmed Simon's journey to rejoin Grusha or what he tells us he remembers of the war and cannot tell (Section 3), then the juxtaposition of the two different types of discourse – dramatic dialogue and film – would draw attention to the fact that both are discourses, not life.

The Caucasian Chalk Circle is sentimental compared to Brecht's other major plays, and it has everything to recommend it to secondary English teachers for class study and production, and I shall use it for my final examples of teaching literature in a way which does justice to that cultural component which recent literary theorists, especially politically committed ones, have demonstrated to be inscribed in literary texts. *The Caucasian Chalk Circle* has themes which make a direct emotional appeal to students – an adoption dilemma and subsequent tug of love, and an arranged marriage. It has caricature villains like a fat prince, a henpecked brother and a drunken monk, and it has a carnivalesque role-reversing people's judge. It has such melodramatic moments as crossing the rotten bridge, Azdak saved from the gallows or Grusha's need to save the child by claiming she is its mother just as her fiancé turns up to see if she is still his virgin. It has separable episodes (in accordance with Brecht's theory of 'epic theatre') suitable for group reading and presentation either as a subcontracted class production or as one-act plays – the final trial or the Bruegelish peasant wedding, for instance.

None of this has to do with teaching the ideological nature of literature, and perhaps *The Caucasian Chalk Circle* is the most popular Brecht play in schools just because it can be taught as an empathy-inducing love-story-in-war. The enjoyment of reading and performing the play would be enhanced by some of the suggestions for developing understanding and interpretation suggested above: set and costume design; diagrams for familiarizing and categorizing the Georgian and Azeri names; 3W diagrams for keeping track of Grusha's and Azdak's movements; pecking orders or lists of 'who's on top/on the winning side/on the run/dead' for appreciating the power see-saws and the move through anarchy to the restoration of a purged Old Order; discussion of the direction on the video.

But without detracting from the enjoyment, a teacher could draw students' attentions to ways in which the play is an artefact for estranging and critiquing social relations, for exposing the historically situated, unnatural and changeable bases of parental and property rights, and for questioning the principles on which justice should be defined and dispensed in a selfish world.

It is important to draw attention to the ending of the play. Grusha gets the baby and her lover (and the fruit-growers get the valley), but Azdak disappears. His reign, like the overturning of values provoked by Oberon and his unruly wife in *A Midsummer Night's Dream*, is temporary. Being less conservative than Shakespeare, Brecht makes the interregnum 'almost an age of justice', rather than a nightmare, but it is '.brief' and 'almost' none the less. It was started by a dynastic squabble rather than a revolution, and it is ended, like medieval institutionalized seasonal carnivals of misrule, by the return of the original ruler. Azdak's chance to issue his final judgement in favour of good mother Grusha is only granted by the restored Grand Duke, and that because Azdak had saved the life of that enemy of the people when he was a fugitive. With Brecht, we and our students should ask why Azdak's justice is temporary, as well as why it is comic and shocking.

It is easy to be ambivalent and rational about Azdak: he is, after all, venal, dishonest, cowardly and a dirty old man, as well as funny. But Grusha is more seductive to student readers and it is too easy to read the play's maternal theme as undramatically one-sided, and not in accord with the offer of debate which I have ascribed to Brecht (who admired Shaw). No one would want to discourage students from feeling for the fate of little Michael, or siding with Grusha in the tug of love, as they would with a contemporary newspaper story. But it would be a pity if they were not moved on to considering the devil's tunes: Natella's mercenary motives for wanting her natural child back (Section 5), the singer's implied criticism of Grusha for taking him at a time when tender-heartedness was foolish (Section 1), Grusha's happy attempted abandoning of him on the peasants' threshold (Section 2), and her implausible good fortune in having her case tried by Azdak. If students' feelings about what happens are not those they would expect Grusha or the singer to have, they should consider why, and possibly see that circumstances influence morality and that therefore changing circumstances can change morality.

Comments on political events are a discourse with which students are less familiar than they are with the interpersonal dilemmas Grusha faces when deciding whether or not to adopt the child, marry the peasant, disown the child or butter up Azdak. Some collecting, paraphrasing and contemporary applying of the slogans would help to bring out the public dimension and start the student audience recognizing connections between what Brecht tells and aspects of their own taken-for-granted social positions and attitudes. Following on from that, they may begin to make decisions of the sort Brecht hoped to provoke. For instance, the way Brecht uses the disputed maternity as a comment on the dispute over the valley should not be ignored (even if a first reading omits it): students may be happy enough to side with the good adoptive mother against the bad blood mother, but would they as easily apply the implied utilitarian principle to property rights and give their bikes to better riders? The fat prince's contemptuous and nepotistic politics need attention, and what about Azdak's wise absurdities that wars are always won by the rulers on both sides and lost by those in whose names they have declared wars, or that the justice you get is in accordance with how much you pay for it?

If the students were also aware of some of Brecht's other works from reading poems or texts or seeing productions or videos, or even from a teacher's paraphrases, then recognizing the common concerns of one author's various exotically set and sited stories might suggest what general issues and what mid-twentieth-century manifestations of them were being suggested for consideration by these distancing parables.

4.5 Loaded language

A text is like a tent. It has internal support from its structures and external support from the guys of culture which fix it in its place (and sometimes open up splits in it). The fabric it's made of is language, and the nature of that fabric influences the shapes the tent takes, the resistance to the external loads, and the experience of being inside it through the colour, smell and so on. It's easy to take language for granted, and treat it as a transparent medium of character, event and value. Some devices draw your attention back to the language, though. They can 'foreground' or 'defamiliarize' it – to use two terms from literary theories. *The Caucasian Chalk Circle* doesn't really begin 'In olden times, in a bloody time . . .', it begins 'In alter Zeit, in blutiger Zeit'. For me, to see a word like 'blutiger' – unfamiliar but translatable – reminds me of a literal, sanguinary meaning behind the too-familiar 'bloody' with its sense of a mild swear-word or just vaguely 'disturbed' as times were in remote history. In one version of *A Midsummer Night's Dream* Theseus's opening speech includes 'Elle retarde mes désirs, comme une marâtre ou une douairière qui laisse sécher le revenu d'un jeune héritier.' In penetrating the opacity of those words I disinterred the buried mercenary metaphor for sexual desire which could have done for me what Eagleton did (and it was reading on in French which exposed the later significance of Lysander's proposal to elope to an aunt who is 'une douairière qui a des gros revenus, et n'a pas d'enfants'). Just as young children best learn to read on texts with familiar content (e.g. fairy stories they have been told), so second-language readers can cope with texts far more difficult than they would normally contemplate if those texts have familiar content: I can't read German, but I can read *Der Kaukasische Kreidekreis*. I'm well aware of the dangers of wishing on-to over-pressed English teachers yet another responsibility in the National Curriculum, but elsewhere I have argued for the efficacy and practicability of looking at texts in two languages, comparing translations, or even some translation work for appreciating literature, especially where classes have bilingual students in them or students studying a second language (Stibbs, in Collins 1990).

So far, especially in Chapter 2, I've tended to discuss literary works apart from their fabric of language, as if they consisted only of the images their readers imagine, their plot-summaries, or such abstract constructs of their narration as 'viewpoint'. But I have pointed out that deciding what was the plot-function of some action, or whether part of a text was a showing or telling, is sometimes only inferable from the context of surface detail. The way that looking at the differences in surface realizations of literary meanings draws attention to their artefactual nature is relevant to what I say about teaching the differences between art and life, at the start of the next chapter. Literary criticism now has a linguistic camp: stylistics is a forensic improvement on the incantations of practical criticism, though I hasten to add that 'stylistics', as generally understood, is not what this section is about. Nor is it about the historical study of language for which literary texts provide excellent material, including records of the interactions and contests of different groups with their different languages. (Though it is problematical material: when literature is often our only evidence of, say, the oral language of a period, it's hard to know what is coinage and what is dialect in *A Midsummer Night's Dream*, or whether the ideologically significant conversational mannerisms in *Jane Eyre* represent what Charlotte Brontë observed as typical or what she individually willed.)

The part played by language in literary meaning is most obvious in a short poem where the formal patterns of sound or spelling are up front. In *Business News* the rhymes are near enough each other to register on the reader's eye and ear. But this may happen subconsciously with longer works – rhymes disguised by enjambment in *Spain, 1809* or the submerged anagrams I describe in *Business News* and 'Spit Nolan'. Then of course, intertextuality works through language at every level. Captain's account of the Charge of the Light Brigade in *Black Beauty* (Chapter 34) has echoes of Tennyson's poem in linguistic content and form, as well as in subject-matter. Basically every word in any text is quotation from previous usage, so that I can't read Enid Blyton without being reminded of niceness and nastiness in *Black Beauty*, nor *Black Beauty* without being reminded of Enid Blyton. (The sequences and mutual influences of readings in readers' experiences in reading-time are not the same as those of influences in authors' writings in history-time – so we can admire Shakespeare for working in all those quotations like 'The course of true love never did run smooth'.)

For the power of surface language to determine meaning, consider the differences which a few changes of vocabulary, word-order or punctuation make to *Business News*, without changing the plot – or the person, tense, voice or viewpoint.

Daedalus and Son
pioneers of man-powered flight
have gone
into the sea

Daedalus and Icarus
pioneers of man-powered flight . . .

> Daedalus and Son
> pioneers of human flight . . .

> Daedalus and Son
> pioneers of man-powered flight
> have fallen . . .

> Daedalus and Son
> have gone
> into liquidation,
> pioneers of man-powered flight

> Pioneers of man-powered flight
> Daedalus and Son
> have gone

> Daedalus and Son
> (pioneers of man-powered flight)
> have gone

Were we to work into the language surface (as we could without altering the plot) that Daedalus made his son's wings, or that Icarus gave his name to the sea he fell into, then we could put new resonances of value into readings of the text.

Here I want to concentrate on the way the language-fabric of literature builds in cultural codes. In our language the use of a single word such as 'black' immediately activates all sorts of value-loaded meanings. Thanks to books like Spender's (1980), we are beginning to be alert to the way in which 'man-made' language – including the language of literary narrative – may systematically stereotype, reify and derogate women. Suppose, in a bodice-ripper, you listed all the verbs used of women and men, respectively – in a whole text or a random sample of pages – what would you find out about their respective roles? More subtly, suppose you did some statistics on the verbs in Jane Austen. Compared to men, how often are women the subjects of active or passive verbs? How often do the verbs used of them suggest that women speak, think, feel and act? If one woman breaks the pattern, why is that – because she's the narrator or because she's an exceptional character? Within the category of saying, are there differences between the genders with respect to who says, replies, asks, questions? Does a character's likelihood to initiate rather than respond to conversation change during the course of a book, and if so why?

Just as the surface features of other languages carry ideological messages (the decoration on architecture, the ornament on clothes, the details of dreams), so the fabric of literary language creates attitudes and values in its readers with respect to many other pervasive cultural assumptions. Note the frequency of words like 'gentle', 'nice' and 'sweet' throughout *Black Beauty*, but especially in the first section about upbringing (10, 18 and 7 occurrences, respectively). And the associations of the words (for instance 'sweet' and 'gentle' with 'ladies' and their voices and hands, or 'well-' and 'good-' with '-bred', '-tempered', '-mannered') is a clue to the nurseriness of its ideology which I hinted at in section 4.3 and will reassert in the next section. So is the Blytonish choice of words for their opposites: 'bad', 'nasty' and 'awful'. Given the right sort of text and the ability to subdivide the work among many workers (and the well-prepared teacher's confidence that the exercise will yield a result and not waste students' time) such word-counting is a simple but effective way into uncovering cultural assumptions of literary texts. Classifying characters from memory then going back to check the effect of adjectives in creating them and their moral tone is another possibility (as with Black Beauty's introducing Jerry's wife as 'plump', 'trim', 'tidy and 'merry' and his son as 'frank' and 'good-tempered').

Suppose you take the passage from 'Spit Nolan' which describes the race between Spit and Leslie and have students pick out what they think are the significant words which apply to each trolley and its driver. Their lists (see section 5.2) provide powerful constellations of some of the concepts which make up the contrasting ideological forces which are pitted against each other in the story. Exton (1984: 18D) shows how underlining '-ly' words in the opening of *Of Mice and Men* showed students that Lennie and George were not as simply and contrastingly 'soft' and 'hard' as they had imagined. Even such an elementary comparison as the words used of Rochester's and St John Rivers's kissing (in Chapters 23 and 34) or the parts of their body mentioned in Jane's first meeting with each of them (Chapters 12 and 29) differentiate their respective functions in the plot of *Jane Eyre*.

A possibility for reversing this sort of 'word-collecting' exercise is providing passages with words deleted for students to complete, as a basis for discussion both of what guides their substitutions and a comparison between their reconstructions and the originals. A more creative reversal is using the well-known 'furniture game' starter for poetry writing on characters in literary narratives. Think of a character. Now, if this character was a piece of furniture, what would he or she be? If a fruit, which one would he/she be? If a weapon? A musical instrument? An animal, drink, garment, vehicle, weather? The word lists produced by this exercise in rapid association can be pushed around to make little characteristic poems (untitled) which furnish a guessing game and more serious discussion about the reasons for certain associations with certain characters and about the function of metonyms and metaphors.

Another way in which a starter for creative writing can be used to develop scrutiny of literary language, and creative and maybe critical insight into texts, is using passages as the bases of collage poems. Ask students to take a part of a story (for instance by directing them to photocopies of some of the more purple pages of the text) and to underline, copy out or highlight 'interesting words' (it's the phrase I use and they seem to understand it). Then they have to assemble the words into a 'collage poem' which evokes the feeling or meaning which the reader takes from the passage. Successive drafts could add and discard words and move as far away as they wished from the original collection of words which – to some extent – had been merely a starting-point for a purchase on the text.

4.6 Beware of the dog: animals as ideological decoys

> When the sharks the sharks devour
> Little fishes have their hour.
>
> He became a wolf to fight the pack.
>
> The plunging wagon
> Drags the sweating oxen down with it
> Into the abyss.

Those are just three of the 'slogans' which, in the previous section, I suggested students might extract and 'translate' in order to appreciate the political significance of Brecht's play (Sections 4, 4 and 1). The import of those words 'sharks', 'wolf' and 'oxen' would provide no more difficulty for their interpretation than they provide linguistic difficulty for the translator from German. As metaphors for types of human being, they are understood the same way in Britain and Germany, even though oxen and wolves long since stopped being part of Europeans' everyday experience, and sharks never were. It's interesting that some animal references are cross-cultural: the human meaning of wolves or lions in literary language-uses such as fables stretches at least from British folk-tales in the West to the *Panchatantra* in India, with Greek Aesop as its fulcrum, even though lions have never been British. However, there are more specific cultural uses of animals: in his introduction to the 1968 Penguin *Poems from Sanskrit* John Brough points out how walking like an elephant is a compliment to a woman in Sanskrit poems: it would not be so in English. Such collection of points of commonality and difference between the languages and literatures of cultures suggests an activity for bilingual groups of students to add to those I hinted at in the last section.

Clichés of animals-as-humans may not be fair to animals, but their use for human meanings has ideological importance. Clichés are coined and become established for good reasons which continue to resonate through their tired and unthinking subsequent over-uses. Beasts stalk through our texts. Literature uses animals as metaphors, as metonyms (Pilot), as psychoanalytical or portmanteau symbols (the Hound) and as disguises.

People's attitudes to animals at different periods have reflected not only their more obvious economic needs (such as looking after horses to help you get about, in Anna Sewell's *Black Beauty*) or modish ideas about animals and society in general, but also people's more embedded values and attitudes, and ideas about themselves and each other. So, for instance, the eighteenth- and nineteenth-century fashion for breeding extreme pedigree animals reflects not only the need to develop more efficient farming industries or more convenient or exotic pets (in many cases breeds of domestic animals have been developed way beyond biologically efficient sizes and shapes) but also a desire in members of a newly self-created aristocracy to symbolically aggrandize or refine themselves – physically, genealogically and culturally. Again, the Victorian surge in zoo-making reflects not just a scientific curiosity but a celebration of the British Empire's collection into its hegemony of so many 'races' (as the Victorians ideologically but unscientifically divided humankind into). We have seen the evidence for that in Mortimer's phrenology and Selsden's alleged degeneracy in *Hound*. One could put a similar case for other recurrent features (e.g. disease, scientists) which inscribe historically specific cultural fears or attitudes or values into literary narratives.

One of my teenage pupils said the people in *Black Beauty* 'aren't characters – the animals are'. I threatened in section 4.3 to justify a claim that *Black Beauty* expressed not just overt propaganda for kindness to animals and implied values about town and country, men and women, low birth and high birth, and so on, but also – in between those two sets of messages as it were -- disguised propaganda about ways of bringing up children. The first chapter contains a lecture on not letting down the family reputation by adopting the rough habits of low-born playmates, which, though ostensibly addressed by a talking mare to a talking foal, sends *frissons* of recognition through a well-brought-up reader like me. There is even an admonition to lift your feet up which provokes in this reader a guilty inspection of my Stick-a-Soles. Chapter 3 is about Black Beauty's breaking-in and, despite Anna Sewell's clear emphasis on the benefits of human kindness, the imperative narration directly preaches unquestioning obedience in a foal, with such uncanny parallels with respectable child-rearing as not running away from frightening novelties, not stopping to talk to your friends, needing to stand still while you're dressed and putting up with wearing uncomfortable tack because that makes you grown up (a bridle, for instance, but it could equally be braces or a bra), and being rewarded for obedience and patience by food. The last point is a telling one for a glutton with a thrifty wartime rearing, and may be one clue to Enid Blyton's infiltration into the intertextuality of my reading: through-out *Black Beauty*, 'good bran mashes' feature as rewards and consolations. Like such inserted tips on health as not gulping cold water when you're hot, the emphasis on diet and healthy masochistic habits is another reason for relating what purports to be a story of a horse to the upbringing of readers of a particular age and class.

Chapter 3 on 'My Breaking In' ends with a mother's advice that the better Black Beauty behaves, the better he will be treated. She also warns him that there are men not as kind and wise as their master who may mistreat him. All she can suggest in that event is 'keep up your good name'. Later in the book we are graphically shown the fate of those who, like Ginger, justifiably rebel and show 'vice'. The plot tells children that the horses with which they are so strongly invited to share experience (and, in the case of the first-person narrator-protagonist, identify with) are powerless, and should feel sufficiently rewarded for their unquestioning obedience, gratitude and stoicism by being awarded a respectable reputation.

Stories about animals carry messages about human beings more pervasive than propaganda for kindness to pets and more direct than incidental sociological information about their settings. Of mice is of men and the fate of Candy's dog foreshadows the fate of Lennie. Carpenter (1985) confirms that the Arcadian nostalgia of *Wind in the Willows* takes its seductive imaginative power from the author's own privileges, prejudices and inadequacies, and influences a reader in the direction of his peculiar priorities and desiderata: the pleasure of escape; the superiority of the countryside and especially of rivers as sites of pleasure; the centrality of meals in security and comfort; the self-satisfactions of the organized solitary life of the bachelor's den; the stupidity of policemen; the vulgarity of the newly rich; the barbarism of the underclasses and wisdom of maintaining a boundary against them; the virtues of modesty and reticence; distrust of new technology. Carpenter says:

> *The Wind in the Willows* has nothing to do with childhood or children, except in that it can be enjoyed by the young, who thereby experience (though they do not rationally understand) what its author has to say, and are able to sense some of its resonances.
>
> (p. 168)

That quotation encapsulates for me the importance of animal stories as signs of life and the way their insidiousness is enhanced by a tendency to classify them as children's books whatever their themes or import. A book like *The Mouse and his Child*, which Russell Hoban did not feel he was writing for children, is recommended to children because superficially it is about toy animals. A better reason for recommending it to them is because of what it's really about: a quest by two (clockwork) mice which

> ... is political as well as personal. They are the houseless vagrants, a placeless people in search of their homeland, the Jew in search of Jerusalem. They are in pursuit not only of territory but of 'self-winding', alias self-determination, independence. And as with all revolutionary causes, they learn that they must fight to achieve their ideals.
>
> (Wilkie 1989: 23)

The danger of the popularity of animal stories and the tendency to classify them as suitable for children just because they are about animals is that they may embody offensive ideas about human beings in the guise of animals. Who would praise Richard Adams's *Watership Down* unreservedly if the furry odyssey was more openly about the Scout Troop fighting its way across country for a gang-bang? And if it's objected that this is how rabbits behave and that Hazel and all are only animals, why do they talk? At least with Enid Blyton the offensive snobberies, sexisms and greed are clearly embodied in human beings and thereby invite inspection and criticism. The danger with animal books is that they pass on human-type behaviour, not as estranged, but as unnoticed.

An example of a children's novel in which animals behave (and talk) as if they were human beings but with attitudes and values which we would find nauseating in human beings and which children would find stranger and less insidious if they were not embodied in animals is Dodie Smith's *One Hundred and One Dalmations*. Though published over thirty years ago (which is well after the rightly derided *The Family from One-end Street*) it remains popular and in print. The dog Pongo admires and protects his beautiful wife Missus but has a laugh with a spaniel ('in a very masculine way') that she cannot tell her left paw from her right (she can't count, either, or understand machines or public – i.e. human – language as well as her husband can). Normally, they live with their parasitic owners and their kept-on nannies in 'the right house for a man with a wife and dogs' fed on steaks brought by page-boys from 'rather good hotels' and protected from the world's unpleasantness by a 'splendid vet' and 'top men at Scotland Yard' (none of your stupid policemen for them). The unpleasantnesses are such as gypsies or low-born knife-carrying villains symptomatically addicted to the television which the dalmations' owners 'do not care for' but allow the nannies to watch in the kitchen. Their puppies are endangered by the only assertive female in the story, the unnatural Cruella de Vil who made her 'small, worried-looking, husband change his name on marriage, but they are rescued by a canine freemasonry of the Home Counties who are all pedigree (a 'courteous' spaniel, a 'handsome' collie, a 'burly' retriever) and – with the exception of a 'graceful' setter who proves the rule by going 'hysterical' and letting them down – masculine. The only estranging of this modelling, naturalizing and moralizing of gender and class roles and attitudes is in a refreshing incident where two of their friends fall in love at first sight, abandon a meal and run into the woods where they make 'swift arrangements for their marriage, promising to love each other always' and, nine weeks after marriage, have babies – eight of them.

There are hints above of the possibilities of exposing the values in some of the animal stories by extracting particular aspects (like primers for upbringing), or of listing words in the manner suggested in the previous section. In Chapter 3 I've argued for rewriting from a changed point of view (such as that of a different species in this case) for estranging literary narratives and exposing their culture-boundedness to inspection and criticism. In the case of anthropomorphic animal books, simply to re-humanize them should be enough.

5 Implications and applications

5.1 Art and life

> By the rules of fiction, with which life to be credible must comply, he was as a
> character 'impossible'.
>
> (Bowen 1989: 140)

In Chapter 1, exaggerating response theory, I wrote as if works of literary
narrative were free plays of readers' imaginations round a few almost arbitrary
hints of text. In Chapter 2 I turned them into elegant puzzles whose appeal might
seem merely formal, like that of abstract paintings or sculptures. Then I turned
them into narrative processes, like the manipulations practised on their victims by
hypnotists. And in Chapter 4 I wrote about them as if they were documents of
deliberate political persuasion or historical information suffering from some
incidental cultural jamming. There is no space here to develop a philosophy of
art, but I will attempt a brief synthesis of the elements in the pattern on the cover
of the book while putting some life into the empty signs. For synthesizing the
signs, in the technical terms of semiotics, I am combining their semantics
(content) with their syntactics (the mutual relationships) and their pragmatics
(the relationships of signs with their producers and consumers). I shall try to
justify the reading of literary narrative by asserting the distinctly literary nature of
the experience while still relating it to humane educational values.

Plots or life

So far, I've tried to make clear some of the differences between plots (in the sense
of literary realizations of quasi-real-life stories) and real-life experience. Plots
purport to be accounts of sets of events – of how a small boy was killed in a trolley
race, or how a Spanish village avenged itself on a punitive army raid, or how two
pairs of lovers were sorted out through a midsummer night in Athens. But a plot –
and this is as true of such 'true stories' as histories, newspaper reports and

eye-witness accounts – is not those events: a plot happens on paper (or screen in the spoken word), or rather in the head of its reader/viewer/listener, not in the 'real world'; a plot recreates only a selection of the events which are supposed to lie behind it; a plot takes the time it takes to read (or see, or hear, or think) it, not the time of its purported events, and puts those events in a different sequence from their sequence in the 'history' it appears to be retelling; a plot is the sum of the data about itself (*A Tale of Two Cities* can't be revised in the light of additional evidence emerging about it in the way that the French Revolution can); a plot describes its events from only one or some of many possible points of view, and points of view are loaded by tellers' purposes and cultures; a plot tells rather than shows, and even if it may try to mimic events (especially if it is in a potentially realistic medium such as film) it always leaves its consumer the possibility of withdrawing. The constructed nature of literary narratives is emphasized by those distinctions.

Plots in life

But it could also be argued that all experience is constructed: our perception of life has some of the features of 'plot' as defined above. This is one reason why narratologists seeking for a definition of a story climb up their own bootstraps. In seeking those parts of, or views of, 'real life' which correspond to the shapes of literary stories – i.e. plots – they are involved in a circular exercise because 'real life' is a mental construct shaped by the same mental aesthetics and economics which create art-stories. Life itself needs reading and we read only those signs and grammatical connections which we recognize – from art! Narrative is a primary act of mind, and we talk about life as meetings, ordeals, trials, transformations and so on. We talk about life in stories (which we call 'true' stories even though they change every time we tell them), we think about life by telling ourselves stories and plan our futures by hypothesizing fictions about ourselves. We know people only from what we infer from the metonymic evidence they give us, as with 'characters' in literature: are these the stuff of art or life? As the head-quotation says; 'to be credible', life 'must comply' with 'the rules of fiction'.

Whether life is like that because art is like that, or art is like that because life is like that does not matter in this context (so it does not matter that the above 'truth' about the fictionality of life is quoted from a fictional character!). Our experiencing of both life and art involves active creation (anticipating, visualizing and so on), provoked by our perceiving structures of events and characters (binaried, troped, forked and so on), rhetorically presented to us (from viewpoints, in voices, shown and told), and coloured by our culture and the cultures of the life-stories' initiators and the values in the language with which we perceive them. So learning to read literature entails learning how we read life. The quotation from Fry (1985) in section 1.4 goes as far as to suggest that children's becoming aware of how they read is to come to understand how they live. Literary theorists since Barthes's *Mythologies* (1957) have talked of life as 'text' and 'read' such life-phenomena as striptease, advertising and car design (to use some of Barthes's subjects) semiotically. That would be a first argument I'd use for the relevance to life of understanding literature literarily: art and life can be brought closer together by asserting the artiness of life as well as the life-iness of art.

Life in plots

But I also think the case can be made the other way round. It can be argued that the signs of art constitute a tribute to life, as well as to other art-signs, without needing to show that life is just other art. I've defined the elements and processes in the model of reading literary narrative in abstract terms, but in operation they are concrete. They are signs and relationships which refer to items and situations which life has valorized. Except for Platonists, the signs have no existence other than in such concrete operation. Intertextualists may say that signs constantly slip from their intended signifieds on to other signifiers, and what we read is quotation, but we need not believe that that is all signs do: the infinite regress for which some theorists argue does not match our experience or practical needs as facilitators of reading, interpretation and criticism. The elements and structures of art do correspond to elements and structures of life, as well as to elements and structures of other art. Grusha isn't a real person (and it makes no sense to empathize with her), but we read her as a person, not just as a plot-plant or a pastiche of Tess, Mandy Rice-Davies and Little Red Riding Hood. So we can sympathize with what happens to her and think and feel about her fictional fate in ways which may make a difference to our lives. That 'fictional fate', like all the others in the examples I've used, is a human fate, not a theorem. If it's a mistake to try to find 'How Many Children Had Lady Macbeth' from the text (Knights 1951), it's also a mistake not to read about or watch the lady without thinking of her as a mother. We may discuss what happens in narratives with such abstract terms as 'peripeteia', 'coincidence' or 'fragmentation', but they are all realized in terms we care about such as falling in love, finding a long-lost sibling, or civil war. They are not realized as chemical, meteorological or linguistic transformations, conjunctions or randomizings. Although characters of people in novels and plays and short stories are artificial and limited, in most cases they still are more interesting even than the lives of their 'real-life' authors (though my selection might include some of the minority cases).

A literary model as a defence against would-be censors

The previous paragraph would not have needed arguing if there was not a danger that my emphasis on literary theories, techniques and terms might seem to take the pleasure and point out of reading. In contrast there is no urgent need to encourage students to see the life in the signs of literary narrative, once they are keen readers of fiction. The tendency to empathize is strong enough, as such metaphors for narrative reading as 'losing ourselves' in texts suggest. However, there is, I think, a need to emphasize that the signs of literature are signs – signs which constitute fictions, not myths or even documentary. Medway and I have argued (in Collins 1989) that literature teachers who justify their work with a simple transparent transmission model of literary reading (like that in Figure A), and pass that model on to children, open themselves to a recurrent danger and open their students to a constant one.

The recurrent danger is that periodically vocal would-be censors complain that teachers give children texts which seem to incite them to elope, steal babies or poison people, as well as, more prudently, keep trolleys off busy roads, avoid man-powered flight and bridge-burning, and marry landowners. Plots thus become either inflammatory or cautionary extensions of experience obtained more cheaply than school trips to the Caucasus, or irrelevant because they have dumb animals as narrators. A colleague who accused me of causing a retroactive pupil pregnancy by the administration of a social realist CSE novel was working with this simplistic model: it does no justice to the idiosyncratic productive role of readers who can find the most innocent pleasures in the most corrupting texts and vice versa.

A more semiotic model, such as I've tried to build up from the implications of the different sorts of literary theory, leaves the teacher the chance to argue that literature offers students thought-provoking demonstrations of ways we might think and feel about experience, not additions to that experience or advocacy of dangerous behaviour or introductions to bad characters. It also, by exercising its hints, structures and rhetoric on recognizable subject-matter, offers critiques of life and hypotheses about how life could be different and better.

Works of literature are games with signs. Games are played with passion, and some of their appeal comes from the correspondences between the semiotics of games and life-living. (So cricket, I should argue, is a ritual estrangement of features of life in a particular culture – a struggle for self-esteem within strict parameters of time and place and in which any venture for gain (like bowling a ball) entails risking a loss (like getting hit for runs). Batsmen get 'out' and bowlers 'taken off'. Although it proceeds within known boundaries, its outcomes are unpredictable, though explicable with hindsight. It's a collective enterprise deploying individual excellences and using cunning, patience, intelligence, force and skill against physical obstacles, the weather, fortune and opponents to whom are extended chivalry and the respect of total opposition within the rules of the game, and for the duration of the match. I hope cricket-loving readers will forgive this gross simplification and trivialization.) There is no benefit or pleasure in playing games half-heartedly – as if they were 'only games' – but if the commitment goes beyond the bounds of the game, it becomes disabling and pathological. I think the analogy with literary fiction is exact.

The version I gave of Brecht's preaching and practice is one I should want to extend to students' reading in general. I should want them to read Brontë in the same way as they read Brecht. But where Brecht does the estranging for them with all the theatrical devices of his *Verfremsdungseffekt* they will have to do their own with Brontë, and oscillate between a proper and passionate engagement with Jane's fate and a critical appreciation of the patterned, rhetorical and culturally saturated nature of the text that tells it. I said the reading journal would help Pierce's pupil reading *Jane Eyre* to do that in section 1.4. The passion should produce the care to think in the face of the text and the critical process should produce some reflection on the importance for women of marriageability in Jane's and the reader's circles, for instance, and an influence on behaviour.

The second danger of the naive model is the constant one of students' vulnerability to the enchanting 'textual power' which texts may exercise over them (the eponymous subject of Scholes 1985). This may be specially so if, as Harding (1967) suggests, 'over-avid' readers may be people with unfulfilled social lives. Literary narratives, as we have seen, have purposes and messages to which entirely enchanted readers are vulnerable. 'Lost' in texts, they confuse 'as' with 'is'. Enchanted readers may not recognize, evaluate and resist the messages. This is a special danger with texts which do nothing to draw attention to their own artefactuality and textuality, especially realist films and novels. One reason why I have used nineteenth-century novels in my illustrations is because the need to deconstruct and estrange them is greatest. Also, realist books on the prestigious Victorian model remain the staple of stock-cupboards, libraries, syllabuses, booklists and our teachers' intertextualities. Ideally, we need a wider canon, as I argue below, but lack of money to buy books and time to find what's available makes that hard. So, while continuing to maximize the range of what's on offer to student readers, we need to be prepared to teach a way of reading which can cope with *Jane Eyre* as well as with *Viz*.

A first teaching implication of empowering readings is the need to draw the attention of students studying or emulating narrative fiction to the textuality of the works. Some of the ways which have been suggested for doing this include attributing the characters, re-viewpointing or transferring the narration to another medium, listing loaded words and considering the social production of the text. Students who have worked on texts like that may be less likely to accept the texts as authoritative slices of real life with unproblematized cultures speaking through them.

A new canon

The second implication is to widen the canon. It is a commonplace that since modernism some of the conventions of the nineteenth-century naturalistic novel have been called into question. There have been movements like surrealism, the nouveau roman and magical realism. There have been experiments with aleatory techniques, multiple narration, pastiche and parody, and typography. It is because of that that in section 3.2 I called Bierce's story, with its shifty viewpoint and tricks with time, 'proto-modernist'.

It is also a commonplace that in what has been called a second 'Golden Age of Children's Literature' (Carpenter 1985: 214), authors as distinguished and serious as many of those in the vanguard of writing for adults have not moved on from the staple nineteenth-century fiction of the slice-of-life story of a sensitive individual. The sensitive individual endorsed in the typical novel for young people is, intransitively, 'sensitive, imaginative, responsive, sympathetic, creative, perceptive, reflective' (Eagleton 1985) – just like Black Beauty. A reader modelled on such a character (what Eagleton would call a 'subject' 'produced' by the technology of literature) learns a way to read as part of learning a way to live. And that reading-style is an intransitively reflective one which would preclude an active response even to provocative literature such as Brecht's plays:

> ... the commitment to individualism as a ... solution to the social problem ...
> remains the long-term position from which most teaching of literature is still
> mounted.
>
> (Hawkes 1986: 114)

The canon, like the teaching styles we use, encourages a naive, absorbed, virtual experience model of reading and produces readers who are tractable people.

To protect children from the adult life-iness in the signs they read is to undervalue and maybe sell them short. So is to deprive them of the types of signifying systems which adults interested in literature read. Except that they are not entirely deprived because parodic, multi-voiced, self-referring textuality features in genres such as comics, pop videos and television adverts and comedies which appeal to the young. They are probably more modernistic than popular material made for adults. For instance the Goon Shows remain popular with generations unborn at the time of their first broadcasts. A typical Goon Show (for instance *The Great String Robberies*, in Milligan 1974) is saturated with parody, plural voices and self-reference. The conventions of the sound medium are mocked by Bluebottle speaking his stage directions (p. 104) and characters travelling by making car noises (p. 94). Artefactuality is emphasized by characters being accused of being figments of each others' imagination (p. 106) or a drowning cartoonist saved by having pencil and paper thrown to him in order to draw himself a life-belt (p. 103). The relationship between the apparent producer and receiver of the literary message is problematized by breaks in sound being explained by one character moving fingers in and out of his ears (p. 99).

There is a similarly up-front textuality in modern comics. Waldeback (1990: 8–9) describes how characters in (admittedly adult) comics such as *Love and Rockets* (Titan Books, 1987) expose, subvert and mock the conventions of the genre which creates them. They ask 'the penciller' and writer to 'give us a brand new wardrobe' and 'exciting new careers like aerobic instructors or private eyes'. One character addresses the reader with 'Eek! Somebody turn the page! You can see my panties!' to which her sidekick gives the literary reply 'That's the stuff comics are made of'. When children are perfectly capable of reading material which is a product of modernism and post-modernism in popular genres, why should they be deprived of it in the literature we teach and provide for them in school and colleges? Some prestigious children's writers in the educational canon do not deserve my implied criticisms, as the Philippa Pearce books or the source of the quotation from Aidan Chambers at the head of section 1.6 would show. Nevertheless I think it is important that writers write and teachers read and buy narrative literature for children which makes a virtue and ploy of its literariness.

In the next two sections I attempt to apply a texty approach to realistic material and show what this would entail in two practical cases. First, I take a justly popular short story for pupils, classes and teachers and explore what some of the theories and their applications discussed above can tell us about the story (without suggesting that all those aspects of analysis should be brought into any one actual reading in a school). Secondly, in section 5.3, I take a longer traditional story and describe the work which a teacher and a mixed-ability class did on it over a period of a month. That report is intended to illustrate some of the theoretically justified approaches which have been suggested throughout the first four chapters, and which are gathered together and summarized in the last section.

5.2   Short story; full treatment

Here I attempt an analysis of some features exposed by literary theory in one of the most popular stories used in secondary (and upper junior) English classes. I certainly don't offer it as a model for teaching the story in the classroom but I do offer it as an example of the sort of analysis which teachers can make in order to spot useful approaches to stimulating discussion, asking questions or otherwise following-up the story. Among the possibilities are: anticipating the course of the story; extracting its shape by summarizing: keeping an eye on how the narration moves between showing, telling, flashing back and dropping ominous hints; recognizing a binary ideology of work; thickening the fabric of words and names and focusing in on them; explicating the references and likenesses to popular, religious, literary and legendary myths and their shapes and iconographies. I have written elsewhere, elliptically, about the different ways I have taught this story in three different decades and in slavish accord with changing fashions in ideology (Jones and West 1988).

'Spit Nolan' is the title, and already we can infer a great deal about the story. The title's a name (which is less usual of a story than a novel though it's more usual for writing for children to be titled by a name than it is for writing for adults – on the evidence of that informal survey of titles I mentioned in section 2.4). So it's a fair guess that the story will centre on the eponymous character (probably a hero?) rather than on some place or event.

The name itself begins to place the work. It's not likely to be by Virginia Woolf, nor, with a name like that, is the eponymous hero likely to be female, aristocratic, foreign or old. For me at least it's not fanciful to take the excuse of the author's game with Madge/*Egdam* to look in a second reading for many foreshadowing suggestions of key words for the rest of the story already embedded in the title as anagrams: anon; split; lost; slain; spoilt.

'Spit Nolan was . . .' begins the first sentence of the story (and by the time we've finished reading we'll know that the last sentence includes 'Spit Nolan had been . . .'). Our first suspicion that this is a pen-portrait is confirmed – with Spit's name titling, beginning and ending the story. And our retrospect might let the tense-contrast between the opening and closing characterize the story as an epitaphic memoir.

'Spit Nolan was a pal of mine.' There, at last we've read to the end of the first sentence, but not before picking up more information and forming more expectations: the tense of 'was' tells us to expect a story, 'pal' puts us into the provenance of small boys, and 'of mine' signals a first-person, small-boy narrator likely to use a boy's viewpoint but (from 'was') an adult voice. Nothing does more disservice to a story than a teacher reading aloud who constantly interrupts (indeed, in this case it could have been complained that the teacher wouldn't let the reader read the beginning, far less the end!). But I for one would not resist a temptation to ask readers or hearers to reflect on what anticipations this form of introduction is creating in them. My assumption is that just being asked to think about their anticipations would provoke those anticipations in some students, and model creative reading.

The rest of the first two paragraphs consists mostly of the descriptors one would expect, but they do contain an appeal to a piece of cultural knowledge (about tuberculosis) which most teachers will have, but may forget that most contemporary pupils will not have. You may think that, at some point, it may be worth passing on this knowledge to place the story historically (and cast a little more light on Spit's nickname), and maybe introduce the author. In the envy for Spit's legitimate absence from school, these paragraphs also contain a confirmation of the particular narrator's viewpoint and boyish values.

Trolleys, then – a technical passage which will enlist the legitimate interest of its implied readers (rough lads and unstereotyped girls? – addressed as 'you' in this third paragraph). The exemplary names of trolleys mentioned in this paragraph are amusing, but also indices of the period and the story's setting ('Dreadnought' etc.). One of them ('Death Before Dishonour') is also a sinister foreshadowing.

The next paragraph is an interesting example of generalized activity acting as description – the sort to erode my distinction between 'forks' and 'descriptors'. Some languages use an 'imperfect' tense for this: here, English uses 'would'. It fills in the picture of Spit, confirms the place and period (dialect 'brew' and horse-drawn coalcarts) throws another shadow forward ('cemetery'), and introduces the momentous Madge, to whom Spit's loyalty is at once comic, touching and very powerful in making the story predictable and intelligible to anyone who has ever read, heard or watched stories in any genre which feature a romantic allegiance made difficult by the circumstances of everyday life (*Rapunzel, Lancelot and Guinevere, Romeo and Juliet, Brief Encounter, Anna Karenina, Hir and Ranjha, Brookside?*). Spit's love and loyalty for the once-met Madge, his carrying her secret and disguised-by-reversal token on his life-defining trolley, *Egdam* – all these place Spit firmly in a tradition of gallant, idealistic, chivalrous, virgin warrior-knights. If you spot that, you'll know what will happen to him and what the author wants you to think of what Spit does and says. And by so doing you'll add to the intertextuality you'll bring to bear on future readings in this and related genres.

The next paragraph builds up Spit's prestige further – his authority, the high standards he sets himself (he rides off scratch), his expertise. And it drops the second of the hints that Spit is more magical, natural and mythical than his mortal companions: he knew the road like the back of his hand. (The first hint, for those who know their stammering, limping mythical heroes, is his disability: his one lung).

Then we have a flashback. A mini-fork sequence in form but again a descriptor in effect. The story of Spit's defeat of Ducker Smith, with its appealing comedy of the borrowed baby's pram-wheel, confirms that invincibility of Spit against which the rest of the narrative must work.

From then on, the main events of the story which string the conventional motifs of hero, challenger and conflict together are narrated roughly in the sequence of their quasi-history, though the narration varies the degrees to which they are compressed or spun out (see Figure 8).

Haddock introduces Duckett. These lads – together with the aforementioned Ducker, the lisping Chick and the narrating Bill – are the only named characters in the story (apart from Spit). Where we have expected Spit, from the time-keeper's use of a pigeon-timing watch, to become a working-class dove, the names of his mortal destroyers build up a strong suggestion of flightless birds and creatures of ambiguous elements (like Grendel) – with which Spit's subsequent flight can properly contrast. It would hardly surprise you if Bill's surname was Platypus. You could play the anagrams game with their names too – Leslie Duckett embodying sell, lie, kill, slick etc. Leslie and Spit, and their corresponding trolleys, make a clear binary contrast: the respectable, solid, smart, man-made boy and trolley against the disreputable, frail, scruffy, self-made boy and trolley.

Next: a sermon (or rather, with hindsight, a valediction to his disciples). Spit's inspection of the meretricious, unnatural, pompously named *The British Queen* – so

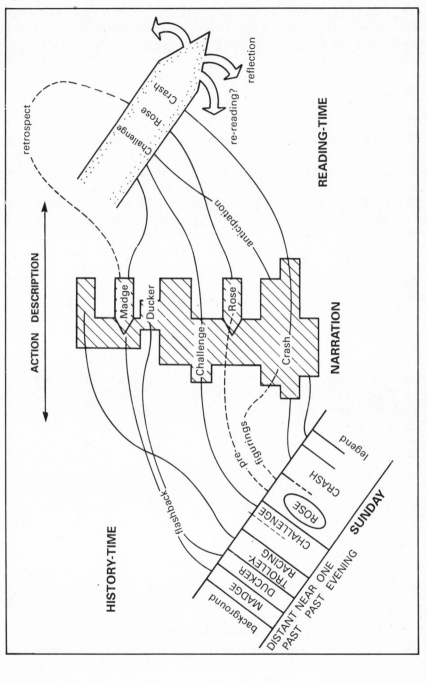

Figure 8   Narration and meaning-making in 'Spit Nolan'

pointedly everything that *Egdam* is not – leads him to a sententious re-statement of Marx's Theory of Value which is utterly implausible in naturalistic terms but utterly central in understanding the author, his motivation in writing, and the romantic-paranoid (Luddite) values which the story's tragic events are to exemplify and valorize. 'You own nothing in this world except those things you have taken a hand in the making of, or else you've earned the money to buy them,' pontificates our hero.

The challenge is the second major fork of the story (I take the first to be Leslie's breaking the rules of construction and introducing the unfair technology theme, the third to be the race, and the fourth the arrival of the charabanc). Then the narration skips a day or two to Sunday (of course) and the race.

The build-up to the race produces a lot more indicators of Spit's qualities. That his 'imperturbability' is 'almost godlike' is now explicit. Not that it needs underlining when he is pulling the cross-shaped wooden instrument of his imminent martyrdom up a hill at the place of the cemetery. His implausibly responsible consideration for Sunday-sleeping society and authority over his gang is established by his rebuking the whistlers. And in the bottle-swigging and calling together of the contestants there is a suggestion for me of the boxing-champs who become bywords for pathos if they survive their defeats.

The incident with Chick (an involuntary Hunfirth and Judas) is indicial too, but it is also a fork. Spit's acceptance of the ominously stolen rose is at once an index of his moral superiority and also a fork on the road to his ruin. In Figure 9 I've tried to show how the rose works as an index and an omen, and also, later, as a metonym of Spit's crash, a metaphor for his defeat, and a symbol of human frailty, all at once. I've tried to show the rose's dual function in Figure 8 which relates the times of the story, the plot, and the reading. On Figure 8 I've made segments of the plot more or less wide according to their significance and extending to the left or the right according to whether their significance is mainly for moving on the action or filling out the description. I've put the rose on the right, as a descriptive trope, but I've made it penetrate the active left, too, in superstitious recognition of its ominousness.

The account of the race itself would make a rich quarry for some after-reading stylistic analysis. A reading-aloud of it takes about the same time as the events it describes would take, and, given a histrionic elocution and allowing for a successful communication of the rhythms of excitement to count, it could be classed as a showing rather than a telling. That's the effect, but it's achieved with a variety of tricks. Naughton varies the texture of the experience like a film-maker, mixing cross-cuts and stills, subjective and objective viewpoints, long-shots and details. Respective instances of those are: the shouts and groans contrasted with the dream-like image of the bird about to soar; Bill's view and the view of the runners alongside; the overall view of the race and the detail of the ball-bearing wheels; the cutting from Spit to Leslie. If students list the most memorable content words associated with the respective racers in this passage

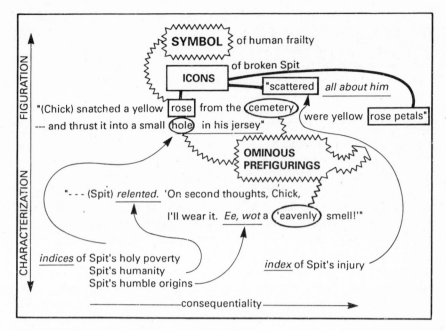

Figure 9 Spit's rose as index, icon, and symbol

(on the one wing 'balance', 'gliding', 'bird', 'poised', 'delicately'; and on the other carriageway 'weight', 'clinging'; 'grimly'; 'thundering', 'forcing') they should need little prompting to spot the author's artfulness or the story's binary ideology. And many pupils may not need the blushing teacher to point out the sexual connotations of Spit's lying 'belly-down' on *Egdam*, 'coaxing her', 'swaying with' her, and 'giving her her head'. (The trolley, like the rose, is a versatile vehicle of trope.)

By the time Nature's Sacred King is dead and replaced by New Technology's Tanist, such textual analysis might lead pupils to spot that the word 'dead' has already been over-used by now, with apparently innocent meanings, although its use with the obvious meaning is saved for the last sentence. Ernie Haddock started the race 'dead on the stroke of ten o'clock'; the last paragraph of the race description begins 'Dead level . . .'; and the paragraph in which the charabanc strikes Spit ends 'stopped dead'. It is not, thankfully, a subtle text.

The contrasting trolley's symbolism will be obvious to children if they read this passage carefully. A bump from *The British Queen*, not just bad luck, puts Spit under the charabanc and into legend; though he does not die before, like King Arthur, he refuses to accept a consoling lie, 'Death Before Dishonour'. And the contrasts between the male charabanc driver's reaction and those of the female passengers who gather like the women round the Cross invites some alignment of a female/male binarity with the binarity of Leslie's technology and Spit's nature.

As I said, I do not intend this exhaustive nut-hammering as a model for classroom exegesis. But to read the text aware of only some of the interests which different literary theories would find in it may suggest one or two appropriate activities to accompany a reading. Teachers might use these in order to enhance the attentiveness, interpretativeness or criticalness with which students might anticipate, participate in, or reflect upon, a reading, hearing or re-creation of this literary narrative. I have mentioned making anagrams of names and collecting words from the race for exposing the power of texts to suggest whole constellations of ideas with a few well-chosen words. Twenty-word group-summarizing is another activity mentioned earlier (in section 2.1) which is suitable as a follow-up to this story: it focuses on what might be the features of stories which give them an excitement and economy instinctively recognized in this one. Alertness to intertextuality might make a learned reader conscious of the parallels between Spit and mythical, legendary or scriptural characters.

Now no one would want to foist those parallels on schoolchildren, but being aware of them might lead a teacher to challenge their students to compare Spit with other characters in comics, TV programmes, films or other short stories in a way which enhances their appreciation of how they get their expectations and recognitions of Spit from between the lines of the text and from their own previous readings. And such an innocent activity as writing rules for trolley races might effectively exhume the moral assumptions and political values underlying this story.

5.3   Opportunities in teaching a legend

To me, *Hir and Ranjha* seemed, to offer plenty of opportunities within a reasonable compass, for some of the theory-implied practical suggestions made in previous chapters: some genre-placing (through prediction); some gap-filling; some analysis of plot through character-attributing and mapping; some attending to linguistic fabric, tropes and its cultural situation. It is a strongly plotted legend of which, so far as I know, there is no edition in English suitable for inexperienced readers. So the presentation would depend on the teacher, initially, with a lot of telling and reading aloud. This would entail 'doing' the text rather like a 'class reader', a practice I should be prepared to defend – including with mixed-ability classes like the third-year I was working with – providing it does not become the staple of the students' work on literature in English. Students read and worked on the story through eight successive double lessons spread over four weeks. In four of the lessons there was also a support teacher helping. By the time I got through it I had a full text typed and copied for the students' own use. They had episodically handed out to them A4 sheets with my pages reduced to A5 and copied side-by-side, with a dramatis personae and a title-page and introduction. Stapled together, these made 14-page books.

The ancient Panjabi legend of Hir and Ranjha concerns the doomed love of noble Hir and proud young Ranjha, a dispossessed young man of a rival clan. It exists in many versions. I used Charles Usborne's early-twentieth-century prose translation of Waris Shah's eighteenth-century poem to make 25 chapters each of which could be typed double-spaced on a single A4 sheet. In summary, the story is as follows:

1 Ranjha, his late father's favourite, is driven from the family land by jealous brothers.
2 Unable to afford a ferry across the Chenab, he sulks and threatens suicide on the banks.
3 Hir comes to the river and finds Ranjha asleep on her private ferry-couch.
4 They fall in love and Hir takes Ranjha to her father.
5 She persuades her father to employ him as a buffalo-herd, so she can secretly meet him.
6 Hir's uncle spies on their forest meetings and exposes them to her father.
7 Hir is to be married off but her father keeps Ranjha because he's good with buffaloes.
8 Hir continues to meet Ranjha, but her father finds her a husband from a distant clan.
9 Hir is forcibly married and carried off to her husband's, with Ranjha following.
10 Ranjha goes into the forest to learn the skills of holy men.
11 Hir pines and gets a message to the 'holy man' to come to her.
12 At Hir's husband's gate Ranjha has a quarrel with Hir's sister-in-law, Sehti.
13 Hir persuades them to let the 'holy man' cast her horoscope.
14 But the quarrel breaks out again and Ranjha is thrown out of Hir's yard.
15 Hir wins over Sehti by offering Ranjha's help to get Sehti to her own forbidden lover.
16 Sehti visits Ranjha, is convinced of his power, and takes his message to Hir.
17 They arrange a secret visit of Hir to Ranjha and the lovers renew their vows of love.
18 Hir pretends to be bitten by a snake and Sehti gets them to call in the 'holy man'.
19 Ranjha, now installed in his rival's house, works a miracle for Sehti to elope.
20 Hir and Ranjha run off but are captured and tried before a local ruler.
21 After a fire raised by Hir's curse, the ruler finds in favour of the lovers.
22 They return to be approved and welcomed by their families, despite continuing plots.

23 The scheming uncle convinces Hir that Ranjha has been murdered by their enemies.

24 Hir faints and the uncle has her poisoned. Ranjha finds out and wades in the Chenab.

25 So they passed away like the water, but their story remains like the river.

In the first double lesson I told and read aloud the material of the first five chapters, with a blackboard display of the names of the characters and their relationships. Then in what remained of the lesson the students made attribute grids of the characters introduced so far (they had made these grids once before, for another story – and later some of them did it for characters in their own stories). I thought it important that at this early stage they worked with names, which were unfamiliar except to the Panjabi minority of the students, so that they did not confuse them as they read on. I also thought it important that some of Ranjha's attributes – not what one expects of a romantic hero in our culture – were established. The attributes they came up with (old/young; male/female; high-born/low-born; proud/humble; etc.) were to provide the divisions which would power the subsequent plot.

In the second lesson, they revised what they remembered of the first five chapters. Then I read them the next two, and asked them, with each other's help, to predict what would happen in the story on the basis of what they had heard (none of them knew the story although it did transpire that one of the students of Panjabi background had seen a video of the story but did not recognize it at this stage). I hoped that this would develop some engagement with and commitment to the story as it unfolded, and that they would deploy some of their existing knowledge about stories to locate *Hir and Ranjha* within a genre, and see how, despite its being set in a distant time and place, it promised to fit a pattern they recognized from novels, magazine stories, soap operas and 'real-life' anecdote and gossip. Again, most found this easy to do well enough, and wrote down their predictions for future reference, some with help from me or the support teacher. For instance:

> . . . So when evening came the following day Hir put a few things in a bag and waited for Ranjha. It was getting very late and Ranjha still hadn't come. Milki asked why Hir was waiting outside the house Hir said she was'nt waiting for anyone she was getting fresh air but Milki knew she was waiting for Ranjha . . .
> [*Milki is Hir's mother*]
>
> (Farhana Siddiqui)

I then produced handouts of a simplified version of the 'story-making machine' illustrated in Figure 10. This – a sort of set of alternative forks stripped of descriptors – attempts to exploit the narratological insight that plots are made by relating a limited number and types of characters and other items into certain relationships. We had feared that this network might seem off-puttingly complex, as it did to us, but the students leaped on it and most asked for the more

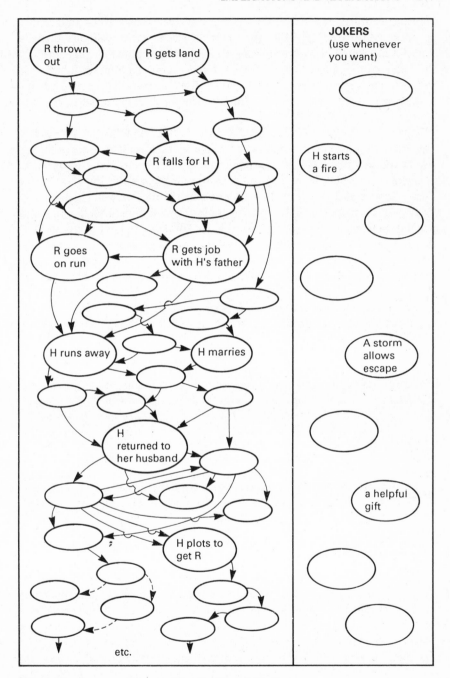

Figure 10   A story-making machine for *Hir and Ranjha*

complicated full version which I'd said was available. They found it an incentive
to write, perhaps because the diagrammatic nature of it reminded them of
domains like games-playing or computing in which they were more at home with
the iconography or algorithmic conventions than we were. Or maybe it had more
to do with the apparently mechanical and small-step-by-small-step nature of the
writing requirement, so much less mind-boggling than the usual freedom to
'write a story'.

Anyway, this was the most enjoyed and successful component of our reading
together of this legend. I asked them, for homework, to start at either of the top
two boxes, and 'flesh out' the narrative kernel in it, by inventing a name and
character for each of 'H' and 'R' and a reason for them gaining land or leaving
home. As soon as their writing had dealt with that or they were stuck, they could
prod on their creation by following one of the arrows leading from their box and
pad out the kernel in the box that arrow led to. And so on. They could dwell on
the contents of any box as long as they wanted and move on anywhere the arrows
allowed. If they became very stuck or bored they could use any of the 'jokers' in
the right-hand column. I did not point out that 'H' and 'R' could well be Hir and
Ranjha, and if any guessed they were they did not say so. But, possibly influenced
by their predictions, some of their (often long) stories corresponded in shape to
the old Panjabi legend, even if they had such surface differences as being pony
romances.

> . . . Ady [*who had been thrown out of his flat for falling behind with the rent*] was out of
> work so everyday he walked until one day he reached a lovely country house and so
> he went and knocked on the door and a beautiful young girl answered the door and
> she said 'Hello, can I help you' in a sweet voice. 'Yes, I'm looking for a job, have you
> got any here?' replied Ady. 'Yes, we have it's in the kitchen, doing the cooking or
> there is another one of working in the stables.' 'I'll take the one of working in the
> stables.' Then the girl introduced herself, 'my name's Joanne, but call me Jo.' 'My
> name's Ady' said Ady. Then Jo took Ady to meet her father and she told him that
> Ady had come to apply for the stable workers job. Her father said that he could do
> the job and so Ady was very happy. At least he would be earning some money . . .
>
> (Neema Shah)

Later in the month I was to get them to use these same networks to trace a record
of the plot of *Hir and Ranjha*.

Next lesson I read six more chapters, and distributed texts, then they had the
option of inventing and writing out only-reported dialogues or writing out letters
of abuse between Hir and Ranjha's brothers which another chapter told of but
did not show. In both cases they were encouraged to fill the gaps and expand the
hints I had put into the text so as to move a telling towards a showing. I had hoped
that the direct speech in the texts of earlier chapters would provide a model for
register and for layout of the dialogues. Their texts were on the whole apt in
content and many were funny, though they tended to be short and coarse and owe

more to the example of their own speech than the speech I'd invented for the characters.

Letter from Ranjha's brothers to say how much they are ashamed of Ranjha

To Ranjha

  You have not only ashamed our family name you have ruined our reputation as well. If you carry on this feasco we will be force to disown you compleatly from the family. If our father was alive now he would tern in his grave. If you retur back to us we will be gladly to put you back down to earth

Yours disgracly
Your family

p.s. Come back to us please

Letter to Hir to tell Hir that she was a fool to take such a young man for a lover

Dear Hir

  You say that you love Ranjha. But if you really loved him you let him return back to his family. Its realy a big laugh how you can take a such a young man for a love. We are try to fider out the real reason why your after him it cart be for money because he hasn't got any but your after something. We'll find out sooner or later what your after don't you worry

Yours
Ranjhas Brothers
(Jason Grant)

Dear Ranjha's Brother

  I am writing to tell you that I will not give up Ranjha because I love him very much. I won't let him go because dead can't be brought back to life by fishing their ashes out of the water.

on behalf of Hir
(Louise Loe)

Next lesson, with another five chapters distributed and the married Hir and disguised Ranjha secretly meeting with the help of Sehti, the students worked in groups with me and the support teacher, in preparing readings aloud of the chapters. Each chapter was the responsibility of one group or pair, and that group or pair could present it, when the time came, in any way they chose. Each group also prepared a script for a short dramatization of any incident in the story so far. I tried to concentrate activities which involved group discussion and reworkings of texts into the lessons in which there were two of us to support the weaker readers or less confident groups. Homework was to write out their own copy of the playscript or continue working on the story based on the 'story-machine' network.

Nearing the end of the story now, we began the next lesson by revising the story-so-far by a sequence of the prepared readings and performances, then they individually worked on 3W diagrams to clarify their appreciation of the plot as a series of meetings and separations tending to move further out from, but eventually back to, two home-bases separated by the all-important river. I gave them five sites of action as rows and hoped that their mapping the main characters' movements between them would be a further incentive to reading the text and might provoke some insights like how the lovers' meetings all have negative associations such as being furtive, disguised or at night.

Next lesson they simply read the final part of the text aloud, in groups, in any way they wanted, and traced the complete action through the story-machine network which I'd based on it and which they'd worked from in their own stories. Homework was to go through the text and make any one of four lists: ways men and women behave differently or are treated differently; references to the river and water and what happens there; references to animals (including comparisons); references in the story which show it's Asian and old, not European or modern. I intended such listing to provoke such awarenesses as how a story from a different culture embodies particular values: 'In the story Hir does not have any choice in who she marries, her father decides. Women are pampered with silk and pearls. When Ranjha's father died his sons had to share the land between them but the sisters did not get any of it . . .' (Stephen Witt). Or how recurrent images or a running theme such as water can give a story coherence and provide tropes (the collage poems which follow or Louise's letter above shows an appreciation of those). On the whole the lists they made were mostly short and did not seem to have provoked many exciting or penetrative insights. By now it was probably time to leave the story and start some new work.

However, writing collage poems next lesson was much more successful. I drew their attention to some of the more purple passages I had deliberately written in to the text for likely word-stocks and subject-matters. One who'd never handed me a completed piece of individual writing before, wrote:

The Reflections pool

The raindrops fell on the waterlilies,
Splashing in the rose cent pool
the sound of bells in the distance
the wind is fierce and blowing cool.

The healthy look upon the river,
reflection showing from the trees,
circles around the floating water,
Flirted softly in the breeze.

(Kelle Marie Russell)

And, with illuminated capitals:

They flowed down the river
like tigers that had drowned
They flirted in the river like
otters in there dam's
The sorrow in her eyes was
like a flowing river

They ended in the garden
where love had first flowed by
The love of hir and Ranja
Will, never die.

(Paul Fernie)

In the same lesson I also tried to get some group discussions going which would indicate that the text was an artefact: what caused the tragedy? People being foolish? or wicked? Or just bad luck? Or the author's manipulations?

In the last session and for homework I also tried to situate the story by going through a short written introduction to its history and significance (as a plea for inter-communal tolerance) and coming clean on my own authorship and asking for their suggestions on how I could improve it (half said cut the descriptions and leave the dialogue and half said the opposite).

They also began (but few finished) one of these: storyboards of the text, with the emphasis on deciding beforehand which six incidents best lent themselves to visual illustration; writing a version from a different viewpoint, such as that of the older people or the clan into which Hir was married and from which she was then stolen back; saucily filling the gap left by the text's allusion to Ranjha getting in to see Hir on one occasion by disguising himself as one of her girl friends. Had I had more time I should have tried to get hold of some of the original versions, especially as there were Urdu and Panjabi speakers in the class, or followed up the fact that one of them had seen an Asian film of the story.

And had I known the class better I should have taken a less directive and didactic approach and allowed for more self-initiated, self-policed and self-assessed work, in the spirit of the poem which heads the next and final section.

5.4   Suggestions categorized

Don't say you are right too often, teacher.
Let the students realise it.
Don't push the truth:
It's not good for it.
Listen while you speak!

(Brecht, *Poems, 1913–56*, p. 436)

At the start of section 1.2 I sketched a history of literary critical and theoretical concerns in relation to changing emphases in English teaching. These can now be written onto two corresponding layouts of the model of reading which has grown through subsequent chapters. Very roughly, writing about literature in English has moved anti-clockwise round Figure H from the biography of authors in the last century (on the left), through a fixation on individual texts of New and Practical Criticism, into a structuralist concern with inter-textual features influenced by mid-century continental developments (see my Chapter 2),

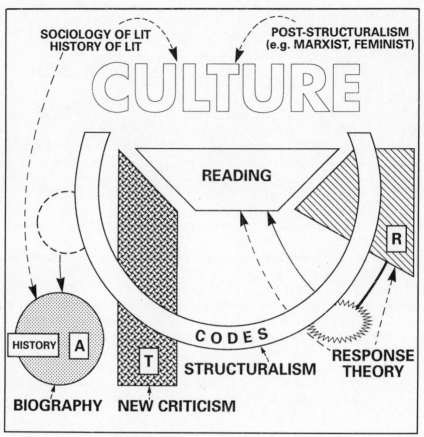

Figure H   Emphases of different literary theories on different components of model

followed by a phenomenological and psychologist centring on the reader and the reader's mental processes in response theory (see my Chapter 1) and now recognizing the cultural and political situation of reading (my Chapter 4). The last in some ways circles back to introduce that historical element into the production and consumption of texts which made a partial, belle-lettrist first appearance a century ago, when the emphasis was on great men (not women) rather than on culture.

This history is roughly repeated, with a time-lag, by the history of English teaching. Shayer (1972) shows: how, before the Newbolt Report of 1921, literature teaching was a history of literature, often without the texts

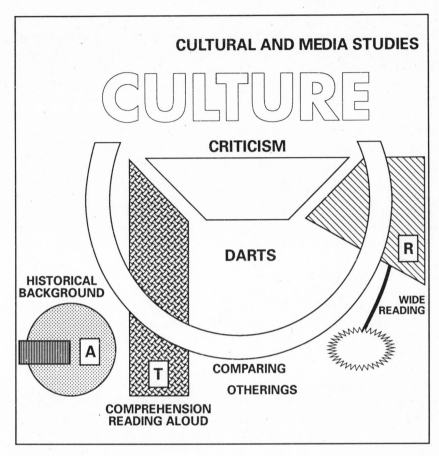

Figure I   Teaching implications related to different components of model

(pp. 33–4); how literary passages were hardly distinguished from non-literary ones in 'comprehension', as in my Figure A; how practical criticism was trickled down by Leavisites from the late 1930s onwards (p. 125); how the fashion for 'relevance' in English, beginning in the 1960s, was predicated on the ease with which young readers could respond as a criterion of suitability and justified by its assumed political and social influence (p. 171). Since Shayer wrote, the part played by culture in producing texts, syllabuses and readers has been developed in many of the materials and *English Magazine* articles originating from the ILEA English Centre (e.g. the *Making Stories* and *Changing Stories* books, Mellor and Raleigh 1984).

In the English Teaching reflection of that Grand Historical Model (Figure I), I've aligned fashionable practices as follows. I've put 'background' studies (e.g.

the lives of Shakespeare or the Brontës) on the left with the biographical approaches to literature. I've put such close study of uncontextualized texts as reading aloud and small-focus 'comprehension' – still a feature of A-level and in diluted form of mainstream class literature study – with New Criticism. With such formalist concerns for codes as structuralism, I've related active playful practices such as DARTs, rewriting and mapping, and also comparative studies which develop an awareness of genre. I've put wide reading in the same place as response theory. And cultural and media studies come in on the coat-tails of current post-structural and materialist theorizings.

I am, of course, aware that this correspondence is rough and ready. It was acknowledged earlier that small-focus study of the work of words in creating literary meaning was the essence of Practical Criticism, yet I chose to concentrate on it in the context of Culture, despite the partisan opposition between many of the Leavisite practical critics and materialist cultural theorists of literature. 'Othering' (rewriting from other viewpoints or in other forms) could equally be counted as visualizing or gap-filling led by response theory. And my model, by shrinking out the 'events' component of its first and most simplistic version, does no justice to the enduring tendency to teach literary texts with 'comprehension', as if they were documentaries.

Now there is a final need to collect the pedagogical suggestions thrown into earlier chapters and recap them in some sort of order. The model will form the basis of that order but I will project it on to a plane with another, more operational, division: Scholes's (1985) reading; interpretation; criticism. If a hierarchy seems implied there (you can't criticize till you can interpret and you can't interpret till you can read), that's not to imply that they should be sequenced in key stages and that the sort of literary reading-processes discussed in Chapter 1 are low-level. The three sorts of operation interact, so that a critical awareness informs subsequent alert, imaginative reading, and so on. All this comes with the reminder that it is no sort of scheme. As the early chapters of Protherough (1986) remind us, there are already enough problems of over-teaching, especially for exams, to take the force and freshness out of literary response. So this is just a repertory of approaches from which teachers might pick one or two theory-informed procedures, matched to the difficulties or temptations of a particular text interacting with a particular reader's interests, needs and reading-style, all leading to a new attentiveness, ability to interpret and willingness to criticize. And also a reminder that the techniques for slowing down reading and making it reflective and suspicious all presuppose that the authors, publishers and librarians have done their work in providing attractive texts for the kill-joy teachers to start estranging and problematizing.

In Chapter 1 I suggested that response theory provides insights into the behaviour of reflective, responsive readers. Teachers could organize their students' literary reading, especially of narrative, in such a way that active, possibly public, outcomes of their reading could model their private silent reading and make implicit knowledge more usable by 'crystallizing' it. The assumption was that if students were required, say, to draw their visualizations or write out their gap-fillings then they would be more likely, in both that and subsequent readings, to visualize and imagine what goes on in the textual gaps. Also advocated (mainly in section 1.4) were: anticipation from early clues – including covers, authors, titles, places and dates of publication, context of presentation (section 1.5) – or the recognition of genre; being publicly open about changes of mind by admitting, explaining and discussing them with others; amplifying each student's attentiveness to the text and its possible meanings and effects by sharing other students' awarenesses and insights. As well as the group discussion, writing and drawing implied by these suggestions, procedures which were advocated for developing responsive reading included: group discussion aimed at comparing different readers' responses and recognitions or for some instrumental purpose such as designing a new book cover; encouraging wide reading to provide a stock of reference and quotation through which to read new texts (section 1.5); keeping of reflective reading journals; doodling and collaging (section 1.5); some of the DARTs techniques, especially, in this context, prediction. In section 1.3 it was suggested that in the particular instance of responsive reading of dialogue students may be helped by discussing how they know who says what, rewriting into other forms of speech representation, and comparing transcripts of in-role improvisations with their textual prototypes.

Chapter 1's suggestions about studying chronology in narratives (by time-lining plots, sequencing extracts or comparing the durations of history-times and reading-times for instance – section 1.6) was a bridge to the more formalist and structuralist interpretative concerns of Chapter 2. Where Chapter 1 provided rationales and models for active reading of narrative, Chapter 2 was more concerned to provide activities which deployed and promoted awarenesses of the structures and workings of texts already read. So, in section 2.1, I suggested isolating plot structures by making 3W diagrams, diagrams of relationships, 20-word summaries, editions for workshop presentations, pastiches, parodies or genre-swops, and identifying plot functions by some genre study. Section 2.1 illustrated Happy Families-type games and section 4.3 looked back to these procedures by showing how devising board games could reveal structure and also the values they embody. Section 2.1 promised an eventual example of students using different forms of visual exploration of a story. Jenny Burgoyne's sixth-formers, having read *The Great Gatsby* and discussed it, conducted the second phase of their exploration by making charts, mostly in pairs, for wall display and presentation to the whole group.

Louise and Vicki set quotations about Gatsby on a time-line, coloured according to whether the statements were true or false. They found most false ones near the beginning and most true ones near the end – a graphic demonstration of how the story works by revealing the mystery of its central character. Sam ordered material related to Nick's attitude to Gatsby in history-time-sequence and arranged it in the shape of a clock. Claire made a board-game of Jay's and Myrtle's fate. The two players were each to follow opposite routes towards what looked like a dream but actually became death, impelled and guided by chance cards which directed them to squares which presaged their fates with items from the plot.

The others all made networks of relationships of some sort, all with quotations: Jenni's showed the relationship between Gatsby and Daisy by surrounding them by grouped statements of what characters said about it; Madasser's filled each of four characters' quadrants with eleven lines coloured according to eleven different attributes ('wealth', 'status' and so on) and ranked with the others in respect of that attribute; Sharon coloured the connections between Gatsby and others according to whether they were from Gatsby's distant past, his recent past, or the period of the book's narrated action; Kaye displayed, and used annotation to compare, carefully chosen blow-ups of early and late passages. Dan made three nets of relationships between the characters in three different sites of the novel's action, again using colour to make distinctions, and each of these networks linked each character to every other by two curved lines, one for each character's relationship to the other, with the convex side of each line labelled with its originator's assumed attitude to the linked character, while the concave side was labelled with Dan's assessment of the real relationship.

All these pieces of work involved a purposive scrutiny of the text, such as I advocated in 'teaching reading', and many involved making discoveries, either in the process of making procedural decisions about the representations or as a result of looking at the finished result. Such discoveries were about themes, developments and relationships in the book. The individual work involved on each one was justified by the opportunity to share the results of others' work.

The subsequent sections of my Chapter 2 introduced some binary concepts from literary theory to develop the idea of narrative structure, and these were used to suggest some comparative and analytical techniques for discovering the workings of plot and interpreting texts. Instances of applying this binary principle included: grouping and comparing different works, storyshapes or characters; recognizing characters as artefacts by attributing them or casting or costuming them; using polarities to structure diagrams of plots (section 2.2). The idea of sequence and correspondence was illustrated by pecking orders and changing Top Twenty charts in section 2.3 and emerged as paths and choices with the suggestion of tracking causes of action through plot sequences or picking out fugued plots with ideas for diagrams developed from 3W charts or time-tracks. In section 2.5, narratologists' contrasts between forks and fillers, proddings-on and paddings-out, suggested principles for segmenting or labelling texts or summaries and for exposing narrative machineries and necessities by exploring the differences which would be made if, where narrative forks, other prongs were followed, or if descriptors were made opposite to how they are in the text. Meanwhile, section 2.4 developed a simple contrast between metonyms and metaphors as symptoms and comparisons and suggested collecting and categorizing these tropes, cartooning 'running metaphors', investigating the titling of texts or the naming of characters in the light of this distinction and making cross-cultural comparisons of the significance of standard similes and metaphors.

Chapter 3 extracted the workings of narrators and their voices and viewpoints. Starting with comparisons of book and film, there were suggestions about: comparing the techniques of books and films and estranging narrative practice by recognizing speedings-up, cuts, zooms and so on and their textual equivalents; discussing the reasons for differences between verbal and visual realizations of the same plots (including those differences inhering in their different social productions); picking out passages of text which would lend themselves to filming; making filmscripts of parts of novels and stories before viewing professional filmings of them. In section 3.2, focusing on narrative viewpoint and voice, I suggested that it could sometimes be useful for readers to rewrite stories or passages from different viewpoints, especially those of characters with social values, genders or degrees of knowledge different from those of the original's narrator, to explore the possibilities and effects of changing the person (in its grammatical sense) of the narration – even to 'you' – and to recognize the function of viewpoint by mapping it on to 3W or other diagrams of the plot. Section 3.3 distinguished between a reader's being shown or told, as well as other experiences such as inferring for oneself or sharing a narrator's ignorance, and suggested that these distinctions may sometimes be useful in segmenting and labelling text, in dividing time-lines into 'shown' and 'told' lengths, in exploring differences between books and representations of plots in films or other media, and in understanding the chronological variations discussed in section 1.6. The final section of Chapter 3 looked forward to the next chapter's section on Brecht and the last chapter's argument for teaching literature as signs rather than life by suggesting looking at production problems and variations in staged or televised stories in order to expose the artificiality of the more ostensibly naturalistic and deceptive forms of narrative.

The introduction to Chapter 4 suggested that, in some cases, a biographical interest in an author could motivate a reader and illuminate and explain a text. It hinted at the utilities of speculating on what author might have written a known text or what sort of text a known author might have made of known events and situations. Section 4.1 raised the possibility of comparing the readings of readers whose cultures differed because of their generation (in the example given) or gender or class or ethnic background or religious or political allegiance, and so on. Section 4.2 showed the values of using critics as other readers to provoke, feed and discipline the growth of a student reader's individual interpretation and critique, and incidentally dropped a hint at the possibility of using famous paintings as a guide to visualizing or illustrating texts or designing productions, and as supportive evidence of the imaginative cultures which produced works of literature. Section 4.3 suggested playing the Martian to estrange the values embedded in narratives and exposing the different potentialities in works by listing what different real or imaginary readers would pick out as the salient events or themes or characters of a work. It showed how some of the techniques of structural exploration such as making games, or techniques for narrational exploration such as rewriting from other viewpoints could be used to expose the ideologies which structure and speak through texts. Section 4.4 took Brecht as a guide to estranging and urged that students should think about what they feel, and should recognize the contradictions within, shockingness of, and the not unchangeably constructed nature of, social relations. Section 4.5 reverted to the language of literature and suggested that students act as suspicious customs officers and pick through the cultural loads of literatures, and that straightforward and apparently technical linguistic exercises could effectively expose the ideological nature of literature. Some of these procedures were: reading, making or comparing translations; discussing the effects of minor changes of wording; listing content words or items associated with characters – parts of speech or parts of body – or surveying their relative frequencies of commanding, asking, replying, thinking or whatever. Finally, and more recreatively, the Furniture Game and word-collaging were suggested as poetry-provokers which, if they used literary narrative texts for their raw material, would draw attention to some of their seductive and maybe insidious power to influence readers morally or politically. Section 4.6 was a warning against animals and contained suggestions that readers might be made wary of them by extracting references to them or rehumanizing furry parables.

There's another warning: the little Brecht poem for teachers which heads this section.

Appendix

Spain, 1809

All day we had ridden through scarred, tawny hills.
  At last the cool
Of splashing water. Then two blackened mills,
  A slaughtered mule.

And there, crag-perched, the village – San Pedro –
  We came to burn.
(Two convoys ambushed in the gorge below.
  They had to learn.)

Not a sound. Not a soul. Not a goat left behind.
  They had been wise.
Those death's-head hovels watched us, bleared and blind,
  With holes for eyes.

Down the one street's foul gutter slowly crawled
  Like blood, dark-red,
The wine from goatskins, slashed and hacked, that sprawled
  Like human dead.

From a black heap, like some charred funeral-pyre,
  Curled up, forlorn,
Grey wisps of smoke, where they had fed the fire
  With their last corn.

What hatred in that stillness! Suddenly
  An infant's cry.
Child, mother bedrid crone – we found the three,
  Too frail to fly.

We searched their very straw – one wineskin there.
  We grinned with thirst,
And yet? – that Spanish hate! – what man would dare
  To taste it first?

Below, our Captain called, 'Bring down the wench.'
  We brought her down –
Dark, brooding eyes that faced the smiling French
  With sullen frown.

'Señora, we are sent to burn the place.
  Your house I spare.'
Her proud chin nestled on her baby's face,
  Still silent there.

'Cold cheer you leave us! – one poor skin of wine!
  Before we sup,
You will honour us, Señora?' At his sign
  One filled a cup.

Calmly she took and, drinking, coldly smiled;
  We breathed more free.
But grimly our Captain watched her – 'Now your child.'
  Impassively,

She made the small mouth swallow. All was well.
  The street was fired.
And we, by that brave blaze, as twilight fell,
  Sat gaily tired.

Laughing and eating, while the wine went round,
  Carefree, until
A child's scream through the darkness. At the sound
  Our hearts stood still.

Dumbly we glanced in one another's eyes.
  Our thirst was dead.
And in its place once more that grim surmise
  Upreared its head.

One dragged her to the firelight. Ashen-grey,
  She hissed – 'I knew
Not even the straw where an old woman lay
  Was safe from you.

'Now you are paid!' I never loved their wine,
  Had tasted none.
I will not tell, under that white moonshine,
  What things were done.

Twenty men mad with drink, and rage, and dread,
  Frenzied with pain –
That night the quiet millstream dribbled red
  With blood of Spain.

Under the moon across the gaunt sierra
  I fled alone.
Their balls whizzed wide. But in each tree lurked terror,
  In each stone.

Yes, men are brave. (Earth were a happier place,
    Were men less so.)
But I remember one pale woman's face
    In San Pedro.

F. L. Lucas

Recommended reading and references

Recommended reading

Of the books listed in the following pages, probably the best value is Lee (1987). It is a rich mixture of articles and chapters on both the teaching of literature and the theory which should inform it, many of them representative of, or extracted from, books I recommend or to which I refer. It contains, for instance, material by Eagleton, Lodge, Benton and Fox, Protherough, Exton, Brown and Gifford, and on adaptations of literature to other media, what literature has meant in the school curriculum, and the assessment of literature in school.

Benton and Fox (1985) is an excellent book on teaching literature, informed by response theory and offering a wide variety of activities all based on a consideration of the nature of literature and reading. Protherough (1983) would supplement Benton and Fox with case histories, as would Protherough (1986) and, for A-level students, Brown and Gifford (1989). Miller (1984) is another source of up-to-date applications to literature teaching of contemporary theory. For a single teacher discussing practice across the age-range, see Jackson (1983).

Exton's hilarious 'The Post-structuralist Always Reads Twice' (1984) is a brilliant and comprehensible short introduction to literary theorists: Culler (1981) is longer and less hilarious but still comprehensible and lively. For response theory applied, Evans in Corcoran and Evans (1987) is good; a more academic introduction to the theories is in the second edition (not the first) of Jefferson and Robey (1987). For structuralist theories, Hawkes (1977) is a good introduction and Rimmon-Kenan (1983) is a terse textbook of narratology. For post-structuralist theories, Griffith (1987) discusses thinkers I have ignored in this book (as well as response-theorists and structuralists) and he applies them to classrooms. Many post-structuralist ideas have been taken on board in the practical suggestions emerging as articles in *The English Magazine* or as booklets such as Mellor and Raleigh (1984) from the ILEA English Centre. Eagleton (1983) is a justly popular introduction with a post-structuralist perspective, and is specially good, I think, on psychoanalytical influences. Dollimore and Sinfield (1985), and both the Zipes titles (1979 and 1983), are stimulating applications of 'cultural materialism' to texts we're all likely to know – Shakespeare and fairy tales respectively. Millett (1969) is a bracing feminist literary polemic, and Tallack (1987) shows different explicit theories applied to a limited number of works.

The one theorist who is sometimes accessible and sometimes amusing and sometimes both – and whose respective works represent all the different 'schools', is Barthes, well represented in Sontag (1982).

References

Recurrent primary texts

Bierce, Ambrose. 'An Occurrence at Owl Creek Bridge' currently in print in:
Bierce, A. (1980). *An Occurrence at Owl Creek Bridge*. Creative Editions.
Hopkins, E. J. (ed.) (1984). *Complete Short Stories of Ambrose Bierce*, Nebraska, University of Nebraska Press.
(1983). *Collected Writings of Ambrose Bierce*. Carol Publications Group.
Brecht, Bertolt. *The Caucasian Chalk Circle* currently in print in:
Brecht, Bertolt (1966). *Parables for the Theatre*, trans. Bentley, E. Harmondsworth, Penguin.
Brecht, Bertolt (1963). *The Caucasian Chalk Circle*, trans. Stern, J. and T. London, Eyre Methuen.
Brontë, Charlotte (1966). *Jane Eyre*. Harmondsworth, Penguin.
Lucas, Frank Laurence. *Spain, 1809* from Lucas, F. L. *From Many Times and Lands* currently in print in:
Newbould, A. and Stibbs, A. (1983). *Exploring Texts through Reading Aloud*. London, Ward Lock Educational.
Naughton, Bill (1968). 'Spit Nolan' in *The Goalkeeper's Revenge and Other Stories*. Harmondsworth, Penguin.
Sewell, Anna (1954). *Black Beauty*. Harmondsworth, Penguin.
Shakespeare, William. *A Midsummer Night's Dream*.
Turnbull, Eric (1982). *Business News* in Stibbs, A. and Todd, J. (eds) (1982). *Behind the Lines*. Brotton, Brotton Writers' Workshop.

Other works referred to or recommended

Adams, Richard (1974). *Watership Down*. Harmondsworth, Penguin.
Bakhtin, Mikhail M. (1981). *The Dialogic Imagination: Four Essays*. Austin, University of Texas.
Bannister, Don, and Fransella, Fay (1971). *Inquiring Man: the Theory of Personal Constructs*. Harmondsworth, Penguin.
Barnes, Dorothy, Barnes, Douglas, with Clarke, Stephen (1984). *Versions of English*. London, Heinemann Educational Books.
Barnes, Douglas, Churley, Peter, and Thompson, Christopher (1971). 'Group Talk and Literary Response', *English in Education*, 5 (3), 63–76.
Barthes, Roland (1957). *Mythologies*. London, Jonathan Cape.
Belsey, Catherine (1980). *Critical Practice*. London, Methuen (New Accents).
Benton, Michael, and Fox, Geoff (1985). *Teaching Literature, 9–14*. Oxford, Oxford University Press.
Benton, Mike, Teasey, John, Bell, Ray, Hurst, Keith (1988). *Young Readers Responding to Poems*. London, Routledge.

Bettelheim, Bruno (1977). *The Uses of Enchantment*. London, Thames & Hudson.

Booth, Wayne C. (1961). *The Rhetoric of Fiction*. Chicago, University of Chicago Press.

Bowen, Elizabeth (1989). *The Heat of the Day*. Harmondsworth, Penguin.

Brecht, Bertolt (1977). *The Exception and the Rule* in *The Measures Taken and other Lehrstücke*. Methuen Modern Plays, London, Methuen.

Brecht, Bertolt (1976). *Poems, 1913–56* (ed. Willett, J. and Mannheim, R.). London, Methuen.

Brough, John (1968). *Poems from the Sanskrit*. Harmondsworth, Penguin.

Brown, John, and Gifford, Terry (1989). *Teaching A Level English Literature*. London, Routledge.

Butor, Michel (1965). 'The Second Case' and 'Second Thoughts', *New Left Review*, **34**, 60–71.

Byatt, A. S. (1990). *Possession: a Romance*. London, Chatto & Windus.

Carpenter, Humphrey (1985). *Secret Gardens*. London, Allen & Unwin.

Carrington, Bruce, and Short, Geoff (1984). 'Comics: a Medium for Racism', *English in Education*, **18** (2), 10–14.

Chambers, Aidan (1982). *Dance on My Grave*. London, Pan Horizons.

Chatman, Seymour (1978). *Story and Discourse: Narrative Structure in Fiction and Film*. Ithaca, NY, Cornell University Press.

Collins, James (ed.) (1989). *Vital Signs I*. Portsmouth, New Hampshire, Heinemann/ Boynton Cook.

Collins, James (ed.) (1990). *Vital Signs II*. Portsmouth, New Hampshire, Heinemann/ Boynton Cook.

Corcoran, Bill, and Evans, Emrys (1987). *Readers, Texts, Teachers*. Milton Keynes, Open University Press.

Cox, Brian (chair), (1989). *English for Ages 5–16: Proposals of the Secretary of State for Education and Science and Secretary of State for Wales*. London, Dept. of Education and Science.

Culler, Jonathan (1981). *The Pursuit of Signs*. London, RKP.

Dickens, Charles (1907). *Bleak House*. London, Dent.

Dollimore, Jonathan, and Sinfield, Alan (eds) (1985). *Political Shakespeare: New Essays in Cultural Materialism*. Manchester, Manchester University Press.

Doyle, Sir Arthur Conan (1988). *The Hound of the Baskervilles*. London, Grafton.

Eagleton, Terry (1983). *Literary Theory*. Oxford, Blackwell.

Eagleton, Terry (1985). 'The Subject of Literature', *The English Magazine*, **15**, 4–7.

Eagleton, Terry (1986). *William Shakespeare*. Oxford, Blackwell.

Evans, Emrys (1981). 'The Act of Reading and the English Teacher', *English in Education*, **15** (3), 34–9.

Exton, Richard (1984). 'The Post-structuralist Always Reads Twice', *The English Magazine*, **10**, 13–20.

Fader, Dan, and McNeil, Elton, B. (1969). *Hooked on Books*. London, Pergamon.

Fish, Stanley (1980). *Is There a Text in This Class?: The Authority of Interpretative Communities*. Cambridge, Mass., Harvard University Press.

Fitzgerald, F. Scott (1950). *The Great Gatsby*. Harmondsworth, Penguin.

Fitzgerald, F. Scott (1960). *The Last Tycoon*. Harmondsworth, Penguin.

Fowler, Roger (ed.) (1975). *Style and Structure in Literature: Essays in the New Stylistics*. Oxford, Blackwell.

Fowler, Roger (1977). *Linguistics and the Novel*. London, Methuen (New Accents).

Fox, Geoff (1982). 'Nineteen Ways to Share a Novel', *Times Educational Supplement*, 9 July 1982.

Fry, Donald (1985). *Children Talk About Books: Seeing Themselves as Readers*. Milton Keynes, Open University Press.

Frye, Northrop (1957). *An Anatomy of Criticism: Four Essays*. Princeton, NJ, Princeton University Press.

Fuentes, Carlos (1988). *The Old Gringo*. London, Picador (Pan).

Garfield, Leon (1971). *Black Jack*. Harmondsworth, Penguin.

Genette, Gerard (1980). *Narrative Discourse*. Oxford, Blackwell.

Graham, Eleanor (ed.) (1958). *A Puffin Quartet of Poets: Eleanor Farjeon; James Reeves; E. V. Rieu; Ian Serraillier*. Harmondsworth, Penguin.

Grahame, Kenneth (1954). *The Wind in the Willows*. London, Methuen.

Greer, Germaine (1986). *Shakespeare*. Oxford, Oxford University Press.

Griffith, Peter (1987). *Literary Theory and English Teaching*. Milton Keynes, Open University Press.

Harari, Josue V. (ed.) (1980). *Textual Strategies*. London, Methuen.

Harding, D. W. (1967). 'Considered Experience: The Invitation of the Novel', *English in Education*, 1 (2), 7–15.

Harland, Richard (1987). *Superstructuralism: The Philosophy of Structuralism and Post-structuralism*. London, Methuen (New Accents).

Hawkes, Terence (1977). *Structuralism and Semiotics*. London, Methuen (New Accents).

Hawkes, Terence (1986). *That Shakespeherian Rag; Essays on a Critical Process*. London, Methuen.

Holland, Norman (1968). *The Dynamics of Literary Response*. New York, Oxford University Press.

Holub, Robert, C. (1984). *Reception Theory: a Critical Introduction*. London, Methuen (New Accents).

Howker, Janni (1985). *The Nature of the Beast*. Glasgow, Collins.

Howker, Janni (1989). 'Janni Howker: an interview', *The English Magazine*, 22, 18–20.

Humm, Peter, Stigant, Paul, and Widdowson, Peter (1986). *Popular Fictions: Essays in History and Literature*. London, Methuen.

Ingham, Jennie (1982). *Books and Reading Development*. London, Heinemann Educational Books.

Iser, Wolfgang (1974). *The Implied Reader: Patterns of Communication in Prose Fiction from Bunyan to Beckett*. Baltimore, Johns Hopkins University Press.

Iser, Wolfgang (1978). *The Act of Reading: a Theory of Aesthetic Response*. London, RKP.

Jackson, David (1983). *Encounters with Books*. London, Methuen.

Jefferson, Anne, and Robey, David (1987). *Modern Literary Theory*. 2nd edition. London, Batsford.

Jones, Michael, and West, Alastair (eds) (1988). *Learning Me Your Language*. London, Mary Glasgow.

Kermode, Frank (1966). *The Sense of an Ending: Studies in the Theory of Fiction*. Oxford, Oxford University Press.

Knights, L. C. (1951). *Explorations*. London, Chatto & Windus.

Kott, Jan (1965). *Shakespeare Our Contemporary*. London, Methuen.

Kristeva, Julie (1980). *Desire in Language*. Oxford, Blackwell.

Leach, Edmund (1970). *Levi-Strauss*. London, Fontana.

Lee, Victor (ed.) (1987). *English Literature in Schools*. Milton Keynes, Open University Press.

Lodge, David (1981). *Working with Structuralism*. London, RKP.

Lunzer, Eric, and Gardner, Keith (1984). *Learning from the Written Word*. Edinburgh, Oliver & Boyd.

Mahy, Margaret (1984). *The Changeover*. London, Dent.

Meek, Margaret, and Miller, Jane (eds) (1984). *Changing English: Essays for Harold Rosen*. London, Heinemann Educational Books.

Meek, Margaret, Warlow, Aidan, and Barton, Griselda (eds) (1977). *The Cool Web*. London, The Bodley Head.

Mellor, Bronwyn, and Raleigh, Mike (1984). *Making Stories* and *Changing Stories*. London, ILEA English Centre.

Miller, Jane (ed.) (1984). *Eccentric Propositions: Essays on Literature and Curriculum*. London, RKP.

Millett, Kate (1969). *Sexual Politics*. London, Virago.

Milligan, Spike (1974). *The Book of the Goons*. London, Robson Books.

Minns, Hilary, Jackson, David, Fry, Donald, and Stibbs, Andrew (1981). *Language, Teaching and Learning 3: English*. London, Ward Lock Educational.

Mitchell, W. J. T. (ed.) (1980). *On Narrative*. Chicago, University of Chicago Press.

Needle, Jan (1981). *The Wild Wood*. London, Deutsch.

Newbould, Anne, and Stibbs, Andrew (1983). *Exploring Texts through Reading Aloud*. London, Ward Lock Educational.

Pearce, Philippa (1976). *Tom's Midnight Garden*. Harmondsworth, Penguin.

Pearce, Philippa (1983). *The Way to Sattin Shore*. Harmondsworth, Kestrel.

Pierce, Andrew (1985). *The Role of Writing in the Development of Literary Response*. Unpublished MA dissertation for University of London Institute of Education.

Pinter, Harold (1981). *Plays: Four*. London, Eyre Methuen.

Propp, Vladimir (1958). *Morphology of the Folk-Tale*. Austin, Texas University Press.

Protherough, Robert (1983). *Developing Response to Fiction*. Milton Keynes, Open University Press.

Protherough, Robert (1986). *Teaching Literature for Examinations*. Milton Keynes, Open University Press.

Pugh, A. K., Lee, V. J., and Swann, J. (eds) (1980). *Language and Language Use: a Reader*. London, Heinemann.

Rhys, Jean (1989). *The Wide Sargasso Sea*. London, Hodder & Stoughton.

Richards, I. A. (1929). *Practical Criticism*. London, RKP.

Rimmon-Kenon, Shlomith (1983). *Narrative Fiction*, London, Methuen.

Rosen, Betty (1988). *And None of It Was Nonsense*. London, Mary Glasgow.

Rosenblatt, Louise (1978). *The Reader, the Text, the Poem: the Transactional Theory of the Literary Work*. Carbondale, South Illinois University Press.

Scholes, Robert (1985). *Textual Power*. New Haven and London, Yale University Press.

Sennett, Richard (1974). *The Fall of Public Man*. Cambridge, Cambridge University Press.

Shayer, David (1972). *The Teaching of English in Schools, 1900–72*. London, RKP.

Smith, Dodie (1975). *One Hundred and One Dalmations*. Harmondsworth, Penguin.

Sontag, Susan (ed.) (1982). *Barthes: Selected Writings*. London, Fontana.

Spender, Dale (1980). *Man Made Language*. London, RKP.

Squire, James (1964). *The Responses of Adolescents While Reading Four Short Stories.* Champaign, Ill., NCTE.

Tallack, Douglas (ed.) (1987). *Literary Theory at Work: Three Texts.* London, Batsford.

Thomson, Jack (1987). *Understanding Teenagers' Reading.* New South Wales, Methuen Australia.

Waldeback, Zara (1990). 'The Revenge of the Bimbo', *Red Letters,* **26,** 8–9.

Welty, Eudora (1987). *The Eye of the Story: Selected Essays and Reviews.* London, Virago.

West, Alastair (1986). 'The Production of Readers', *The English Magazine,* **17,** 4–9.

Wilkie, Christine (1989). *Through the Narrow Gate: the Mythological Consciousness of Russell Hoban.* Cranbury, NJ, Associated University Press.

Wilks, Brian (1975). *The Brontës.* London, Hamlyn.

Willett, John (1964). *Brecht on Theatre.* London, Methuen.

Yeazell, Ruth (ed.) (1986). *Sex, Politics and Science in the Nineteenth-Century Novel: Selected Papers from the English Institute. 10. 1983–4.* Baltimore, Johns Hopkins University Press.

Zipes, Jack (1979). *Breaking the Magic Spell.* London, Heinemann.

Zipes, Jack (1983). *Fairy Tales and the Art of Subversion.* London, Heinemann.

Index